PRAISE FOR *HOW TO GET A JOB YOU LOVE*

'Alongside the various editions of *How To Get a Job You Love* and his other titles, John is a regular speaker at member events. His real-world approach and engaging style of career coaching have made him the obvious choice to launch AMBA's webinar series. Business schools repeatedly welcome John to dispense highly practical advice to MBA students so that they become more employable in the right role sooner, while MBA graduates find his invaluable wisdom and experience sound counsel to develop the next stage of their careers.'

Steve Gorton, Trustee Director,
Association of MBAs

'John's ability in this book, to unlock the secrets of finding a satisfying job have been invaluable to me and many others. His practical, no-nonsense, common sense and simple techniques help bring clarity and order, and demystify one of the most important steps that any of us will take towards finding a more rewarding life.'

Tim Franklin, Coach, Consultant, Non Exec
Director of The Post Office
and HM Land Registry

'I've had the pleasure of working with John over several years where he has been a regular speaker at **I Am** events on the theme of finding a job you love. John's talks never fail to inspire; the advice he gives is always very well received, insightful and most importantly, of a practical nature. From both my own personal perspective and that of our delegates, I can't recommend *How to Get a Job You Love* enough!'

Debbie Hockham, Director,
I Am Enterprises

'As a career coach, this is a great book to have by your side – and one to recommend to those you work with. It consistently stimulates, encourages and inspires people to think in new ways about their career.'

**Derek Osborn, Business and
Career Coach, Whatnext4u**

'I frequently recommend job seekers or those at a career crossroads to read *How to Get a Job You Love* as it offers practical and easily accessible advice from someone with vast experience in the area.'

**Joëlle Warren, Managing Director,
Warren Partners Ltd**

'Having changed career three times, I was introduced to this book by an outplacement consultant. I was an IT specialist then, working with the world's largest IT services company. As a careers education manager now, I have enjoyed learning and applying many of the tools and techniques in the successive editions as well as passing them on to countless career changers and more recently students and graduates. This edition will offer you the comfort, assurance and much needed guidance from a trusted friend in these confusing times that you too can find, get or keep … a job you love.'

**Ajaz Hussain, Careers Education Manager,
GSM London and Visiting Tutor (Careers),
Lancaster University Management School**

'John Lees' approach works, because he gives readers simple, practical steps to help flip their mindsets into the more daring, exploratory and confident mode needed for career transition success.'

**Stuart Lindenfield, Head of Transitions Practice,
Reed Consulting**

'This practical guide is a well-thumbed book in our school careers library. John Lees' advice and guidance is as useful to young people as it is to adults.'
James Brittain, Head of Careers and Higher Education, Millfield School

'John Lees' latest revision of his seminal book both brings it firmly up to date and reinforces its now established special position as a place of reference and unusual insight'.
Stephen Bampfylde, Chairman, Saxton Bampfylde Hever Plc

'I love John's really practical "how to" guides – over the years I have recommended them to clients, family and friends, as they are full of ideas on how to unlock the potential opportunities you have when seeking a job or career change. Life is too short not to love your job and this wonderfully practical book will help you secure the perfect job for you. It is filled with a number of creative tools and techniques that are fun to work through and will provide you with new insights and ideas that will encourage you to think in a whole new way.'
Brigit Egan, Director, Oakridge Training and Consulting

'A wealth of practical suggestions on how to land your dream job.'
Suchi Mukherjee, Managing Director, Gumtree.com

'John Lees advice on careers is always useful and interesting and often surprising and even fascinating. From getting ahead to changing your career completely, this book is great guide to navigating the treacherous waters of the modern workplace.'

Rhymer Rigby, writer of the FT's
Careerist column and author of
28 Business Thinkers Who Changed
The World** and **The Careerist

'When I read John's writing, two things happen. First, I feel as if he's standing right there, personally advising me. And second, I always come away thinking over the issue in a new way. It's a rare, but very useful, gift.'

Sarah Green, Associate Editor,
Harvard Business Review

'I know first hand the joy that being in the right career can bring and I commend John Lees for his books and seminars which help other people do just that.'

Rosemary Conley CBE

'John Lees is the career professional's professional; the doyen of careers experts. His books and advice have helped countless numbers of people to enjoy better, more fulfilling careers.'

Dr Harry Freedman, Career and Business
Strategist, Hanover Executive

PRAISE FOR *KNOCKOUT CV*

'A comprehensive and practical guide to building a relevant, evidence-based CV which will win the recruiter's attention. Looks afresh at the role of your CV, the pitfalls to avoid and shares invaluable recruiter insights.'

Liz Mason, Associate Director, Alumni Career Services, London Business School

'You write a CV for a purpose – to get a job. *Knockout CV* works backwards from the desired result, analysing each feature of the CV from the perspective of impact on the decision-maker. No frills, no diversions, simply full of practical help.'

Shirley Anderson, HR Director, Talent and Reward, Pilkington Group Limited

'John has produced an honest and authentic approach to creating a winning CV which speaks to your strengths, and will make the difference to getting noticed and in front of the selection panel. Yes, you can expect to work some, however John's advice plus your investment in time will produce a great result with the critical bonus of mental and emotional clarity over your next (right) career move.'

Angella Clarke-Jervois, Big 4 Partner Recruiter and International Career Coach

PRAISE FOR *JOB INTERVIEWS: TOP ANSWERS TO TOUGH QUESTIONS*

'As a careers adviser, I often find that clients know that preparation is the key to a successful interview but are unsure where to start. John Lees deals with this clearly and comprehensively. This book is based on real evidence gained from employers and this new edition has been comprehensively updated. I would recommend the book for anyone who is anxious about interviews and to people applying for any level of job, regardless of how much interview experience they may have.'

David Levinson, Assistant Director, Newcastle University Careers Service

'Once again, John shows how to be at your very best in front of a prospective employer. This latest edition covers every aspect of interview preparation and is a must-read for anyone in job search. As ever, his advice is eminently practical and accessible, delivered in a caring and supportive voice that will resonate with all readers and encourage them to embrace every job search opportunity.'

Sophie Rowan, Coaching Psychologist at Pinpoint, author of *Brilliant Career Coach*

'John's book is a great asset to anyone who fears the interview process. As well as some very practical and useful exercises, designed to help capture powerful information and to get you thinking, he gives a fascinating insight into the psychological processes, making it much easier to understand and put yourself into the shoes of the interviewer. John's style is very accessible, demonstrating his years of experience and translating it into an easy-to-read collection of hints, tips and guidance. I suspect a lot of interviewers will also want to use this book to help them raise their game!'

Kerwin Hack, Consultant Director, Fairplace Cedar

FURTHER PRAISE FOR JOHN LEES' WRITING

'For years, John Lees has been the smartest voice in career coaching. His insight and advice are a must-read for anyone entering today's competitive job market.'

Rebecca Alexander, Dossier Editor, *Psychologies* magazine

'John Lees is a purveyor of sound, no-nonsense career advice which delivers results – whatever your age or status.'

Carol Lewis, Business Features Editor, *The Times*

'The popularity of John Lees' writing lies in his ability to connect with the sense many people have that they can be more than they currently are, and deserve greater job satisfaction than they currently have. What makes his work distinctive is his use of his wide experience in careers coaching to provide tools and ways of thinking that any motivated individual can easily use to take control of their working life.'

Carole Pemberton, Career and Executive Coach and author of *Coaching to Solutions*

'You can't buy this kind of valuable intelligence ... very accessible and free of the jargonistic tripe that all too often fills career books.'

able *Pathfinder* magazine

How to Get a Job You Love

2015–16 Edition

John Lees

The **McGraw·Hill** Companies

London • Boston • Burr Ridge, IL • Dubuque, IA • Madison WI • New York
San Francisco • St. Louis • Bangkok • Bogotá • Caracas • Kuala Lumpur
Lisbon • Madrid • Mexico City • Milan • Montreal • New Delhi • Santiago
Seoul • Singapore • Sydney • Taipei • Toronto

How to Get a Job You Love
2015–16 Edition
John Lees

ISBN: 9780077164096
e-ISBN: 9780077164102

Published by McGraw-Hill Professional
Shoppenhangers Road
Maidenhead
Berkshire
SL6 2QL
Telephone: 44 (0) 1628 502 500
Fax: 44 (0) 1628 770 224
Website: www.mcgraw-hill.co.uk

British Library Cataloguing in Publication Data
A catalogue record for this book is available from the British Library

Library of Congress Cataloguing in Publication Data
The Library of Congress data for this book
is available from the Library of Congress

Typeset by Gray Publishing, Tunbridge Wells, Kent
Cover design by Two Associates

McGraw-Hill books are available at special quantity discounts.
Please contact the Corporate Sales Executive

Printed and bound by CPI Group (UK) Ltd, Croydon, CR0 4YY

Foreword

You would not believe how many career and job-hunting books cross my path each year. New ones appear at my door week by week. All of them have some good ideas, of course, but only a few really stand out. John Lees' classic work here, now in its eighth edition – yes, eighth – is one of those. I cannot recommend it highly enough. It is thorough, inventive, truth-telling and helpful. I have known John, and this book, for a long, long time. John was a student of mine, twice in fact, back when dinosaurs were still roaming the earth. He was already well known for his distinguished career, but since then he has, as we say, gone from strength to strength. We have stayed in touch all these years, in spite of the fact that I live across the pond (in San Francisco Bay area, to be exact).

John is one of those people in life who is thoroughly worth staying in touch with. His integrity is rock-solid, he is always anxious to help as many people as possible, he is thoroughly grounded in a faith that means something, and he is an expert in his field. You want a book from such a man, you *hope for* a book from such a man. And, thank the good Lord, here it is.

Now used by countless numbers of people who found themselves helped by the wisdom in these pages, this book is a treasure. Read it, devour it, use it, and find that job you once dreamed about but had almost given up on. Time to revive your dreams. This book will give you chariots to ride.

Richard Nelson Bolles, author of
What Color Is Your Parachute? A Practical Manual
for Job-hunters and Career-changers

About the author

John Lees is one of the UK's best known career strategists. *How to Get a Job You Love* regularly tops the list as the best selling careers book by a British author, and along with *Job Interviews: Top Answers to Tough Questions* has been selected as WHSmith's 'Business Book of the Month'.

As a career and outplacement coach, John specialises in helping people to make difficult career decisions – difficult either because they don't know what to do next or because there are barriers in the way of success. John Lees Associates helps career changers across the UK, and John has presented at conferences and events in the USA, Switzerland, South Africa, Australia and New Zealand.

John is the author of a wide range of career titles. His books have been translated into Arabic, Polish and Spanish. He has written a regular column in *Metro* and *People Management* and thought leadership pieces for *The Guardian* and *The Times*. He is regularly featured in the national press and his work has been profiled in *Management Today, Psychologies, Coaching at Work* and *The Sunday Times*. John broadcasts widely and has contributed to the BBC interactive *Back to Work* series programme, BBC2's *Working Lunch*, Channel 4's *Dispatches* and ITV's *Tonight – How to Get a Job*. He is a regular blog contributor to *Harvard Business Review* online and in 2012 wrote the introduction to the *HBR Guide to Getting the Right Job*.

John is a graduate of the universities of Cambridge, London and Liverpool, and has spent most of his career focusing on the world of work. He has trained recruitment specialists since the mid-1980s, and is the former Chief Executive of the Institute of Employment Consultants (now the IRP). John Lees Associates provides one-to-one career coaching in most parts of the UK. John has worked on career management projects with a wide range of organisations including: British Gas Commercial, The British Council, the Chartered Institute of Personnel and Development (CIPD), Fairplace, Harrods, Hiscox, the House of Commons, Imperial College, the Association of MBAs, Lloyds Banking Group, Marks & Spencer, NAPP Pharmaceutical, Oakridge, Tribal, as well as business schools across the UK. John is a Fellow of the CIPD and an Honorary Fellow of the Institute of Recruitment Professionals, and was a founding Board Director of the Career Development Institute.

Alongside his careers work, John serves as an ordained Anglican priest. He is married to the poet and children's writer Jan Dean, sharing time between Cheshire and Devon (with occasional visits from their two adult sons).

Contact John Lees Associates for details of our career management services and John's workshops at the website **www.johnleescareers.com** or follow John on Twitter **@JohnLeesCareers**.

johnlees
associates

Acknowledgements

With age comes, perhaps later than it should, a realisation of those many people I haven't thanked enough.

I owe a huge debt to Richard Nelson Bolles, author of the world-famous *What Color Is Your Parachute?* My work as a career strategist was inspired by the creativity, wisdom and generosity of 125 hours' teaching from Dick at two of his summer workshops in Oregon, USA, and over a decade of encouragement and support.

My thanks go to everyone who has published my thinking about careers in the media since the last edition including: Rebecca Alexander (*Psychologies*), Daniel Allen (*The Times*), Tom Banham, Ted Lane, Ed Vanstone (*Men's Health*), Rachel Burge (*Career Builder*), Elizabeth Eyre (*Training Journal*), Alexander Garrett (*Management Today*), Amy Gallo, Sarah Green, Tim Sullivan (*Harvard Business Review* online), Will Ham Bevan, Nick Morrison (*The Telegraph*), Rhymer Rigby (*Financial Times*), Martin Stevens (*Metro*), Neil Boorman, Thomas Watson (*Total Jobs*), Kate Hodge, Clare Whitmell (*The Guardian* online), Alison Dixon (*Career Matters*) and Linda Whitney (*Daily Mail*).

I'm also grateful to those who have let me road-test ideas with different audiences: Liz Baldwin (Harvard Business Press), Jane Chanaa and Jennie Courtney (University of Oxford), Paula Eccles (Aston Business School), David Eade (Nottingham Trent University), Mark Burbridge and Brigit Egan (Oakridge), Janice Chalmers (Kingston

Business School), Julian Childs and Matthias Feist (Regent's University London), Lindsay Comalie (Imperial College), Laura DeCarlo (CDI, USA), Jan Ellis (Career Development Institute), Graeme Dixon and Steve Gorton (AMBA), Lizzie Gossling and John Bound (RCA Fuel), Liz Hall (Coaching At Work), Deborah Hockham (I Am Events), Marcia Hoynes (Durham University Business School), Stuart Lindenfield and Ian Nicholas (Reed), Rosemary McLean (Career Development Institute), Kim Morgan (Barefoot Coaching), Gillian Stark (3 Monkeys), Phil Steele (Hiscox), Rob Nathan (CCS), Janie Wilson (Can Do It Now), Clare Witheycombe (British Council) and Penny de Valk (Fairplace/Penna).

My appreciation goes out to everyone else who has shared great ideas or asked good questions: Steven Benson, Roger Bicknell, Jo Bond, Richard Braybrooke, Marie Brett, Jim Bright, Catherine Brooks, Simon Broomer, Claire Coldwell, Zena Everett, Peter Fennah, Helen Green, Peter Hawkins, Barrie Hopson, Caroline Humphries, David Levinson, Stuart McIntosh, Brian McIvor, Amiel Osmaston, Bernard Pearce, Carole Pemberton, Daniel Porot, Stuart Robertson, Robin Rose, Sophie Rowan, Sital Ruparelia, Michael Spayne, Philip Spencer, Joëlle Warren, Ian Webb, John Whapham, Ruth Winden, and fellow members of the LinkedIn Career Coach Forum.

My special thanks go to several people. To Kate Howlett, Managing Consultant at John Lees Associates for all her perceptivity, good business sense and encouragement. To Gill Best for everything she does as friend, wise counsel, and fellow traveller. To Trevor Gilbert for being a great business mentor earlier in my career. To my brother Andrew Lees for his insights into the way scientists think. To Stephanie Clarke for her diligent research, and to Jane Bartlett and Stuart Mitchell for reviewing the first edition of this book. To the whole McGraw-Hill team for their creativity in coaxing this eighth edition into daylight, particularly Priyanka Gibbons and Katherine Wood, with continuing appreciation to my first commissioning editor, Elizabeth Choules. To my agent James Wills at Watson, Little for his unstinting support. And, with sadness, to friend and talented publicist Sue Blake (1961–2012), without whom it wouldn't have been half as much fun.

This book, like all previous editions, is dedicated to someone who has been special to me for a very long time. To my wife, Jan, for giving me space to find out.

Other careers books by John Lees published by McGraw-Hill Professional

Knockout CV: How to Get Noticed, Get Interviewed & Get Hired **(2013), £8.99, ISBN 9780077152857**
Building on an extensive review of what employers love and hate about CVs, helps you to decide which CV format will work best. How to write CVs and covering letters that convey your strengths quickly and get you into the interview room.

Job Interviews: Top Answers to Tough Questions **(2012), £7.99, ISBN 9780077141608**
Lists 225 interview questions typically asked by employers and recruiters, including the kind that will throw you completely unless you have prepared carefully. Also, a range of tips about multi-strategy job search and using your CV in the interview process.

Career Reboot: 24 Tips for Tough Times **(2009), £6.99, ISBN 9780077127589**
Packed with quick-read, practical tips for rejuvenating your job search, this book is a must for anyone striking out into a difficult job market after redundancy or simply looking for new opportunities in a difficult market.

Take Control of Your Career **(2006), £12.99, ISBN 9780077109677**
How to manage your career once you've got a job, learning how to read your organisation, avoid career traps, renegotiate your job role and enhance your future without losing control of your life balance.

Contents

Foreword by Richard Nelson Bolles   iii

About the author   iv

Acknowledgements   vi

How to use this book   xi

1   Can you really get a job you *love*?   1

2   What problems are you trying to fix?   14

3   First steps towards change   31

4   Thinking around corners   44

5   Your career hot buttons   58

6   Making sense of your skills   70

7   Your House of Knowledge   90

8   The personality dimension   96

9   Matching yourself to work you will enjoy   121

10   How do I change career?   144

11   Job searching creatively and effectively   166

12   Online presence and searching   189

13   Networking and information interviews   206

14   Job interviews: tipping the odds in your
          favour   224

15   Your first 90 days and beyond   244

16   From part-time to portfolio: rethinking   253
          career choice

17   Starting your career after finishing study   265

          Appendix 1 CV and covering letter tips   281

          *Appendix 2 People who have transformed
                       their careers*   289

          Appendix 3 Useful websites   298

          Index   304

How to use this book

Who is this book for?

This book is written for anyone who is trying to make conscious, informed decisions about career choice. This book can help you if you are:

- feeling 'stuck' and looking for new challenges, and wondering 'what on earth can I do?'
- ready to plan the next stage of your career
- facing redundancy and asking 'what do I do next?'
- leaving full-time education or seeking work after bringing up a family
- unemployed and looking for better ways of identifying opportunities
- seeking work and are short of ideas about job possibilities
- discouraged because you believe that you have little to offer the labour market
- exploring the idea of finding a completely new career.

How this book might help you

There are many 'how to' books about career change and job search. If you're looking for boxes to tick, 'to do' checklists, model CVs or letters, look at one of the hundreds of books available that will give you an organised, left-brain solution to career management. We all need good advice when it comes to managing our job search. These books work well if you have a clear sense of direction, and all you need is a more effective job search technique. However, they don't help answer the most common career statement: 'I know I want to do something different, but I don't know what it is.' And just as important, the question: 'How do I take the first step towards making a change?'

The chapters ahead do something different. In these pages you will look at the way businesses and individuals generate ideas about products, services and organisations, and apply that creative energy to career planning. It will challenge your perceived limitations and help you to discover your strengths.

This book aims to unlock your hidden potential and apply it to your career and life planning, to make the way you spend your waking hours more creative, more meaningful, more enjoyable. Its focus is not on job change for its own sake. Quite simply, the aim is to help you to make connections between your natural creativity and the way you plan your life's work. As a result of reading it, you may discover tools to improve your present job and create career opportunities where you are now. Alternatively, you will find practical advice about making your chosen future happen.

Does the approach work? Appendix 2 looks at people who have used the book to help them to make significant career changes.

You may find that a single exercise unlocks your potential, or you may gain multiple insights from using several ideas or exercises. One word of advice: if the exercise doesn't work for you, don't feel you have 'failed'. All it means is this: *the exercise doesn't work for you.* Put it aside and move on.

Maps for the journey ahead

Chapter 1, **Can you really get a job you *love?*,** asks important questions about balancing work satisfaction against job market reality, taking a sideways look at work in a competitive market. Chapter 2 asks **what problems are you trying to fix?** What's preventing you from getting a job you love? and Chapter 3 moves you forward in your **first steps towards change.** Chapter 4 invites you to begin using creative strategies to revive your career by **thinking around corners.**

Chapters 5–8 offer you an opportunity to understand yourself better and catalogue your **career drivers,** your chosen areas of **knowledge,** your preferred and hidden **skills,** and the key aspects of **personality** that will shape your career.

If you're thinking about career change, look at Chapters 9 and 10, including the **Field Generator** – a ground-breaking tool to generate potential fields of work (Chapter 10). Check out Chapter 16 on the range of working models you might consider, including a portfolio career.

Next, some highly practical advice on getting results in the job market: Chapters 11–13 give you a complete overview of creative job searching, the pros and cons of using the internet, and how to broaden your network. Chapter 14, **Job interviews: tipping the odds in your favour,** does exactly what it says on the tin.

Career development is about much more than job search, so in Chapter 15 you will read about managing the first 90 days in the job and also longer term career management, including tips for renegotiating your job.

Chapter 17, **Starting your career after finishing study,** is written specially for those who will shortly be graduating or leaving full-time education.

We close with three appendices covering CV and covering letter tips, stories from people who have changed their careers using this book, and a list of recommended websites.

New in this edition

This new and substantially revised edition provides the biggest update to *How to Get a Job You Love* for over a decade (even the title has changed very slightly – 'you'll love' simplified to 'you love'). It gives even greater emphasis to the big problems people experience when they ask the question 'what kind of career would suit me best?'

Brand new in this edition:

- Features of the new marketplace as we emerge from recession – staying in a dull job too long, and how you explain putting your career on hold since 2008.
- Changes in how people find jobs – coping with the complexity and opacity of the job market.
- Material on what will shorten (or extend) your job search.
- How and why people make the same mistakes as first-time job seekers.
- New exercises to draw out **skills** and **values**, and a revised **career hot buttons** exercise.
- New material on how employers prefer to recruit and their risk avoidance strategies.
- Up-to-date advice on interview preparation from recruitment experts.
- Expert advice on handling formal assessments and dealing with executive recruiters.
- Update on CVs and how they are constructed and read by employers.
- Refreshed overview of portfolio careers and self-employment.
- Refreshed and updated material on using the internet and social media.
- New thinking on personal branding and the way we plant key pieces of information about ourselves to build personal reputations.
- Advice on your first 90 days in a new role.
- Up-to-date advice for those leaving full-time education and embarking on a job search for the first time.

Can you really get a job you *love*?

'There is no point in work unless it absorbs you like an absorbing game.' **D.H. Lawrence**

This chapter helps you to:

- Look at what has happened to career thinking in a flat economy
- Understand how self-managed careers are becoming increasingly necessary
- Explore how you make career decisions
- Start to think about talking about where your career went during the recession
- Learn creative career management

Managing your career in demanding times

This chapter provides an overview of what work is about in the second decade of the twenty-first century, and whether we can hope to be happy in it.

I have occasionally had the interesting experience of standing next to someone picking up a copy of this book and showing it to a friend. 'A job you love ... hmm.' It's fascinating to hear what comes next. One of these two people is quite likely to say something along the lines of 'get real!' The other is likely to carry on reading the contents page.

Writing a book titled *How to Get a Job You Love* requires a little nerve as we gradually emerge from an extended downturn, this period that Americans call the Great Recession. I'm humbled that the book still sells. My firm belief is that in difficult times it's important to hang on to more than a sprinkling of optimistic thinking – having a sense of what an ideal job might feel like provides the energy to drive the long slog of exploration and applications. Besides, as a number of readers kindly remind me every year, looking for the right job is important, whatever the state of the economy.

Where are the jobs hiding?

At the beginning of the recession I was asked to write a New Year essay for *The Guardian*. In it I looked not just at the state of the market, but also at career strategies. When the stock market is buoyed up by mergers and acquisitions and employers are expanding, there are usually enough jobs around. Even the relatively passive job seeker will usually find something. Jobs are visible, because many of them are advertised.

When organisations started to shrink, jobs seemed to disappear suddenly. In fact, they went underground. One of the confusing features of today's marketplace is the way that jobs are increasingly filled by low-cost, low-visibility, informal methods (see Chapter 11 on the hidden job market). Today far more responsibility falls on the shoulders of individuals to take the helm and set their own career direction.

Everyone knows someone who has experienced redundancy or coped with cutbacks. Some have been forced to change jobs, often with difficulty; others have had to apply for the job they already hold. Redundancies have hit all sectors and regions. This has its positive side: employers see many candidates who have experienced redundancy, so the stigma of being 'let go' has largely disappeared (unless *you* make an issue of the topic, as discussed later). Some parts of the working population have taken a real hit, particularly 16–24 year olds, but the market has been tough on workers over 50 too. Underemployment is as big a problem as unemployment.

Confidence about long-term job security has certainly weakened. The *Employee Outlook* published by the CIPD in Autumn 2013 stated, for example, that 23% of workers in the public sector felt it was likely or very likely they would lose their jobs. Unsurprisingly, those who felt insecure in their jobs also felt less engaged. However, times appear to be changing as the report adds that 'planned redundancies, pay freezes and reduction to employee benefits are all on the decrease' in the private sector. The report concludes: 'the findings are showing real indications that talent is preparing to be on the move again and that employees in general are feeling more optimistic about the jobs marketplace – a signal which organisations should not take too lightly'.

Where organisations have restructured extensively, the psychological contract has clearly been weakened, if not torn up. As the market picks up we are likely to see a considerable increase in job movements. The UK recruitment industry grew by 3.5% in the year to April 2013. At November 2013 there were 1.1 million agency temporary workers, about 4% of the total workforce. According to the Recruitment and Employment Confederation, the UK recruitment market was already predicted to surpass its pre-recession peak by the end of 2014.

Seeing the whole picture

Every job market has its paradoxes. It's also important to distinguish between what has actually happened and the way we feel about it. Many employers have complained of the skill shortages throughout the recession (a CIPD survey in 2012 revealed that no less than 82% of employers were experiencing 'recruitment difficulties'). Some sectors run against the trend and have experienced continuous growth throughout the past decade.

Although newspaper headlines are perpetually gloomy, the UK maintained relatively high levels of employment during the recession. In June 2013, for example, there were 40.2 million people in the UK aged 16–64, of whom 28.2 million were employed – a high proportion of the working-age population compared to other countries (Office for National Statistics data). Although unemployment increased during the recession, the UK experienced levels of employment that many of our European neighbours would have envied during the boom years. According to the Institute of Employment Studies, approximately five to six million people begin new jobs every year in the UK. This includes job changers as well as market entrants, but the truth is that even in a downturn a lot of people are moving in the jobs market.

New conditions, new thinking

The downturn has had a positive effect for some people. Some people are saying 'if I'm going to lose my job I might as well find something interesting'. Naturally, there have also been a good number of people saying 'I just need any kind of job', but often that simply reflects a low point in their job search cycle – they quickly discover that this undifferentiated message puts them at the bottom of shortlists.

What's happening inside organisations is in some ways a good indication of how we should operate when trying to get into them. Organisations have become leaner, with fewer rungs on the ladder and therefore fewer options for promotion. Individuals often have to make lateral moves to new divisions or teams in order to advance, often relying heavily on inside information and the support of champions and mentors. These pathways are certainly not textbook, and not clear when you join an organisation. Lateral moves require lateral thinking, and your employer probably won't do it for you.

Compared to a generation ago, few employees believe that their organisations will manage their careers for them. In every recession an increasing number of people turn to self-employment, and the recent one has enlarged our interest in 'alternative' careers (see the discussion on portfolio careers in Chapter 16).

What did you do in the Great Recession, Mummy?

During the extended downturn in our economy people have adopted a wide range of career strategies. Some have kept their heads down, hiding inside large organisations and working just hard enough to make sure they were retained. For the past three years or more they have probably not been stretched very much. Others have taken lower status or entry-level jobs to pay the bills. For many, the strategy has been to lie low and ride out the storm. We are good at avoiding career responsibility, so the recession has become the nation's new favourite excuse for passive career behaviour.

As the market picks up many of these candidates are going to find it hard to present their CVs. While others in the marketplace have been keeping their skills up to date and gaining the right experience, some have effectively allowed their careers to stand still for a number of years. When asked about their learning, their challenges and their career plan, their answers will be variants on 'I played safe', sounding very passive.

If this describes your career history for the past few years, how are you going to handle it? There are ways of making your choice sound less passive, less defeatist. You can, for example, focus on the benefits of continuity, and the things you learned by staying with projects over the long term. You may have to dig deeper to find evidence of where you have developed your skills – just because evidence is hard to find doesn't mean it's not there. Present what you did as a conscious choice ('I decided it would be better to remain in the role and see how I could develop it …') so you don't sound like one of the many people who are coming back to the market after being in hiding for five years or more.

Watch this space: when employers are desperate for staff again and it becomes a seller's market for candidates, we will find other excuses for living an indifferent career.

Is work that important?

Judging by the amount of time spent complaining about work, it must be. If it wasn't for work, we would have far less to moan about. We put a huge amount of energy into work, and rely on it for a large chunk of our self-esteem. For this reason alone, unemployment and underemployment are damaging. Being underemployed is as worrying as being jobless: people who are underemployed or in the wrong kind of work become demotivated, depressed or even ill. Work matters. Finding the right kind of work matters even more.

If we begin with life and work, we should ask ourselves one question: do you **work to live** or **live to work**? If you believe that you **work to live** you may be more motivated by the things you do outside work than the things which earn you a living. You are living out your dream in a different reality, and your salary is there simply to fund your dream. A lot of people live that way, and can be happy.

The problem is that this ignores the huge amount of time that work consumes. If you work full-time hours, you spend more of your life in work than in any other waking activity (if you live for 70 years, you'll spend about 23 of those years asleep and 16 years working). Accounted for in another way, you will spend about 100,000 hours in work. (That's just what Americans call 'face time', the time when your jacket is on the back of your chair. Just think about all the other hours that go into preparing for work, worrying about work, complaining about work and so on.)

If you feel that you **live to work**, it may be that you've found the best job in the world, or perhaps you haven't explored enough to find out what life has to offer. Perhaps work plays too important a part in your life? Those who suffer the greatest impact of redundancy are those who have made their work their only focus, perhaps at the expense of family or personal development.

One definition of the word 'career' is *move in an uncontrolled direction*, as in 'the steering failed and my car careered across the motorway'. Random movement in an uncontrolled direction. Does that sound familiar?

The days of your life

In the past decade or so we have got used to the idea that we can make life choices – about how we live, the things around us, the activities that fill our days. Here's another perspective. In an average lifetime (according to the Office for National Statistics), a woman will live for about 29,800 days. Men get rather less, about 28,200 days. That's around 29,000 days to learn, work, play, raise a family, leave your mark on life and acquire wisdom. It doesn't sound many days does it? Certainly not a lot of time to be saying 'this isn't what I wanted to do when I grew up …'. How you spend those days matters, no matter what your spiritual perspective.

Why should people be happy at work?

It's easy to believe that work is not somewhere you are supposed to enjoy yourself. You can easily create a world of compartments: *This is the compartment where I work. This is my family compartment. This small compartment in the corner is where I really enjoy myself.* It's all part of that either/or thinking we're so good at. I have *either* a job that pays the bills, *or* a job that's fun. I can't have both.

Career development specialist Carole Pemberton talks about the Faustian pact we make in our careers – a deal you make that allows you to think in these either/or terms, like Faust's pact with the devil. A pact typically says 'I can only be successful if …'. Here are some examples: 'I can only be a top salesperson if I work long hours and eat badly.' 'I can only be a great manager if I don't empathise with my staff.'

Why should people be happy at work? Work isn't fun, your friends will tell you. Work is real. If this all sounds reasonable, look at the people who seem to have most fun in their jobs. They're often running their own businesses, making new things, meeting new people, sharing what they know and inspiring people. Sometimes they are in jobs that directly improve the lives of others. For some, it's about producing brilliant ideas, products or great experiences for customers. Are these workers poor as a result? Sometimes. However, some of them are richer and more successful than most. Happiness and success don't always come hand in hand, but on the other hand being unhappy is no automatic route to success either. Unfortunately it's often the unhappy, unenthusiastic, low-energy people that companies get rid of first.

Why should people be happy at work? Take a deep breath. Read that question again. Work is where you spend most of your waking life. It's where you put about 80% of your personal energy. It may be one of the things in life that contributes most to self-esteem and a sense of fulfilment. Work matters. For today's workplace, choosing how you spend Monday to Friday is probably one of the most important life decisions you make.

So the question *why should people be happy at work?* really means why should people be happy? What do you think?

Do happy people live longer, have great children and make a difference? You know they do. So let's stop that all-time Faustian deal: 'I can only get a great job if I forget about being happy at work.' That's a self-fulfilling deal. Be careful what you ask for in life, you might just get it.

'One of the symptoms of an approaching nervous breakdown is the belief that one's work is terribly important.' **Bertrand Russell**

Happiness – goal or accident?

Are some occupations more satisfying than others? We seem to have a constant fascination with the worst jobs in society, but research published in 2007 by the Economic and Social Research Council's Future of Work Programme identified that some jobs are more likely to lead to job satisfaction. It seems that medical secretaries, childcare workers, cleaners, clergy, various managers and those offering personal services such as healthcare, travel and catering get top place. Low job satisfaction levels are recorded among journalists, mining surveyors, postal workers and civil service executive officers. (For what it's worth, telecoms engineers declared themselves Britain's unhappiest employees.)

It's worth saying a little more about happiness. Many of us think that happiness is a vague, subjective and entirely individual state of mind. Others believe that we can do very little to influence or adjust happiness.

Richard Layard's book *Happiness: Lessons from a New Science* (2005) is one of several that reflect on the research undertaken into what makes some communities and some nations happier than others. This research begins with the principle that when people say they are generally happy or very happy in life, this is something that can be measured. Layard looks at the major factors in life that contribute to happiness, and the results are fascinating. First, being happy seems to contribute directly to good health. Second, being rich doesn't make people any happier. Many countries in the developing world with low income levels per capita are just as content as developed nations, and in some cases happier. Internationally, as Layard writes, 'above $20,000 per head, higher average income is no guarantee of greater happiness … extra dollars make less difference if you are rich than if you're poor'.

Layard defines his 'Big 7' factors that affect happiness:

1. **Family relationships** – countries with the highest rates of divorce and family break-up have relatively unhappy populations.
2. **Financial situation** – not earning enough for your needs, or feeling pressurised to earn competitively for reasons of status, tends to lead to less happiness.
3. **Work** – being underemployed or economically inactive makes us unhappy; doing relatively fulfilling work acts as a positive. Layard writes: 'When people become unemployed, their happiness falls much less because of the loss of income than because of the loss of work itself.'
4. **Community and friends** – having active friendship groups and being involved in community activity and associations increases happiness.
5. **Health** – ill-health, particularly where it involves pain and distress, naturally leads to unhappiness.
6. **Personal freedom** – having some independence in our life decisions helps us to be happy.
7. **Personal values** – being of service to others, contributing to society and having a personal faith are all factors that increase happiness.

It's worth revisiting what Layard has to say about work:

'Work is vital, if that is what you want. But it is also important that the work is fulfilling. Perhaps the most important issue is the extent to which you have control over what you do. There is a creative spark in each of us, and if it finds no outlet, we feel half-dead. This can be literally true: among British civil servants of any given grade, those who do the most routine work experience the most rapid clogging of the arteries.' **Richard Layard**, in *Happiness: Lessons from a New Science* (Allen Lane, 2005)

Exercise 1.1 – Time balance

How would you like your time to be balanced in your ideal job?

Starting with the job you're in now (or one you left recently) estimate what percentage of your time you spend in each activity over the course of a month or so. Then in the right-hand column state your ideal percentage. Each column should add up to 100.

Experienced reality (%)		Ideal reality (%)
	Working entirely alone Working on my own without distraction. Working things out, being given space to sort out a problem or finish a piece of work, writing something, having time to reflect ...	
	Working independently but close to colleagues Being responsible for own results but having colleagues around. Having ready access to the ideas and encouragement of other people ...	
	Working 1:1 Explaining, persuading, influencing, selling, coaching, managing, teaching ...	

	Attending meetings Meeting to deal with agendas, share information, and make collective decisions …	
	Working in active teams Group problem solving, planning brainstorming ideas, reviewing, getting things done, training, motivating …	
	Extending your network Telephoning new contacts, networking, meeting plenty of new people, going to conferences, seminars …	
	Working with an audience Public speaking, performing, entertaining, giving talks, informing larger groups …	
100%	**Total**	**100%**

When you have completed the time balance exercise above, compare your experience with your ideal picture. This isn't self-indulgence or fantasy – it's a healthy recognition of how you work at your best. Look at the activities where you spend most of your time. Which would you like to increase or decrease, substantially? What difference would that make to your effectiveness?

'Must do' list

- ✓ Reflect: have your career decisions been made consciously, or have you largely responded to opportunity and chance? How much of your career is about regret or missed opportunity?
- ✓ Think about how you can use this book to help. Begin a hardback notebook to jot down your discoveries and the results of the exercises in this book. Write down the steps you need to take in the next two months. Then take step one.
- ✓ Plan ahead. Look at the chapter headings and decide how and when you are going to set aside time to go through this process.
- ✓ Use the **time balance** exercise to get a broad picture of what your ideal job would look like in terms of activities.
- ✓ Identify someone you know who has very clearly taken control of their career. Find out their first steps, how they made change happen, and how they sustain their energy.

What problems are you trying to fix?

> 'The minute you begin to do what you really want to do, it's really a different kind of life.' **Buckminster Fuller**

This chapter looks at the following:

- The reason careers go off-line
- Why people follow careers they hate, and fail to get careers they would love
- Working out how far you are from your dream job – and what you can do about it
- The blocks between you and a great career
- Overcoming personal barriers

I don't have time for a career crisis ...

How many times have you heard someone talking about where they have 'ended up'? The truth is that most people are very passive about their career choices and leave job satisfaction very much to chance. It's easy to shrug off responsibility with a phrase like *A job's a job. It pays the bills.* We are getting used to the idea of job mobility, and some people are changing jobs ever more frequently. New occupations are opening up all the time, and people are sampling a whole range of them during the course of a single 'career'. Does this mean that people are happier in work or better at choosing career paths? It seems not. According to the US writer Studs Terkel, work is, for some, 'a Monday to Friday sort of dying'.

Where do the days go?

One of the impacts of the recession on working life is that some people are working fewer hours than they would like. However, the CIPD reported in 2010 that 'around one in five people work 45 hours or more per week'. Research published by recruitment firm Randstad in 2013 found that only six out of ten workers are happy with their life–work balance.

Studies on job satisfaction show that over the past 20 years or so we have become increasingly unhappy at work, and one of the most common reasons quoted is long working hours. There are other factors too: people seem to have increased expectations of what their careers will provide; others are fazed by two decades of downsizing and job uncertainty. While some people are burdened by overwork and in danger of burnout, others have no work. It matters more than ever that we have a toolkit to help us to find a job we enjoy.

The good, the bad and the just plain awful

In 2013, Gallup reported that worldwide only 13% of employees are engaged at work; that is, psychologically committed to their roles and unlikely to leave if an opportunity presented itself. In Western Europe the comparative figure was 14%. Interestingly, the same Gallup survey also indicated that two-thirds of engaged US workers would continue in their jobs if they won a $10 million lottery. Clearly work motivation is a complicated arena.

What are the things at work that give you the greatest buzz? The sort of things you go home and talk about? Write them down. It's worth recording the good things. Take a blank piece of paper and divide it into three. Write down everything that matters under each heading:

1. **The really good stuff.**   Things you find stimulating and enjoyable.

2. **Things I could live without.**   When do you find work boring or dull?

3. **Things I put up with at work that I need like a hole in the head.**   What aspects of work fill you with dread or loathing?

Exercise 2.1 – How happy are you in your work?

Which category describes your situation best?

Dream job

I can't wait to get into work. Work is the place where I grow and learn most, where I am set healthy challenges, where I am valued and appreciated. A great deal of fun and self-esteem is centred in my work, which fits my values, talents and personality. I know that I make a difference. I express who I am in my job. The rewards are right, and I would be happy to be paid less if necessary. I love the part work plays in my life.

Thumbs up

I enjoy work most of the time, but sometimes there are headaches and problems. My work feels useful and contributes to my self-esteem. My contribution is clear, acknowledged and significant. My career is a good match to my talents, personality and values. I am appreciated by others. I feel that I make a difference, and that I add something positive to the organisation. I find supervision helpful, but my boss is more a mentor than a supervisor. I lead a satisfying career which contributes to all parts of my life.

Mustn't grumble

I accept the work I do. Sometimes I feel valued, other times exploited or ignored. Work is stable, largely unexciting, doesn't interfere with my inner life too much. New ways of doing things are sometimes discouraged. I may be in the right line of work, but in the wrong organisation. I am valued for some of what I do, but not always the most important things.

Someone's got to do it

I work because I need to. I don't feel I owe a great deal to my employer. Several parts of the job are unpleasant/boring/demeaning/pointless. Real life begins at five o'clock. I'm not learning anything. I try to make a contribution but sometimes hit a brick wall. My skills are getting rusty. I would just like a quiet life.

Clock watcher

There are days I almost have to drag myself to work; every day and every moment is miserable. I feel a huge mismatch between the person I am and the person this job requires me to be. I feel trapped. Each day makes things seem worse. I dread the prospect of Monday morning. I take all my sick leave because the job makes me ill.

If you're in the first category, congratulations. Recognise what's good about your work and ensure that it remains that way. Generally, only 30% of people place themselves in the top two groups. Indeed, surveys repeatedly show that as many as 70% of people are unhappy with the work they do. If you're in the 'clock watcher' box, make a review of how you can change things. Soon. You may not find a dream job tomorrow, but moving up the scale is possible for most people in work.

Your world view

Careers specialists have long talked about *motivated skills*; in other words, the skills you relish using, the skills you would exercise for next to nothing, even for free. There's a huge difference between doing something because you know how and doing something because you actively choose to do so. That difference is the power of motivation. Motivation turns a task into a joy, an errand into a quest, a job into a vocation.

The key ingredient in your career exploration is the degree of motivation you apply to the process. *You get out what you put in*. Read that last sentence again. Your success in gaining a stunning career depends as much on your own personal motivation as it does on any other combination of factors, internal or external. And that's not all. Some of the satisfaction you will get from career exploration and success will be about meeting other people, finding out about them, making connections and – occasionally – helping others out. So here's another important reminder in a rather self-focused age: one of the strongest factors affecting happiness is about having the opportunity to help other people. As you set out on the journey this book offers you, consider from the start that some of the best parts of the process will be those moments when you help someone else.

You will, of course, be more use to others when you are able to help yourself. Let's start by looking at your career motivation. Think about your **world view** – your internal working model of how life operates. What makes up that picture? It is built from your earliest influences, memories, the world view held by your parents, and the ups and downs of life. It is often constructed as a reaction to the way that you have been treated. Your world view contains your preconceptions, your fears, your values. A world view is made up of sentences as well as pictures. We have an all-too familiar script running most of the time: 'charity begins at home', 'if you want a job doing properly, do it yourself', 'keep your cards close to your chest'. This world is strongly influenced by the media's constant flow of bad news, but in every generation you will find people who, looking at the same evidence, can justify any world view that appeals – scarcity or abundance, conflict or co-operation, doom or hope. Look closely at the picture you hold of yourself and the script you run in your own personal soap opera. Do you see the glass as half full or half empty?

Ah, that depends … And it does. It depends on the way you look. Look at the signals you receive during the course of a day. How many times do you receive praise and ignore it? How many times do you hear neutral or objective data and take it the wrong way? How often do you hear criticism and clutch it to yourself as the last, final and totally accurate picture of *you*? The reality is that most of us have an impressive talent: to ignore positive information, distort neutral information and attach ourselves to negative information.

Where you put the energy matters. If you put your energy into believing the glass is half empty, what you see is emptiness, absence, insufficiency. If you choose to put your energy into seeing the glass as half full, you will see fullness and abundance everywhere.

Information is neutral. But where do you put your energy and attention? You fill your personal bubble with evidence of what you lack: 'I can't do that …', 'I've never been good at …', 'Nobody's interested in me when I …'. You have a natural, inexhaustible ability to hang on to these favourite ideas. Those who understand the secrets of motivation are generally masters of two areas of personal growth:

- They know who they are, and what they are good at.
- They know when to ignore negative data, when to accept a neutral picture as simply neutral, and when to remember and act on all the good things they ever learned about themselves.

At this point you may be hearing two words in your head: **'yes, but …'**.

About now the **yes, but** area of the brain is kicking in. We all do it. It's a part of the human psyche that psychologist Ned Herrmann called the *safekeeping self,* an idea much beloved and promoted by Richard Nelson Bolles. The safe-keeping self is the senior committee member who faithfully attends every meeting in your brain and says: 'We've heard all this stuff before', 'It'll never fly', 'I'd be taking a risk', 'It might work for somebody else', 'Show me the statistics', 'It might work in London, but …'.

'Yes, but' thinking is the biggest block to career transition. Saying 'yes, but' is a good way of avoiding an issue and avoiding change: 'Yes, but I have to earn a living', 'Yes, but in the real world …'. It's often a sign that the speaker is not listening positively – it's a classic defence mechanism, a way of avoiding having to face issues.

'Normal is getting dressed in clothes that you buy for work, driving through traffic in a car that you are still paying for, in order to get to the job that you need so you can pay for the clothes, car and the house that you leave empty all day in order to afford to live in it.'   **Ellen Goodman**

Problems for the career doctor

Time to discuss your various 'yes, but' symptoms. The career doctor will see you now.

It's a recession, stupid …

Ah yes, the nation's great new excuse: *because we're in a downturn there's no point looking at my career.* No point trying to find something just a little more exciting when everyone has long faces. *And there aren't any jobs out there anyway ….*

At the time this book is going to press it's looking like the real picture is that we are in the process of emerging rather slowly from recession. Finding a job you love for at least half the week is clearly tougher in a restricted economy. Yet there are people making small changes, sometimes even big steps. Every day people leave jobs or retire and new roles are created. What's important is this: *the economy isn't in your head.* If it dictates every choice, every action, your reaction to every opportunity, then you're buying in to the majority view that it's not worth exploring.

I'm indebted to Marie Brett, who told a story at one of our masterclasses for career coaches. She overheard two women on a bus in Northumberland talking about one of their daughters. 'These days,' one explained, 'it's not about what you *want* to do, it's about what you *can* do.' Marie could hear the poor daughter's career derailed in one sentence.

Too long in the same job

The 'same job' could have been a 20-year history of change, variety and development. We're not demotivated by being in one job or one organisation. We're turned off when things start repeating themselves and we're not learning or changing.

Even if you're in a great job that you love doing, you may not want to do it forever. Most careers need a reboot from time to time.

The side benefits are good

In one firm, an employee stayed on for several years because somebody in the office brought in an excellent cake every day. We all have our reasons for staying and our reasons for leaving. The million-dollar question is: are these the *real* reasons? People are very good at finding excuses for avoiding the real issues, or justifying decisions. If you find yourself saying 'the pension scheme/the medical insurance/the gym is so good …' , then the question should be: *but is this why I'm here*? Side benefits go quickly in times of trouble.

Talk to people about their careers after they have retired. Do they talk about the salary and benefits, or do they talk about the good relationships, the fun, the excitement, the feeling of doing meaningful work? When your last day on earth arrives are you going to say 'I wish my pension had been just a bit bigger' or 'Why did I waste 20 years in that office watching the clock?'

I'll stick at it for the moment

'The job's okay, and a lot of things are good about it, and even though it's boring it's a good place to ride out the storm …'. There are a lot of people in the workplace today thinking that way. The problem is that dull jobs create dull people. Once your learning curve has flattened out and the job is no longer challenging, you've accepted another kind of Faustian deal: *I will trade boredom for security.* In addition, you may be setting yourself up for future problems.

If you've kept your head down a bit too long and you're finding it hard to explain why you put your career on hold during the recession, look again at Chapter 1. How will you explain this period of inertia in five years' time when you are in a job interview?

I can't move on

It's all too easy to believe that the only solution to unhappiness at work is job change. Often, all that work dissatisfaction can show you is that there's a mismatch between who you are and what you are doing. That mismatch shows, if not to ourselves, to others. But the real answer is **career growth**: moving towards a closer match between yourself and the work you do. Career growth may be something you can achieve exactly where you are already. Review your current job carefully and ask yourself:

- What parts of the job do I enjoy?
- What parts do I *really* enjoy? When does the time pass quickly?
- If I could change something using a magic wand, would it be the people, the place, the rewards, the tasks I do? Make a list, then look at what you can actually change, and be aware of the difference between what can be changed, and what can't.

I'm too old

Yes, employers are wrong-headed about age. But time and time again they buy experience, know-how, reliability. Employers sometimes think that younger people are more adaptable, learn more quickly and have more energy to dedicate to work, but they also recognise that older workers are often more committed, more reliable, and have wisdom and common sense. Look at the information the employer is sending in the job description: do you hear steadiness and reliability or short-term energy?

Try to match who you are and what you have to offer against the job, and be careful that you don't build age barriers by the way you present yourself. All too many older workers proudly say something like *All this social media stuff is beyond me ...* and don't hear the door slamming shut.

Remember this: employers who discriminate on the grounds of age are either too young to appreciate that anyone can have an original idea over the age of 30 (so show them ...) or old and tired and assume that everyone over 40 is equally old and tired. If the employer wants a 21 year old he can burn out in two years, do you want to be there anyway?

Here's some of the best advice around, from John Court's, former head of search and selection firm John Court's & Partners:

Too young? Too old? Does your age matter?

- Only if you keep on about it.
- Only if you look it.
- Only if you bring it up and apologise for it in your covering letter.
- Only if the photo you've attached to your CV makes you look significantly older/younger than the chronological date would suggest.
- And last – only if you don't distract the reader of your CV with all the *good* things you have to offer – recent relevant achievements, unique selling points, etc.

I don't have the qualifications

Formal qualifications are often far less relevant than people think, particularly in flexible environments like the UK and the USA. Two considerations here: there are now so many young people obtaining degrees, diplomas and certificates that employers can't tell one from another, and they have no idea whether any qualification equates to workplace performance.

In the (rarer than you might think) event that a particular qualification is a non-negotiable requirement, then get it, or a recognised equivalent. With most roles you can explore the alternatives, other ways to prove your acceptability. Can you train on the job? Can you buy the training somewhere? What kind of parallel experience might be accepted?

Where an employer mentions a specific qualification you don't have, don't despair, and don't send in your application anyway, saying nothing, hoping that the gap won't be noticed. Ask yourself, 'why do they need this? – what problem will it solve?' – and then address the issue directly by communicating what you know and what you can do: your answer to the problem posed by this job.

I'm not IT literate

If you are even tempted to use this statement, do something about it. At one time, using a PC, the internet and email was a specialised skill. Now it's common currency. It's not rocket science. As a minimum target, get yourself connected and get an email address that you check at least once a day.

There are a million things the web makes easier: research, finding people to speak to, discovering new ideas, tracking down former colleagues, seeking recommendations and endorsements. Doing all this and keeping others in the loop without using the internet is hard work, like trying to cook a three-course meal over a candle flame by avoiding those dangerously modern tools, electricity and gas – an unnecessary challenge which leads to indifferent results very, very slowly.

I'd need to retrain/go back to university/college

Almost every time a journalist rings me for a quote about career change, they usually say 'don't people have to retrain?' It seems they think that someone can only have a bright future if they stop working to retrain full time. This is another example of old-world thinking struggling to cope with twenty-first century reality. In the past, almost every career path required an apprenticeship or qualification, now the majority don't. Even those occupations which require entry qualifications often allow alternative ways in. Ask, and keep asking, and don't let 'I'd need to retrain' become a job myth that stops you finding out.

Your second line of defence might be 'I don't have the time or energy to study'. Is that true? If the job you do takes so much out of you and leaves nothing left for learning, maybe it's the wrong job, or maybe you're doing the right job the wrong way?

If retraining is required, look at the range of options available, from home study through to full-time education. Information on courses and qualifications is widely available. Bookshops have miles of texts telling you how to do things; YouTube will show you. There are thousands of choices in education today: part-time study, open and distance learning. Talk to tutors and past students to find out whether the course is the passport to success the college brochure claims. Take soundings from recruiters about whether the qualification is going to improve your employability or simply put a hole in your bank balance. (Chapter 17 has more discussion on saying useful things about your qualifications.)

'The trouble with the rat race is that even if you win, you're still a rat.'   **Lily Tomlin**

I'll never earn what I earn here

This one's the kiss of death, because it's really saying 'I'm overpaid here and nobody else will let me get away with it.' This is usually wrong-headed. Very few people are overpaid for more than a short period. Whatever you're earning (or have earned) is a reflection of what someone, somewhere, feels is the justified cost of your presence and activity.

I might be found out

It's surprising how many people in senior jobs share a common fear: that they are only pretending to be good enough to do the job, and one day they'll be found out. It's known as the **impostor syndrome**. This was first recognised in the 1970s, and it's widely experienced. A significant number of senior staff believe they have got a job largely through luck, they are 'faking it' daily, and one day their boss will say: 'OK, we know it's been a big pretence. Just leave now and we'll say nothing more about it.' A worrying number of people would leave the building without protest.

Insecurity is everywhere. The strange thing is that everyone seems to assume that people who are more senior in the organisation are immune to it. In fact, many senior staff feel so isolated that they spend more energy than anyone else coping with their impostor syndrome.

I can't get motivated to make the change I need

You don't have to make a big change on day one, but you need to do something. It's true that sometimes we can't get round to doing the very things that we know will make life better. Why do we fail to take the first step? If it's a direction you know you want to take, then the usual answer is fear of failure, which can include fear of rejection. There's a simple trick I use with many clients: imagine you are making enquiries for someone else. A colleague has offered you several thousand pounds to find *her* ideal career path. If you accepted that brief you wouldn't be going back every five minutes saying 'this won't work for you', 'this isn't as exciting as I thought' or 'this is a difficult sector to get into'. You'd keep exploring, keep looking for variations and angles, press on by asking questions like 'what else is there?', 'who else could I talk to?' and 'what are the unconventional ways into this field?'

I don't interview well

What does *interviewing well* really mean? If it means that you're negative, that you talk yourself out of every job you apply for, then this isn't a matter of technique, but just a trick you play. The trick is this: you think you'll fail, so you set the game out to ensure that you do. That way you won't be disappointed. Employers, in general, buy experience, but they also love enthusiasm. That's not the same as false confidence, but conveying a simple statement: *I like what I do. I do it well. I can do it here, for you.* Chapter 14 has a wide range of tips but help is also at hand in my book *Job Interviews: Top Answers to Tough Questions.*

I have other constraints

If candidates get past the above barriers, they are usually capable of finding others (see Exercise 2.2 below).

Exercise 2.2 – Understand your constraints

We all have constraints, but each of us thinks that our constraints are uniquely limiting. Tick the constraints that you feel apply to you.

- ☐ I am too old
- ☐ I am underqualified
- ☐ My experience is all in one industry
- ☐ Travel-to-work distance
- ☐ Travel as part of the job
- ☐ Nights away from home
- ☐ Lack of information about the job market
- ☐ The stigma of unemployment
- ☐ No clear career goals
- ☐ Financial commitments
- ☐ Family/personal problems
- ☐ Fear of approaching people
- ☐ Few measurable achievements
- ☐ Attitudes/needs of family members
- ☐ Lack of confidence selling myself in person
- ☐ I worry about taking risks
- ☐ I worry that I will repeat old problems

- ☐ I worry that I will be out of work for a long time
- ☐ Fear of employer's attitude to redundancy or unemployment
- ☐ I have health problems
- ☐ Lack of up-to-date skills
- ☐ I am out of touch with the market
- ☐ Fear of rejection
- ☐ Lack of relevant qualifications
- ☐ I worry about having to retrain/go back to full-time study
- ☐ My job search to date hasn't worked
- ☐ I don't want to make the wrong decision at my time of life
- ☐ I want to get a job that looks good on my CV

☐ I don't interview well   ☐ I want a safe job
                                  ☐ I have never had to apply for
                                     a job before

Look at the constraints you have ticked. Take a highlighter pen and mark the ones which you think are most critical or most limiting. Record against each one a time when you overcame this constraint in the past, and the steps you can see to help you to overcome this barrier in the future. If you feel you have constraints that you can't overcome, that's a good reason to find help.

Some constraints are actually helpful to you because they describe correct limits. These might be about location, travel distance, hours of work, and sometimes about minimum income levels. These are worth defining so you have a strong sense of the key elements that need to be in the mix.

Other constraints are psychological, but these often exert an even more powerful grip, like that line *I don't want to make the wrong decision at my time of life*. These thoughts really do constrain – by limiting your performance. You can spot these constraints a mile off – these one-liners pop into your head when you consider something different or risky, or keep you awake at two o'clock in the morning. (If they do, don't act on them. One school of psychology tells us that the voice you hear in your head in the small hours of the morning is a child's voice, speaking from fear. That's why things often look better in the morning.)

'Must do' list

- ✓ Career problems are sometimes concrete, but usually strategies for avoiding the issue of change. What are your favourite 'yes, but' defences?
- ✓ You can be happy at work. What would be the first step you could take to achieve that? How would your friends and colleagues notice the difference?
- ✓ Look at your CV, your interview style, your attitude to work. You complain that employers see negative things about you. How many of these messages are actually composed and delivered by you?

First steps towards change

'Furious activity is no substitute for understanding.'
H.H. Williams

This chapter helps you to:

- Look at the mix of accident, luck and design in your career
- Understand that a new career direction will probably require new kinds of thinking
- Learn how to work smarter rather than harder at shaping your career
- Imagine possibilities for change

Decision making

My colleagues and I specialise in helping people to make difficult career change decisions. They are difficult for a variety of reasons: people don't know what they want to do next, they can't see a way out of where they are now, or they know where they want to be but don't know how to get there.

If you manage your career, actively and consciously, you will make it work better for you. We've already discussed the false security of a long-term career plan. We need to think smarter: planning ahead is far less important than being *awake* now – awake to the possibilities of change and the urgency of doing work which is more fulfilling.

A critic writing about Jane Austen once pointed out that the author makes a distinction between people who live and *people who see themselves living*. Reflecting on what you do every day means an openness to learning from it, and doing things differently. The truth seems to be that people who make conscious decisions about their working lives are more successful and more satisfied. They have thought about the work that they want to do and are actively pursuing it. Some have sought out the right job. Others have learned the skill of redesigning the jobs that they do, so that they play to their strengths. Sometimes what matters is recognising the value of the things you do outside work. Career development doesn't always mean changing jobs.

Career management has many dimensions, including:

- Discovering the kind of work you find most stimulating and enjoyable.
- Discovering fields of work (including jobs you didn't know existed) where you can make a difference.
- Striking a balance between what you are looking for and what the world has to offer – setting out the steps on your journey.
- Setting goals – these may be financial, learning or personal goals.
- Achieving the right life–work balance – making room for learning, family, relationships and the things that matter most.
- Making sure that work provides the things that motivate you most – status, recognition, independence, learning, and so on.
- Renegotiating your job so that you can do more of the things that energise you.
- Planning for changes of lifestyle, possibly including portfolio working, or planning an active retirement.

What is creative career management?

Valuing creativity

Before you skip this paragraph, let's establish one ground rule. We're all capable of inventing creative solutions to life's problems. Most of these problems are everyday: taking children in opposite directions in one car, paying this week's bills with next week's money, or mending using old bits and pieces rather than buying an expensive component. Sometimes it's a task we take for granted, such as taking an engine apart and putting it back together, perfectly, without a diagram, or caring for three or four difficult children at their most unpleasant, or making dinner out of six things in the cupboard. We are all creative. We have to be: that's how humans have survived.

You will have come across different ways of describing the way people think. However, for many of us lists, plans, diagrams and flowcharts don't work. We don't read life that way. We're inspired by conversations, by people, by stories and poems, by movies; our natural creativity needs a different kind of kick-start.

The important thing to remember at this stage is this: we are all given a particular kind of creativity. Career choice is about unlocking what makes *you* a creative, energised person.

Why logical planning doesn't always help

Anyone asking themselves what kind of career path they should follow normally tries to deal with the problem logically. That's the kind of thinking we're trained in on any science or business course. We try to solve problems in sequence. So you plan to take the right courses, apply for the right jobs, gain the best experience .... Did this kind of planning get you the right results? (See also A to Z thinking in Chapter 4.)

Experience shows us that process-thinking works fine if you have a clear goal in mind, but as soon as you develop an interest in doing something different, it lets us down badly. We need another method, and here's why. Every day, business executives wake up and have to think of new ideas: new names for brands, new ways of selling old products, new ways of communicating with people. Where do ideas come from? The age-old question of the tired mind. Writers, designers, inventors and advertising executives all have the same dread: the blank piece of paper. Yet there are ways of learning how to generate ideas. We normally look for the 'right' solution, but creativity works better where we seek multiple solutions: first one idea, then another, then another. Creativity thrives on abundance.

The important thing is not to confuse idea generating with decision making. How many meetings have you been to where the first good idea is shot down in flames? Ideas are tentative, fragile things that in their early stages can't stand up to the strong light of decision making. It's no use thinking 'I wonder about medicine ...' if you immediately say 'Do I want to be a doctor or don't I?' Forcing a decision too early simply crushes creative thinking. Maybe not a doctor – maybe a medical journalist, or a pharmacist or a physiotherapist.

When a business enterprise is in decline and heading towards oblivion because it has nothing interesting to offer the market, it needs to find a new way of thinking. Right now this business needs some smart thinking: how can it reinvent itself and turn things around? At times like this some businesses throw out the rulebook and become hungry for ideas that will generate new products and services. If your career is in the doldrums you may benefit from the same kind of thinking: you need to reinvent yourself, rediscover what you are capable of doing and being.

Many years ago I heard a motivational speaker in California deliver a great one liner. I've tried to track down the name of the speaker, without success so far, but I thank him anyway. He said: 'if you only live half your life, the other half will haunt you forever'.

Why do people avoid having great jobs?

There are more varieties of jobs out there than ever before, yet we still generally let our careers be shaped by accident, or accept second or third best because it's easier to stand still than to move forward. Most importantly of all, we insist on using the most limited kind of straight-line thinking in career planning and job search. Why? Essentially, we like to do what feels safe, even if that means being unhappy. There's a powerful part of the brain that says *Stop here. It's dull, but it's comfortable. Out there looks difficult and strange.*

And then you find evidence to support your position. You focus on stories of people of your age and background who tried to make a change and failed. I have a theory. At times when change threatens, we develop a personal radar that scans the horizon for information. Radar, as you know, is hungry for enemy objects. And we find them. You suddenly discover people who were made redundant and never found a job again. People beat a path to your door to tell you *Don't do it … it will all come to tears.*

As you'll discover from reading this book, we come up with all kinds of negative messages to act as blocks to growth and change. If you believe 'I'm not an ideas person' or 'I'm not a leader', your brain is capable of making sure this is a self-fulfilling prophecy. If a golfer says, 'I bet I slice this ball', she probably will.

Adaptability

One of the odd reasons that we avoid doing the kind of job we'd love to do is that we are adaptable. Human beings have evolved to become highly adaptable creatures. We can live in climates ranging from Arctic to sweltering. We can survive in the most demanding, unhealthy and difficult conditions, and families can work, raise children and live good lives even under the most brutal political regimes. Perhaps because of this built-in survival instinct, some of us have the capacity to do something that modern society finds odd and most of history saw as the norm. We can hold down an uninspiring job for decades. Given a world of choice, the fact that we can doesn't mean that we should.

I don't want to make the wrong decision

Planning a career that has no risk is a consoling fantasy from the 1950s of finding a job that will take you safely through to a comfortable retirement. The idea that 'I don't want to make the wrong decision' sometimes reflects what we have seen happen to others, but far more often speaks of our fear of doing something which will make us look foolish. Being motivated by safety is not being attracted towards something, but is about being motivated *away* from danger. Sadly, this means that all your energy goes into avoiding the first steps which will lead to exploration, and trying to conform to some internal picture of a life that is sensible, low risk and conventional.

How many successful brands or products started life by being *conventional*? It is true that people have constraints: bills to pay, mouths to feed. It's important not to underemphasise that fact. However, what matters is that these basic requirements are seen for what they are: problems to be solved, not reasons for living. See also Chapter 8 on the word 'realistic'.

Put another way, incremental thinking only gets you incremental results. But if you don't take even the small steps, you can pretty much guarantee that nothing will change at all.

'I just need a job'

By now you may have come to the conclusion that creative career management might be a good thing for somebody else. Why not you? Because you feel that reality is harder and tougher than that. You need something real, right now, that pays the bills. You just need a job. This might be because you're unemployed, or because you're not paid enough to make ends meet. This places you in a vulnerable position in the labour market. It forces you to become a job beggar, going round with your hat in your hand saying just one thing: I need a job. Desperately.

I spent some time in early 2000 working with a group of job seekers from one of the townships in Johannesburg. One of them, Gugu, was aged 17 and had given up looking for work. Why? 'There are no jobs in South Africa,' she said. But new jobs are being created in that country every day. 'Yes, but so many people are chasing them,' she said sadly. Talking to her I realised that all over the world too many people fall into job-beggar mode. Fortunately, Gugu and her fellow job seekers all found jobs as a result of a programme which encouraged them to focus on their strengths and actively talk about them to employers.

'No, it's true: I just need a job'

Do you really? How long will it be before you're back asking the same questions: *What am I doing this for? Where's my life going?* Soon you end up saying that there's no point thinking about your career, your skills, your future, *because there are no choices.* There are very few occasions when that's true. Just get some perspective on that statement. Compared with most of the world's population, past and present, people in today's developed world have a huge range of life choices, and more protection against failure. If you need money, just earn it. Don't pretend that's all there is. We all have choices.

Perhaps an inner voice is saying *'get real* – choosing a job because you enjoy it is self-indulgence, a daydream'. If you want a concrete and practical reason for not taking just any job, it's this: in five years' time, how will you explain this job on your CV?

How many excuses do you need to have to ensure you stay miserable at work? Listen to successful people talking about the work they do. They don't often say 'Well, the money's good'. They talk about work being like a 'game', being 'fun' or they talk about the privilege of doing for a living what they would gladly do for nothing. During the decade up to 2008 the UK enjoyed low unemployment, and more people were employed than at any time in its history, yet people still said 'this is a really bad time to be unemployed'. We should remember that some people continue to get brilliant jobs even in the depths of recession.

Effective career planning is about finding a job that works for you, matching who you are to the life you are going to lead. That's not a luxury: that's the clearest reality there is. Doing that provides you with a great career, and gives you a greater chance of contributing to life.

Working smarter rather than harder at career building

Some say that the right job is somewhere out there looking for you. Beware: this sounds like a strategy of 'I'm not getting excited until the perfect job comes along', but even if there's a job out there which is great for you, you can't sit at home and wait for it to knock on the door. The majority of us have to rely on a mix of good judgement, inspired guesswork and a pinch of luck. Luck has been described as two mathematical laws working together: chance and averaging. We can't control chance, but we can increase the odds in our favour.

Invest in your future. Use your precious thinking time care-fully, and learn to think openly, because a moment's inspira-tion can sometimes take you far, much farther than a year's dull planning.

Setting objectives is a vital part of the process. Ideas without activity are daydreams. The danger is that we move too quickly to activity without really taking the opportunity to reinvent our careers. Equally likely, we may continue to have career daydreams without making the first step to find out anything at all about the possibility of change. You don't need to wait for a master plan, an original idea, a lucky break-through or great contacts (although any of the last three will shorten the process). What you do need is to plan what you are going to do very soon, and then take the first step, and the step after that. That's what makes change happen.

Be experimental

Setting out means being prepared to make mistakes, and – ultimately – being prepared to make a change. However, the first step is simply finding out, and trying on new ideas to see if they fit.

Adopt the habit of being experimental. To think 'it's all experimental' is a great approach to life. It's an approach that values finding out and avoids blame when experiments go wrong. Experiment and failure, 'making mistakes', is a necessary part of creative thinking. It's a well-known fact that behind every new business idea there's a long list of things that didn't quite come off. Before every new invention comes a history of failed attempts. You can't make progress without getting things wrong some of the time. If you are going to focus on failure, then fail forwards rather than backwards; in other words, make your mistakes positive learning steps. Every successful product brought to market required a thou-sand near misses. Experiment away.

'No one can persuade another to change. Each of us guards a gate of change that can only be opened from the inside. We cannot open the gate of another, either by argument or by emotional appeal.' **Marilyn Ferguson**

Exploring is an opening-out process. We tend to think along tramlines, moving logically from one stage to the next. Divergent thinking works rather differently. Let your imagination fan out: rather than making decisions too soon, look at possibilities. Try on ideas.

Look at the **career transition triangles** shown below. The first phase of career transition is the lower triangle – this is all about opening out, experimentation and idea building. It's important not to find early reasons to say 'no' to ideas during this phase. After proper investigation you gain enough information to start closing things down. For example, you might decide to target a small number of fields for investigation (see the Master Sheet on page 142). Now you're in the top triangle which closes down helpfully, a time when you make choices and move towards specific outcomes.

Career transition triangles

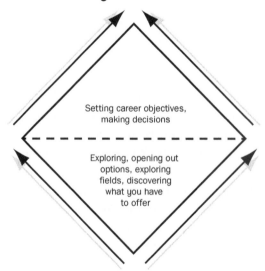

Setting career objectives, making decisions

Exploring, opening out options, exploring fields, discovering what you have to offer

Look again at the **career transition triangles**. Notice the dashed line that separates the two triangles? This is an important transitional point to watch out for. This line marks the transition between reflection and action, the point where you stop examining yourself and your ideas and you start to place your attention on what's 'out there'. Instead of hunting through this book for more career exercises, this will be the moment when you pick up the phone and arrange your first exploratory discussion (see Chapter 13 on networking and information interviews).

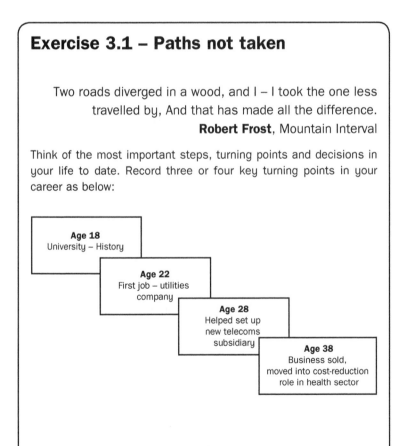

Exercise 3.1 – Paths not taken

> Two roads diverged in a wood, and I – I took the one less travelled by, And that has made all the difference.
> **Robert Frost**, Mountain Interval

Think of the most important steps, turning points and decisions in your life to date. Record three or four key turning points in your career as below:

Age 18
University – History

Age 22
First job – utilities company

Age 28
Helped set up new telecoms subsidiary

Age 38
Business sold, moved into cost-reduction role in health sector

Now think about the **paths not taken**. Look at **one** of the turning points you have outlined above and – as in the diagram below – pull out in what you believe the alternative paths were ('the things I nearly did/could have done').

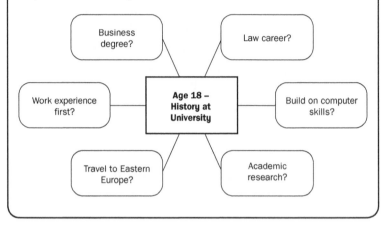

Questions to address on completing the 'Paths not taken' exercise

1. What choices were available to you at these critical points?
2. How did you make a choice?
3. How have you made career choices since?
4. What difference would a change of path have made to you?
5. Where have you adapted and shaped your career?

Exercise 3.2 – Mind mapping your future

You might find it helpful to use a **mind map**. This is a technique pioneered by Tony Buzan that provides a tool for individual brainstorming. Place a topic at the centre of a large, blank piece of paper, and draw a line out of it to record a new idea. Start a new line, like the branch of a tree, to represent each new idea or connection as it comes up. A completed example is shown opposite.

Mind mapping your future

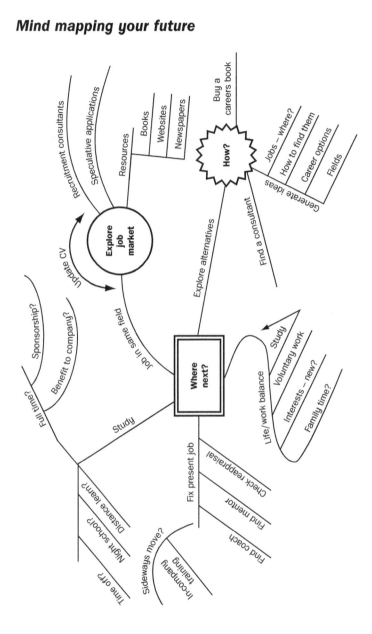

4

Thinking around corners

'What happens when there is a mismatch between your talents and your work? For creatures other than us humans, the answer to this question is extinction. Because we are so adaptable, we survive, but at a terrible cost. What gets extinguished is the pure joy of doing something that comes perfectly naturally. The further you get from fully expressing your talents and abilities, the less likely it is that you will enjoy your day on the job.'

Nicholas Lore

This chapter looks at the following areas:

- Rethinking the way you solve problems
- Breaking out of A to Z thinking
- Aiming for career breakthrough
- Moving towards positive solutions

Problem solving, and what goes wrong

How can you solve the problem of your career? Well, if you use the strategies you have learned so far in your life, you'll probably try a structured approach such as undertaking research and working out possibilities logically and systematically. Such *structured* approaches usually rely on what you have learned about organising information and ideas. We categorise problems. We write out lists. We prioritise.

We time plan. We write out pros and cons. That's a sound, business-like way of working things out, isn't it?

A to Z thinking

In school and in work we learn *straight-line thinking*, a logical progression from one step to the next. This is the mindset that says every book must be read from front to back, from A to Z, as Chapter 3 discussed when looking at planning. From problem to solution: this was the language of a great deal of post-1945 management training. Analyse the problem and work out a logical sequence of actions to form a solution.

Businesses all over the world are discovering that this kind of thinking doesn't help in every situation. Sometimes survival depends on thinking very differently. Many businesses have taken non-linear thinking to new heights: they turn problems on their heads. They seek innovative solutions. They invent new concepts, not just new products. In the twenty-first century, this is the kind of thinking to apply to our working lives.

This might be about being a little less subject to tunnel vision. Accept that you can come up with new ideas for your future, and just try things out. For some it's about being open to *inspiration*. When you are inspired something larger than you moves within you. How are you going to plan to be inspired? This sounds absurd, like planning to be spontaneous. You *can* plan inspiration, in the sense that you can open yourself up to possibilities, and you *can* learn to use both conscious and unconscious techniques to teach you how to break down barriers and begin to grow.

Varieties of creative thinking

Chapter 3 introduced you to the fact that everyone has their own form of creativity. It's important to remember that there are several kinds of creative thinking. Some of them come naturally to some people, but most can be nurtured or actively learned.

Different styles of creative thinking

Straight-line creativity

This is step-by-step, detailed, methodical. It's fairly close to A to Z thinking, but ensures that you don't jump to one immediate conclusion. It's about defining a problem and looking for a variety of effective outcomes. This kind of creativity is great for questions such as 'who can I talk to about physiotherapy?' or 'what should I remember to take to the interview?' It can be done alone or in groups. Used in career decisions it ensures that you use research, investigation and the full range of tools and techniques available to you.

Provoked creativity

This derives largely from the work of Edward de Bono. The idea is that you can use an unexpected and unrelated prompt or provocation to make the mind switch gear: this may be an analogy, a metaphor, a word chosen at random or a picture. For example, think of your favourite pop song. What do the lyrics of that song make you think about? How can that help to solve your problem or create a new approach?

Used in career decisions it helps you to make unexpected connections. It's great for exploring fields, and for overcoming the 'yes, but' barriers described in Chapter 2.

Freestyle creativity

This is free-flowing, fast, exciting. It relies on open-ended, discontinuous thinking. What else can be done? What other ways are there of looking at this? What happens if I turn the problem on its head? Examples include brainstorming and idea creation. This kind of thinking tends to work best with other people to bounce your ideas off. This is the kind of thinking found in organisations that claim to be creative. Used in career decisions it generates positive possibilities and connections, and it's great for generating ideas for sectors and possible employers.

'The best way to get a good idea is to get lots of ideas.'
Linus Pauling, Nobel Prize winning scientist

'Flash' creativity

Sometimes known as 'Aha!' or 'Eureka!' moments, these are times when you get a sudden insight or moment of illumination. These often happen at a time when we are doing or thinking something entirely unrelated to the problem at hand, possibly having a bath or digging the garden. Flash creativity results in totally new ideas, approaches, products and ideas that did not exist before. There are no steps, no rules, no predictable outcomes. One way of aiding the process, however, is to clear your mind, stare out of the window, and see what comes up.

Used in career decision-making the vital thing is to recognise the tangible possibilities that can come out of daydreaming, and test them out.

Combine and conquer

It's important to realise that these kinds of creative thinking are not exclusive; they work best in combination with each other. Brainstorm possibilities using freestyle creativity. Use provoked thinking if you get stuck. Explore the range of positive practical outcomes using straight-line creativity. Reflect on a problem unconsciously by doing something that engages other parts of your brain: jogging, listening to a piece of music, stripping down an engine, etc. (See Exercise 10.4 on discontinuous thinking on page 164.)

Career breakthrough tools

Here's a range of tools from different sources that work well to help you to achieve career breakthrough.

Get unstuck

First, review where you feel a sense of dissatisfaction at work. Perhaps it's about knowing you could do more, or you would like to be valued more. A feeling that you don't quite match the life you're leading. A vague sense that there is more to life than this, that your work should have some meaning.

People often say they are stuck in a career rut. The worst kind of rut is the *velvet rut*: you hate its confines, but it's just too comfortable to move. You may also get stuck in your thinking. You know that something needs to change, but what? What's needed is breakthrough thinking, a great idea to move you forward.

Distinguish between goals and dreams

We're all great at having 'safe' dreams: ideas we like to play with, assured that we will never have to do anything about them. They are daydreams that keep us warm on cold winter evenings. Goals are things we can do something about. For some people dreams become goals when logical/planning thinking is applied to them: 'What do I do next?' However, it's important to remember the dream as well, or the original impulse is lost.

Think in a forward gear

> 'Whether you think you can or you can't, you're right.'
> **Henry Ford**

There are a few ground rules for idea building:

- Believe that the solution to your career block exists, either within you or somewhere out there.
- Allow yourself to generate a range of ideas, without self-criticism.
- Learn how to focus on both questions and solutions.
- Don't restrict yourself to tools that you find easiest or the most comfortable. Stretch yourself.
- Believe in your ability to succeed.

Behave and believe

Rule 1: **Behaviour follows belief**. The greatest barriers between you and an inspired career are not in the marketplace or on your CV, but in your mind. And if getting your ideal career requires positive thinking, then getting the ideas to put your career plan together takes even more; it's vital that you learn to accept your brain's own ability to create ideas, possibilities, connections. Accept that this is not only a natural gift for the chosen few, but (as thousands of businesses have discovered) something you can practise and train your mind to do.

It's often said that the creative mind can hold contradictory ideas at the same time. So to Rule 2: **Belief follows behaviour**. This is certainly true in the very first stages of working on your self-belief. Richard Nelson Bolles, author of *What Color Is Your Parachute?*, has said: 'It is easier to act your way into a new way of thinking than to think your way into a new way of acting.' This has all kinds of implications. For example, if you have to make a public presentation, then decide to act, walk and talk as if you already have the full attention of your audience. Sometimes the thing that works is to act and behave as if you are already successful. Walk the walk, talk the talk, and something happens – you physically act your way into a new way of looking at yourself. That's why it's easier to have authority if you are dressed professionally, and why people are more assertive on the phone when they stand up. If you act confident or proficient, eventually you become it.

Shift your language

A huge jump in understanding demonstrated in career clients is that they, and only they, are responsible for their happiness.

Try a change of vocabulary. Describe the glass as half full, not half empty. Practise a register shift, from no to **yes**.

The language of NO	The language of YES
It'll never work	Let's look at our alternatives
It's how I am: I was born that way	I can try a different approach
She makes me behave like that	I control my own feelings
It's against the rules	I'll invent a new rulebook
I'm forced to	I will choose
It's just not me	What shall I try next?
In the real world …	I make my world real by …
Another mistake …	How interesting …
If only …	Let's try …
Never	It's all experimental

Find new life in the old clichés

Too many businesses misuse the idea of creativity, and pay lip service to the idea of genuinely open thinking. Even the word 'creative' can become a cliché.

Clichés have their usefulness. 'Thinking outside the box' was a term used in the advertising industry to think outside the rectangular frame of an advertising billboard. 'Pushing the envelope' comes from the field of aviation. The 'envelope' is the boxlike shape on a graph representing an aeroplane's maximum speed and range. Behind the tired language lie some highly useful concepts.

Focus on what's working, not on what isn't

Trainee airline pilots are taught, in an emergency, not to focus on what parts of the aeroplane aren't functioning. Instead they ask themselves, 'What do I have left working which will get me safely on the ground?' In the same way we need to learn to put our attention on everything we're doing which is working – and what we have in our toolkit that can be used. Otherwise it's easy to spend all your time and energy focusing on conversations that haven't worked, applications that fell at the first hurdle, or people who won't return your call. Everyone gets knock-backs. If you are the kind of person who takes rejection personally, don't beat yourself up about it – recruit some support.

Set real goals

Stephen Covey's book *The Seven Habits of Highly Effective People* advises us to 'begin with the end in mind'. Many people believe that all you need to make the future happen is to set long-term objectives and stick to them with fanatical commitment. In his inspirational book *59 Seconds*, Richard Wiseman debunks a great deal of the theory of goal setting.

Wiseman demonstrates that it's a myth that writing down life-changing goals has a recordable effect. However, there is evidence to suggest that another kind of goal setting is very effective indeed.

Real goals require a first, second and third step. Active commitment to short-term goals that have long-term ends in mind is the most effective strategy. If you break tasks down into mini-objectives and reward yourself for achieving them, you're more likely to make progress.

Take happiness seriously

If you have reached a career crisis, you'll already be in tune with this point. It's fairly central. If you don't believe in being happy, you probably don't believe in enjoyable work. If you're unsure, look at it this way. As the work of Richard Layard and others has demonstrated, happiness isn't a passing fancy but is measurable, and there are things you can do to improve it. Being in work which feels worth doing *and* which you have some control over is one of the key factors. Second, be pragmatic: if you are in work that makes you happier, you will probably be more motivated, more productive and potentially better paid. There really isn't much of an argument in favour of prolonging misery.

Going with the flow

Psychologist Mihaly Csikszentmihalyi coined the term 'flow' to describe a mental state when you feel totally absorbed in an enjoyable and fulfilling activity.

Being absorbed in your work

1. Your concentration is entirely focused on what you're doing – you are absorbed, fully engaged.

2. The activity feels worth doing, purposeful.
3. You feel you're doing something purposeful.
4. You learn or discover skills to meet the challenges you face.
5. Time seems to pass quickly.
6. You enjoy the process as well as the outcome.

Remember times when you felt like this? Ask yourself 'what was I doing?' Record them – they make great CV evidence and provide solid evidence of motivated skills (see Chapter 6).

Start with your natural talents

The highly successful fashion designer Ozwald Boateng was interviewed on BBC Radio 4 in March 2012. He mentioned that his father's career advice was 'if something comes easy to you, stick at it'. So he did, switching from a course in computer studies to fashion. His father quickly said that this wasn't what he had in mind, but Boateng stuck at it and has built a highly successful business with an international reputation. Your talents are not always evident until you discover them, but if you discover something that 'comes easy', it's often a great place to start.

Aim for 70%

Once you know what you're looking for, try to resist offers that really don't match. However, don't get carried away with the idea of the perfect job. Believing that only 100% will do is in fact a great excuse to stop looking. Understand that work is all about making deals, and *good enough* can work for you.

First of all, look at yourself until you're pretty sure about the kind of role that suits you best, and the skills you'd like to use. Many chapters in this book will help you with this, and you can summarise your findings on one page in the **Master Sheet** (see page 142).

Next, look hard the employer's shopping list. This means going way beyond job descriptions – dig deep to find out what the organisation needs and wants. When you know this clearly (it will usually involve at least one conversation with someone who knows the organisation well), then look for overlap between you and the job:

The 70% overlap

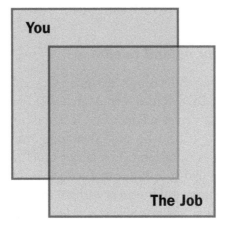

If you identify a genuine overlap of around 70%, the job is probably a good match – you'll be happy in work about 3½ days out of 5, which is plenty. If it feels more like 50% or 60% the role may be an acceptable stepping stone. If the match is 50% or less, watch out.

Look for synergy

Make it a life habit: look for connections. Carl Jung talked of *synchronicity*, a sense of things coming together in a pattern of significant coincidences. Once you start to make connections, patterns in life start to emerge, and you become more aware of synergy. At a most basic level, the more you discover about yourself, the more you discover that many others around you are on a similar journey, with anxieties very similar to your own. Such people make good support partners.

Recruit a support team

Few things are achievable without the right tools and the right people, yet all too many job seekers try to manage careers alone. Get support. First of all, have experimental, 'what if?' conversations with as many folk as you can who can give you a different perspective (but make sure the feedback is at least objective, and preferably upbeat). Second – and do this before you finish this book – build a support team.

Find *two* other people who will help. They don't need to be in the same situation as you, but they do need to be curious about people, jobs and the world. One other person will do, at a push, but a coach/pupil relationship often happens when there are only two people. With a trio meeting together regularly you get two perspectives on everything that's said. The conversation doesn't need to be just about you – you can help each other in turn. You'll often find that a trio discussion over a cup of coffee or a bottle of wine works very nicely.

Recruit the two members of your trio carefully. They should be people who can:

- Support you in the ups and downs of career transition.
- Give you honest, objective advice about your skills, and help you to see the evidence you use to back them up.
- Give you ideas for exploration and connections with other people who can help.
- Use 'yellow hat' thinking (see page 105) to support your ideas. If you say 'I'm thinking of becoming an astronaut', they will be the sort of people who will say 'How would that work for you? What would be the spin-offs? What first

step could you take? How can you get to speak to someone who's been into space … ?'

Warning: if you hear a friend say 'yes, but, in the real world …' or 'it's not that simple …' or even 'that won't work', don't invite them to be part of this process. There are thousands of people out there who will be all too happy to pour cold water on your ideas. Career success is as much about motivation as it is about strategy. Choose people who will give you encouraging feedback and positive support.

Exercise 4.1 – The ideas grid

Once you have generated a number of tentative goals or career ideas, you'll need to find some way of focusing on those that will really work for you.

This idea originates with the 7 × 7 technique, developed by Carl Gregory. Use blank cards that you can pin on a notice board or Post-it notes on a wall or a mirror.

1. Begin by writing out all the goals that seem important or attractive. Don't exclude anything because it seems unrealistic. Write them all on separate cards.

2. Combine ideas that are virtually the same. You might have both 'serving the community' and 'putting something back into society'.

3. Sort your draft goal cards into columns. Give each column a heading (for example, Financial, Learning, Personal).

4. Place the most important column on the left, the least important on the right.

5. You might want to apply a timescale; for example, discard anything that you can't achieve within two years. So 'Find time to write my novel' might have to go on the back burner for a year or two. It's up to you.

6. Put the ideas in rank order within each column, with the most important at the top.

Now stand back and look at your results. Better still, go away and do something else for an hour, then come back and look. What you have is a draft *prioritised* grid, with the most important, critical or immediately relevant ideas in the top left-hand corner.

You can use the same technique to come up with ideas to solve a problem. For instance, if your problem is 'How can I change my career without going back to full-time study?' you can come up with a range of potential ideas and solutions, without self-criticism or feeling forced into a decision too soon. Reward yourself for off-the-wall ideas. Sort, re-sort, reflect.

'Must do' list

- ✓ Record times when you were totally absorbed in tasks – either in work or outside it. What skills were you using?
- ✓ Practise using different modes of thinking. Try a range of techniques for idea generation and problem solving (start by using them on everyday problems and then adapt them to career planning).
- ✓ Take dreams seriously, and see which ones will translate into goals. Write them down, somewhere, and tell someone you've done it.
- ✓ Write a Plan A for the next 12 months. Things to include: first steps on the journey, measurable goals, the critical steps you need to follow to make things happen (writing articles, going to conferences, talking to people, getting your CV rewritten, finishing that book ...).

5

Your career hot buttons

'In order that people may be happy in their work, these three things are needed: They must be fit for it. They must not do too much of it. And they must have a sense of success in it.'

John Ruskin

This chapter looks at ways of:

- Identifying workplace turn-offs
- Measuring your career satisfaction
- Looking at money and motivation
- Piecing together your jigsaw job
- Discovering your career drivers

Turn-offs in the workplace

Go back to 'The good, the bad and the just plain awful' on page 15. Think about your hate list: the ten things you would like to change most (about the work you do, or the way you are at work). Write them down.

You might find it helpful to categorise some of your dissatisfactions: physical work environment, location, colleagues you work with, management style, status, recognition, people, tasks, variety, values of the organisation, and so on. Make sure you have recorded all the things that demotivate or irritate you.

'I need the money'

Psychologists will tell you that money is rarely the primary motivator in changing jobs. People are often persuaded to take only a minor increase in salary, or even a pay cut, in order to get the 'right' job. Money only motivates in the short term: once you've got your fast car and the key to the executive washroom, the buzz fades pretty quickly. However, poor rewards can quickly demotivate, particularly where there is a sense of injustice. The thought 'I'm worth more than this' may begin from an awareness that you are underpaid.

How do you have any sense of what you are worth? I have known individuals being interviewed for £40,000 and £80,000 jobs in the same week, with little real difference in responsibility or complexity. Markets often do very odd things with salaries. Have you ever calculated what you really cost your employer, including overheads, and then calculated what value you add to the bottom line, whether actual in terms of profits or metaphorically in terms of your invisible contribution?

'You ask what is the proper limit to a person's wealth? First, having what is essential, and second, having what is enough.' **Seneca**

When asked 'How much money do you need to feel that you have enough?', I'm told that most people name a figure which is double their present income, whether they earn £15,000 or £150,000 a year. However, most careers books ask you to work out the minimum you need to pay all your bills and to eat. Unfortunately, far too many people confuse this figure with what they are worth.

Write down a figure in answer to each question overleaf.

What do you need to earn?

When you have added up all your monthly bills, travel, insurance, health and food costs:

What do you need to live on?   £ [   ]

What would you need to earn to be relaxed about what you spend each month?

What would be ENOUGH?   £ [   ]

How do you value your skills, knowledge and commitment? What do other people like you earn in your chosen field? If you know the earnings range, what do you have to do to be in the top 25%?

What are you worth?   £ [   ]

Now think ahead. Assuming you keep motivated, keep learning, and move forward in your career:

What do you really want to be earning in five years' time?

£ [   ]

What *really* motivates you?

Recruiters will tell you that the first answer to this question is usually 'money'. The reason is that it's easy, convenient shorthand. In my interview training programmes I always try to get interviewers to probe to the next level. You may not be motivated by money at all, in fact. Throwing money at a problem does not make satisfied workers. Once money issues are resolved, deeper motivators kick in, such as being respected for what you know, seeing the job through to the finish, variety, making a difference, learning and work–life balance.

What recruiters know is that everyone has career hot buttons, but most of us are not good at identifying them (Exercise 5.2 on page 64 will help). If you're asked why you want to leave a job, it's convenient to use shorthand: 'the job stinks', 'the money's rotten', 'it's the way they treat you'. We all have our convenient shorthand for the things that go wrong in life: work, car, house, marriage. To build on that experience it helps to ask 'What went wrong? What parts did I find uncomfortable or unhelpful?' and then actively seek the positive.

Knowing what you don't want is helpful, but only as a first step. This book is here to help you to discover what you do want in your career, and to help you to get it.

Exercise 5.1 – Your jigsaw job

Here's a way of building your ideal job, bottom–up, from the smallest components.

People find it difficult to describe their ideal job because it requires too big a commitment: a job title, a field of work, a potential decision. An easier way in is to use the jigsaw job technique.

Imagine that you buy a jigsaw puzzle from a charity shop, but the puzzle comes in a plastic bag: you have no box, no picture, no title. You have no idea whether you have a picture of a cottage, a seascape or a kitten. So, in order to make the jigsaw you have to use other rules. You'll probably begin with the edges and the corners, but in the early stages of assembly you have to let go of the question 'what is this a picture of?'

Defining your 'jigsaw' job is like making a jigsaw without a box or the picture. You begin by making recognisable shapes. The analogy in career terms is that you forget about job titles and fields, and build the job up from the inside.

So, imagine you are in a reasonably fulfilling job, and you've been in the job for at least a year (well beyond the novelty stage). Forget for the moment the job title that might appear on your business card. Looking at one ingredient at a time, build the picture, as shown in the example below. Use the same list of ingredients on a blank piece of paper to build up your own jigsaw job.

Example jigsaw job

My jigsaw job will contain the following ingredients:	
Location, setting	Urban. Aesthetically pleasing. Flexible. Involves travel and meeting people
Hours	Generally Monday to Friday, but hours flexible
General details	A firm that's large enough to help me grow, small enough to support people
People	A role where I am mentored. Trusting, co-operative environment. Team-working environment. Sharing ideas, thinking collectively
The way I manage other people	More a mentor than a supervisor
The way I am managed	I am given opportunities. My boss is direct, honest, sees my potential. Keeps me on the straight and narrow
Skills I use	Being the face of the organisation. Liaising, explaining; translating complex ideas into straightforward terms. Communicating/influencing. Using creative and analytical thinking

Problems	Trying to help people with their problems. Completing work on time
Challenges	Competition: something to drive me. The job is testing/stretching. Learning about managing/leadership
Values expressed	Strong ethos. Clear sense of purpose/ meaning
Likely/attractive outcomes include	Getting a team result. Bringing the best out of people. Delighting the client
The job will be rewarding because	I will be achieving something. It will be fun
How work contributes to life outside work	Comfortable lifestyle. Health. Well-being
Work will allow time and energy for me to do these things outside work	Spending time with family and friends. Enjoying the theatre and cultural events again

Exercise 5.2 – Discover your career hot buttons

Read all the questions and then circle the overall score you feel is right in each category. Use the full scale rather than bunch all your scores in the middle.

Career hot buttons

---

1. Financial rewards

How important is the money, really? How much would you be re-energised if your salary increased by 10%? 20%? How long would that feeling last?

How motivated are you by financial rewards such as bonus payments?

If you could do more of the great things about your job and fewer of the dull things, would you be just as happy with less money?

When you're at a party and people talk about their jobs, how much do you think about what they earn? How much does it matter if you feel you're earning less than your peers?

Financial rewards are:

1	2	3	4	5	6	7	8	9	10

Unimportant	Moderately important	Very important

---

2. Influence

How much do you enjoy leadership and persuasion (high influence)?

How much control do you like to have over people, situations, problems?

How much does it trouble you when you have little influence over decisions?

Do you prefer to be in charge (high influence) or are you happy to follow a good leader (low influence)?

How much do you like to have a say in change?

Influence is:

1	2	3	4	5	6	7	8	9	10

Unimportant	Moderately important	Very important

3. Expert

How much do you like the feeling of being knowledgeable, skilled, an expert?

Are you happy knowing a lot about one focused area of knowledge?

Do you enjoy a reputation as a specialist (high expert) or a jack of all trades (low expert)?

Do you enjoy people seeking you out to ask for your advice or special knowledge?

Being an expert is:

1	2	3	4	5	6	7	8	9	10
Unimportant			Moderately important				Very important		

4. Independence

How far do you prefer a mentor to a supervisor?

Are you a self-starter? How much do you like to set your own deadlines?

How much control do you like over how you will allocate your time in achieving a task?

How much does it matter to you that you decide how you spend your time?

Do you like to have control over what you do (high independence) or are you happy to accept intelligent supervision (mid to low independence)?

Independence at work is:

1	2	3	4	5	6	7	8	9	10
Unimportant			Moderately important				Very important		

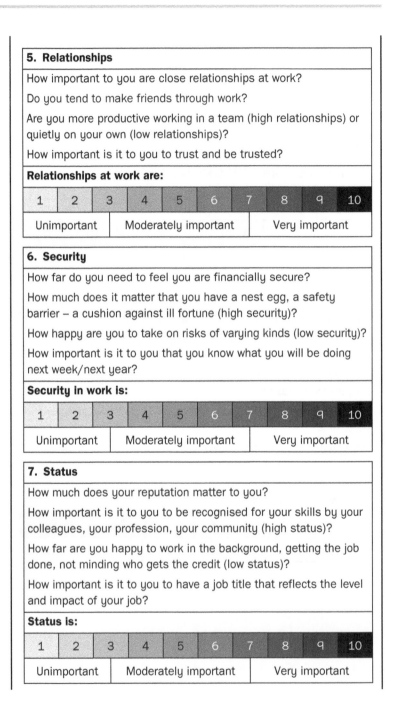

5. Relationships

How important to you are close relationships at work?

Do you tend to make friends through work?

Are you more productive working in a team (high relationships) or quietly on your own (low relationships)?

How important is it to you to trust and be trusted?

Relationships at work are:

1	2	3	4	5	6	7	8	9	10
Unimportant			Moderately important			Very important			

6. Security

How far do you need to feel you are financially secure?

How much does it matter that you have a nest egg, a safety barrier – a cushion against ill fortune (high security)?

How happy are you to take on risks of varying kinds (low security)?

How important is it to you that you know what you will be doing next week/next year?

Security in work is:

1	2	3	4	5	6	7	8	9	10
Unimportant			Moderately important			Very important			

7. Status

How much does your reputation matter to you?

How important is it to you to be recognised for your skills by your colleagues, your profession, your community (high status)?

How far are you happy to work in the background, getting the job done, not minding who gets the credit (low status)?

How important is it to you to have a job title that reflects the level and impact of your job?

Status is:

1	2	3	4	5	6	7	8	9	10
Unimportant			Moderately important			Very important			

8. Meaning and purpose

How strongly do you feel about the value your work adds to society?

How aware are you of the damage your work might be doing to others, or to the environment?

Do you hear yourself saying that your work should be meaningful (high meaning)?

Are you happy to seek meaning outside your working life (low meaning – as far as work is concerned)?

My search for meaning through work is:

1	2	3	4	5	6	7	8	9	10
Unimportant			Moderately important			Very important			

9. Imagination

How good are you at discovering new ideas, new ways of doing things?

Do you prefer to let others come up with ideas while you do the detailed planning?

Do you prefer to follow a system or set of rules (low imagination)?

Do you like to invent new solutions to problems (high imagination)?

Using imagination at work is:

1	2	3	4	5	6	7	8	9	10
Unimportant			Moderately important			Very important			

Career hot buttons scores		
Career hot button	**Score**	**Rank order**
1 Financial rewards		
2 Influence		
3 Expert		
4 Independence		
5 Relationships		
6 Security		
7 Status		
8 Meaning and purpose		
9 Imagination		

Write down your total scores, and then work out a rank order for your career hot buttons, so the button with the highest score is No. 1.

If you have given equal scores to more than one button, test to see if one is stronger than the other. For example, if your scores for 2 (Influence) and 7 (Status) are the same, ask yourself 'Would I prefer a job where my ability to influence or control others was *marginally* more important than my status?' If you have 3 or 4 equal, play 1 off against 2, then 3, then 4. It works, but if you have equal scores for some headings, no matter.

What are the implications? Match your top three career drivers against your present or most recent role. What is the degree of overlap? What is missing that you would like to add into your present job, or you will be actively seeking in your next post?

Occupational psychologist Stuart Robertson has been kind enough to build on my career hot buttons when designing his very interesting **Career Motivation Indicator**. See www.careermotivation.co.uk.

'Must do' list

Now you have identified your career hot buttons, look at what you will discover elsewhere in this book:

- ✓ What really motivates you?
- ✓ What do you find unstimulating, unacceptable and demotivating?
- ✓ What might move you up the career satisfaction grid?
- ✓ How will you deal with 'yes, but' and the limits it puts on your life?
- ✓ How far does your present job match your top three career hot buttons?

6

Making sense of your skills

'When love and skill work together, expect a masterpiece.' **Charles Reade**

This chapter helps you to:

- Map your hidden skills – the parts of your experience you took for granted
- Discover your potential, undiscovered, uncharted and motivated skills
- Communicate your skill set to your colleagues, managers or potential employers
- Identify your achievements and express them as mininarratives
- Compose brilliant presentation statements

Rediscovering your skills

You use and observe skills every day, and you may think you're expert at cataloguing your own skills. Ask most people and they'll tell you 'it's obvious … it's just a matter of knowing what you are good at'. One of the greatest reasons people fail to achieve motivated careers is that they only ever see half the skills they actually possess. They only really know and develop 25% of those skills, and they only communicate a fraction.

If you want to make sure you never get a great career, one of the best strategies is never to reveal your full set of gifts. If you're determined to continue doing work that fails to stretch you or match your aspirations, that will do the trick.

Also, we are not simply what others see in us. It's too easy simply to accept the skill set that others describe – your friends see and affirm the skills they value; they don't always see the skills that motivate you.

Example: Bill uses his computer every day, but his real interest is natural history. He gives time freely to his local school, which asks him to come in to fix computer problems or advise on software. If he is invited to do anything with the children, it usually involves explaining something about computers. He's great at it: probably the best person the school can find. But what he really wants to do is to talk to the kids about pond life.

Exercise 6.1 – Skills catalogue in ten steps

Take a pad of paper. List your skills in the ten steps below. Make sure you write down *skills* (for example, organising, planning, negotiating), not aspects of personality (for example, enthusiastic, reliable, calm).

1. Think of the most enjoyable job you have ever done. What skills were you using most of the time?
2. Remember projects which you found a stimulating challenge. What skills were you using?
3. Imagine it's Sunday night and you are looking forward to activities and projects in the week ahead. What skills do you see yourself using?
4. Think about a time when you surprised yourself by doing something you didn't know you were capable of doing. What was the skill you were engaging?
5. Imagine you're having a brilliant day at work. If someone was following you round with a video camera, what would the recording show you doing in terms of activity?

6. Think about times when you have received praise for your work performance. What skills were mentioned?

7. Remember a time when you went out of your way to help someone or solve a problem. Again, what skills did you use?

8. Write down any other skills you are good at *and* you enjoy using.

9. Look at all the skills you have recorded in steps 1–8. If you could choose only one skill from this list, which skill energises you most?

10. Finally, think about a day at work when you were entirely absorbed in what you were doing, time passed quickly, and you went home feeling a 'buzz'. Find someone to talk to about that day, and ask them to make a list, while you are talking of all the skills you were using. Add any new skills to your list.

When you have completed Exercise 6.1 you should have a fairly comprehensive list of your main skills. This list should provide a useful mix of the skills you have noticed and those which have been valued by others. If you want to cross-check this list or find better phrases to describe your skills, try the **JLA Skill Cards** (see page 89).

Now you have a good basic list of your skills you might find it helpful to see how these skills fit into different **skill categories**, for example:

- Skills connected with **information** (research, data, analysis).
- Skills connected with **imagination** (creating, designing, building).
- Skills connected with **planning** and **systems** (structures, processes, organisation).
- Skills connected with **growth** and **enterprise** (making new things happen, being an entrepreneur).
- Skills connected with **influencing people** (leading, driving change, managing stakeholders).
- Skills connected with **developing people** (coaching, training, mentoring).

Unwrap your gifts

Few of us see what a well-equipped skills toolbox we've been given. We use skills without recognising or crediting them, and we fail to bring out our latent talents, blinking, into the light. You have been given a unique set of talents. Unique not because of one, primary, virtuoso skill that commends you to the world, but because of the way all your skills are uniquely combined in you. Unique because you are the only person with your skills, exercised through your personality, your history, your viewpoint. No one else can be you, in your particular situation in life. You can always find somebody who can employ a particular skill better than you, but they can't be *you*.

However, be careful of the idea of *transferable* skills. A lot of people assume that all they need to do is to list their skills and an enlightened employer will make connections between their past and the role on offer. In practice, you are likely to be excluded from any selection process early if you don't have the right skills or you don't describe your experience in terms which are immediately meaningful to an employer. Skills don't transfer on their own – you have to explain how what you have done is relevant.

The skills below your radar

The experience of helping career changers suggests to me that most of us have skills that we know well and are comfortable with, but there are huge areas of unmapped territory. How many of your skills fit one of the following categories?

**Unconscious   Undeveloped   Unsung
Unfulfilled   Unpolished**

Unconscious skills

Unconscious skills are the skills you use so frequently they have become invisible to you. I sometimes call them 'wallpaper skills'. When you put up new wallpaper you're very aware of it for a month or so, and then you gradually stop noticing it once you get used to it. It springs back into focus when someone walks into your home and says nice things about the way you have redecorated. Therefore, you notice your 'wallpaper' skills when others see them. It's generally useful for people to remind you what you're good at, but especially so when they spot skills you no longer see.

Example: Maureen's great skill is untangling messy personal situations. She works quietly in the background, helping people to see things clearly, encouraging the parties to put anger aside and seek common ground. Others see her do it: it's oiling the wheels, building community. She was entirely unaware that she has these skills until a friend said, 'Do you know what you do most of the time? You're the cement between the bricks of our community.' She never gets the opportunity to use these skills at work, so she says nothing about them in her CV.

Example: Norma has never been able to walk past a piece of fabric without touching it. She has a good eye for texture, colour and pattern, and for matching materials simply and cheaply to make a room look great. She has a knack of walking into a room and knowing how to make it look more welcoming, more 'together' by making a few simple changes. Last year her friend brought out these 'wallpaper' skills and found a set of undeveloped and marketable skills underneath – becoming a 'house doctor', helping other people to sell their homes quickly by reading the mind of the buyer and offering a series of low-cost, high-imagination solutions to make a home look great and sell quickly.

Sometimes these are skills you use only occasionally, perhaps under pressure or in special moments. You often don't notice yourself exercising these skills in the heat of the moment, or you don't claim ownership: things just happened. In an emergency, for example, there is often someone present who has great clarity of mind, organising people, calling an ambulance and preventing panic.

Undeveloped skills

We're generally very good at talking about the skills we don't possess, or the things we're not very good at. You might gain more by focusing on skills that you have never really had the time or opportunity to develop, skills you instinctively feel you might be good at if you only had the chance.

How do you know they are there? One way is to catalogue your experience, project by project, constantly asking yourself 'what did I do?' Another is to follow your curiosity – what skills would you like to have a go at? Watch any craftsman demonstrating a skill and you will often see a small handful of people secretly thinking 'I wouldn't mind having a go at that …'. You may see only the beginnings of undeveloped skills in yourself. Look for potential, small seeds that may grow into something stunning. Stretch yourself. Read books and go on courses on new subjects.

Example: Nick is a keen photographer but a novice in terms of the digital age. He looked at the images produced by others but felt that he had no chance of equalling some of the work they did using expensive software. He decided to follow his curiosity, and asked some of his photographer friends to demonstrate the software they were using to process images from their digital cameras. His most important question each time was 'how long did it take for you to learn this?' When he found a quality but entry-level program that he liked, he bought it, catalogued all his photographs, and learned how to make basic images into great prints.

Undeveloped skills are often revealed by moments of surprise – particularly where you learned something new very quickly. Alternatively, you may have discovered you could do something (a) you hadn't tried before or (b) you found difficult when you were younger.

Unsung skills

You know you possess these skills, but you feel they are of little value. You enjoy using these skills, but you feel they have little currency, so you don't cultivate them or talk about them.

Example: Sue's hidden passion is ballroom dancing. She has never put it on a CV because she feels it is entirely irrelevant. One day, she heard of a college lecturer who taught business skills through ballroom dancing. Formal dancing teaches timing, responsiveness, leading and following, reading signals, anticipating change and paying attention to personal space. Sue realised that using these skills at work was what made her a brilliant PA.

We often think of skills like this as 'hobby skills'. They could include horticulture, craft skills, fine hand-to-eye co-ordination, being good at crosswords, being a great sports coach. Job-changers often say 'I talk to my friends about this stuff all the time, but I don't know how to fit this kind of stuff into my CV or talk about it at interview.'

Example: Sally has held a number of voluntary positions, connected with school, church and Scouting. In the past ten years she has acted as treasurer, leader, resource manager, transport co-ordinator, catering manager and team leader. She condenses this into a throwaway phrase on her CV: 'voluntary interests'.

This category often includes so-called 'soft' skills. Many have a skewed idea of the business world: hard skills are seen as relevant, soft skills as 'nice to have' or ten-a-penny. The paradox of course is that some of the most difficult tasks are achieved through well-crafted soft skills such as useful persuading, influencing and negotiating. Yet many candidates are worried that their 'soft' skills don't have a place in today's workplace.

Look for those moments when you say 'things just happened … it all came together at the last minute'. Who made it come together? If it was you, how did you do it? The clue for a skill that has value is that something changed because of your involvement. Ask someone who saw the event what it was you did, and then think about how you can build on that experience. If the skill is valuable to you, reveal its value to others. Make better connections between the skills you love using outside work and what you do best 9 to 5.

Telling others about what you do is a good way of rediscovering your skills. Tell two friends about a time when you did something important, and ask them to write down all the skills they hear mentioned in your story. Every opportunity you can take to get people to remind you of what you do well boosts your confidence.

Unfulfilled skills

Your unfulfilled skills are the things you'd love to do. Listen to those dreams calling you: *I always wanted to … paint watercolours, ride a horse, write my autobiography, run a soup kitchen, build my own house … .*

How do we turn these fantasy scenarios into real opportunities? Sometimes by not taking them exactly at face value, but by interrogating them for clues. If you've always fancied being a long-distance lorry driver, for example, this may be a specific calling or may be a strong indication that you like to have a great deal of freedom in your job. Sometimes the fantasy is a simple invitation. If you've always dreamed of being a novelist, take a writing class, write the opening paragraph, read more novels … do anything, but do something.

The real test of longing is that the idea won't leave you alone until you do something about it. The crunch comes when impulse needs to translate into action. Want to be prime minister? Join a political party, achieve some kind of elected office, take the first steps towards becoming an MP.

Watch for activities that quite literally fill your dreams. I sailed as a boy, not particularly well. I often dreamt about sailing again, and in the dream I usually felt I had no idea what I was doing. At the age of 40, I took up sailing again, and because I had practised sailing so often in my head, I was actually better at it. I've heard this phenomenon called 'learning to ski in the summer, learning to swim in the winter'. All kinds of sports research has also confirmed that training by visualisation is almost as good as the real thing. If that's true, then imagined skills are more powerful than you think.

Nothing is as damaging as a ruthless policy of ignoring your unfulfilled skills. Try things out. Try a job on a short-term basis. Work for nothing just to get the feel of it. Shadow someone doing the job to find out if it's what you'd really like to do. Take a short course rather than a three-year degree.

Warning: These skills are most easily dampened by others. People will try to steal or suppress your dreams.

'A new idea is delicate. It can be killed by a sneer or a yawn; it can be stabbed to death by a joke or worried to death by a frown on the right person's brow.' **Charles Brower**

Unpolished skills

Unpolished skills are rather like undeveloped skills, but with one important distinction: you are fully aware of these skills and value them, but you have settled for competence when you know you are capable of far more. The skill is stuck at a fixed level. It's not growing, and nor are you.

Example: Maya learned through her job in customer services to deal with complaints, and when to refer difficult calls to managers. She had learned the job inside out, but hated any change: new products, new support services. She had failed to stretch herself, to see what she was really capable of, because she had never looked at the underlying master skill: *keeping customers happy*. Once Maya learned to develop that skill, to invent new ways of helping people, she began to grow and was promoted to supervisor.

Example: When you learn to swim, you begin by thinking of it as organised movement. Somewhere, you think, there's a special combination of movements that will keep me above water and move me forward. The barely competent swimmer achieves that, and no more. *That'll do. I can swim.* Bill broke through that stage when he realised that swimming wasn't about movement or power, but a form of guided floating. With that idea in mind, he progressed to swimming several lengths. Then he discovered that it was also about timed breathing. Control the timing and breathing, and you can continue swimming just like you can continue walking. The first skill breakthrough will rarely be the last.

What if I don't get much out of the skills I use?

Sometimes you get the biggest breakthrough by spotting the activities where your competence level is high but your satisfaction levels are low; in other words, skills you're good at but don't enjoy using.

If you are in demand for skills you don't enjoy using, you may still be able to learn to love them, but you'll probably need to find ways of stretching yourself. People who dislike what they do have often hit a flat patch in terms of their learning curve. If not, it could be that you feel the skill is not worth using – in which case look at the **Values** exercises in Chapter 10 (see page 152).

Alternatively, learn to say no, and learn to negotiate opportunities to spend more of your time using skills you enjoy. You might also train someone else who will have a great time doing the things you find dull.

Exercise 6.2 – Skill clips

If your life is a movie, when you talk about yourself in a job search you've got to decide on just a few frames. Movies are promoted through trailers – the whole plot condensed into 3 minutes. The **skill clips** exercise sends you back to the cutting room to create a condensed, all-action version of you.

In the movie of your life, what are the key moments? Your best action scenes are the ones where you're doing things, getting results, interacting with people, starting or finishing projects.

Home movie rules for editing and composing your skill clips

1. **Zoom in as tight as possible** – avoid long sequences. One day is good. One hour is better. Keep it concise. Like a movie clip, it's got to convey a lot in a short space of time.

2. **Use slow motion** – reveal the action as it happens by thinking about what you did and how you did it.

3. **Use a good screenplay** – does this scene convey a message about skills, about overcoming obstacles?

4. **Keep the star in shot** – make sure this scene is about the hero: you.

5. **Make sure the clip has a happy ending** – an achievement or a skill revelation.

Fix on one event. Start with an occasion when you felt a great sense of success or achievement. Picture your 'clip', and give it a title. Then ask yourself the following skill discovery questions:

What obstacles did I have to overcome?

What was the task or challenge?

What planning did I need to do?

What skills did I see myself use?

What skills did others see me use?

What did I have to do to achieve this?

How did I work with others?

What was my best moment?

How did I surprise myself or others?

What did I do personally?

Some prompts for your skill clips:

- Think of times when you achieved something you are proud of. This doesn't need to be a work-related achievement. How did you do it? What difference did you make? Turn the event over in your mind until you see skills, particularly those you don't normally claim for yourself.
- Now look at your achievements from your non-working life. Times in the past when you overcame the odds, did something that surprised you.
- Think about work-related clips that demonstrate the full range of skills: things, people, information, concepts, etc.

Keep drawing up these skill clips, either alone or, even better, with a fellow career developer. If you show a series of movie clips from the work of famous film director Alfred Hitchcock, you see similarities of style and content. After five or six skill clips you'll start to notice a pattern of skills, or a set of *master skills*, and you'll get a strong sense of what you are really good at *and* enjoy doing.

Example skill clip

Title: 'Top of the World'			
INTRODUCTION: I've always been frightened of heights. I was pretty unfit. My work team challenged me to climb Cwm Clogwyn in Snowdonia.			
[Scenes] **Opening shot:** **The problem**	**First step**	**Main action**	**Ending**
Panic! Fear of failing. Sponsorship for a good cause convinced me to go ahead	Weighing up the problem. Deciding what I needed to learn and practise	Setting off – the real thing. Putting theory and training into practice. Scary!	I made it! Photograph at the summit. Elation
Skills I used Recognising my limitations. Overcoming fear	**Skills I used** Learning from friends, practising on a climbing wall. Learning to climb and belay, understanding equipment. Risk management? Anticipating and measuring problems	**Skills I used** Working as a team, learning to rely on others. Responding (fast!) to instructions. Helping others to cope with their fear. Keeping people's spirits up with humour!	**Skills I used** Celebrating – enjoying what we had achieved as a team, and my special role in our success. Reflecting on what I had managed by overcoming fear and relying on my colleagues. Insight: new ways of working together

Express achievements as mini-narratives

You can build on the skill clips exercise by learning how to remember each achievement as a mini-narrative. A good story is short and memorable, and has a clear topic. A good statement of your achievement has the same structure, as outlined below: a short explanation of the problem, a brief overview of what you did, and an indication of the outcome.

Achievement as mini-narrative

Story: Beginning	Middle	End
The problem	**What I did**	**The outcome**
My company needed to simplify its accounting system and save money	Identified, researched and introduced an off-site central accounting function	25% savings, and the new accounts centre came on line to budget and on deadline

Using mini-narratives has great advantages. First of all, it's easier for you to remember at interview and far less risky than improvising. Second, a rambling tale bores the interviewer and you may start to include negative information. Third, a well-constructed story is easier to listen to (people remember stories far longer than they remember facts).

Trying to remember good examples during an interview is hard work, because you have to apply several filters at once ('Will this sound interesting/relevant/impressive ... ?' 'Will it come out right?' 'Can I remember enough detail to answer supplementary questions?'). Having this information ready in the front of your head means you can give more attention to using your interview radar, working out the *real* agenda (see Chapter 14 for more on interviews).

Presentation statements

I am indebted to my colleague Bernard Pearce for his brilliant concept of presentation statements. At interview and when networking it's vital to give brief, upbeat responses to key questions. Being brief prevents you getting bogged down in difficult details. Being upbeat focuses the listener on the positive (interviewers are good at remembering negatives). A presentation statement also allows you to communicate your skills and successes. Work on them carefully before you go anywhere near a decision maker.

Compose a short answer to each of the following difficult questions:

1. **Why do you want to change career?** Explain why you are looking for a new opportunity. Don't dwell on past problems or uncomfortable relationships, but discuss positive reasons for change.
2. **Describe your career to date.** It's important that your career history comes across as a coherent story. The role on offer should sound like the next obvious chapter in that story.
3. **Tell us about yourself.** Compose a brief summary of who you are, what you do, and what skills and experience you have: encapsulate traits, skills and accomplishments to build a positive image in the mind of the listener.
4. **Why are you interested in this role?** Describe the job you are looking for and why you find it exciting. Say why you believe you are suited to this kind of work, and stress how what you have to offer will help a prospective employer.
5. **What are your strengths?** Give a concise overview of the skills and abilities that are likely to be of most interest to prospective employers. Remember that this is not a list of the job titles you have held or the companies you have worked for, but a shortlist of your main skills.

6. **What are your weaknesses?** This is always the toughest question. You can usually admit to pushing yourself too hard, but otherwise avoid giving away any huge negatives. It's generally safe to talk about skills you want to improve, and to emphasise the fact that you're a swift learner.

7. **What are you proud of?** Learn how to communicate achievements – learn them as mini-narratives (see above). Explain what you have done so the benefits to the new organisation are clear.

8. **What motivates you?** Be prepared to talk about what you have to offer rather than what you want to gain – talk about valuing the chance to use particular skills, opportunities to learn and grow or try out ideas. Stress the benefits to the organisation. Show rather than tell – don't just say you are committed, give an example which proves it.

9. **Why should we hire *you?*** Describe how your skills, know-how and experience combine together in a unique way. This is your unique selling point (USP) – the reason(s) why you are the best person for the job.

10. **Why do you want to leave your present job?** Alternatively, this may be a question about why you left your last job. Whether you were pushed or decided to leave for your own reasons, keep your answer as short and upbeat as possible. If you were made redundant, a phrase such as 'the organisation restructured and laid off a number of staff' usually works. Talk about what you want to do next as soon as possible. Avoid saying anything negative about a previous employer.

(Also see **Your two-breath message** in Chapter 13, page 209.)

How employers see skills

Employers see too many candidates who claim to be skilled but fail to provide supporting evidence, for example: *I am a good communicator.* What kind of communication? What do you mean by good? Say something about the level of skills you possess, and about the context: *I regularly communicated difficult messages to team members, keeping them informed and motivated – resulting in improved staff retention over a three-year period of organisational change.*

Exercise 6.3 – Motivated skills

What skills do you really enjoy using? Think about a time you were so engrossed in a task that you lost all track of time – moments when you felt completely yourself.

Look at skills you have identified in Exercise 6.1. Try putting them into a grid laid out as below:

Your motivated skills

	Skills I love using	Skills I quite enjoy using	Skills I don't enjoy using
Skills I perform well			
Skills I perform reasonably well but need to develop			
Skills I do not perform well			

Skills in the darker areas are those you should probably be using and developing. How many of these skills do you use in your current role?

Exercise 6.4 – Skills circle

Go back to your list of skills from Exercise 6.1. Use a highlighter pen to pick out your top 12 skills and write them in a circle, like the 12 points of a clock, as in the **Skills Clock** below.

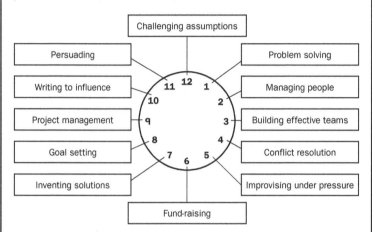

Try combining skills at different points of the clock face. Ask yourself, 'When have I used these two skills together? What sort of work would benefit from a combination of these two skills?' You might, for example, combine 2 *Managing people* and 7 *Inventing solutions*. This might mean: inventing new management systems, devising new ways of looking at management issues, such as giving people the tools to solve their own problems.

Combining 12 *Challenging assumptions* with 6 *Fund-raising* might make you think about turning the whole idea of fund-raising on its head. You might look at the question, 'how can we persuade more people to give us money?' and turn it around: 'how can we get people to persuade us to take their money?' Your fund-raising campaign may find a way of empowering people to select charities that exactly match their values.

'Must do' list

✓ Find the best way for you of discovering your hidden skills. Enlist the help of a good listener, a patient friend or a professional career coach.

✓ Look at the connections between your dreams, your interests and the skills you love using. There's a magic combination somewhere.

✓ Try at least four **skill clips**. Write out the skills you discover. Look at the skills that keep coming up time and again.

✓ Identify achievements for the different stages of your career.

✓ Plan, write down and then rehearse your **presentation statements**.

Further help to identify your skills and achievements

It's difficult to capture all your skills without the assistance of a skilled career coach. John Lees has developed a set of skill cards you can use to sort through a full list of skills used in today's workplace, and then work through a series of exercises until you have a shortlist of your motivated skills and linked achievement stories.

The **JLA Skill Cards** can be used by individuals as well as career coaches – they come with a full set of instructions and exercises to provide achievement evidence for your CV and job interviews, plus advice on communicating skill evidence to employers. See **www.johnleescareers.com**.

For further tips on communicating your skills at interview, see *Job Interviews: Top Answers to Tough Questions* (McGraw-Hill).

7

Your House of Knowledge

'My work is a game – a very serious game.'   **M.C. Escher**

This chapter helps you to:

- Tap your hidden knowledge
- Understand how your preferred interests provide huge clues about career satisfaction
- Make new connections between what you know and what you can do

What do you choose to know about?

Just as we all have hidden skills, we have concealed, but vital, areas of knowledge. What's powerful about your hidden knowledge is not just what you know, but why you know it. A certain amount of knowledge is imposed on us in school, but from the age of 14 or so we begin to make choices about our academic subjects. All the subjects we read, learn and think about in our own time tell us a huge amount about our personality, aspirations and interests.

Don't reject the possibility that there are new areas of knowledge you have yet to discover. One of the benefits of a demanding and eclectic education system is that it forces students to be exposed to subjects, materials and ideas that, at first sight, don't seem to be interesting at all. It's one of the reasons why exercises focusing on skills and knowledge don't tend to work with young people – they just haven't explored enough yet.

Exercise 7.1 – Your House of Knowledge

This exercise helps you to identify, record, value and communicate the things you know about. It is also a vital step to help you to identify your areas of interest that may provide strong links into fields of work. What we choose to learn about is a vital part of who we are.

What do you know about? Ask that question of someone you meet on a train or in a pub, and most people talk first of all about the areas of knowledge most frequently used by their current job. They will often talk about their educational specialisation. Therefore, 'My degree was in Spanish, but I'm an accountant now.' This is merely scratching the surface.

Look at the three-storey house shown below. It has a ground floor, first floor and second floor. It has an attic and a basement, and a garage at the side. Each level of that house represents something of what you know.

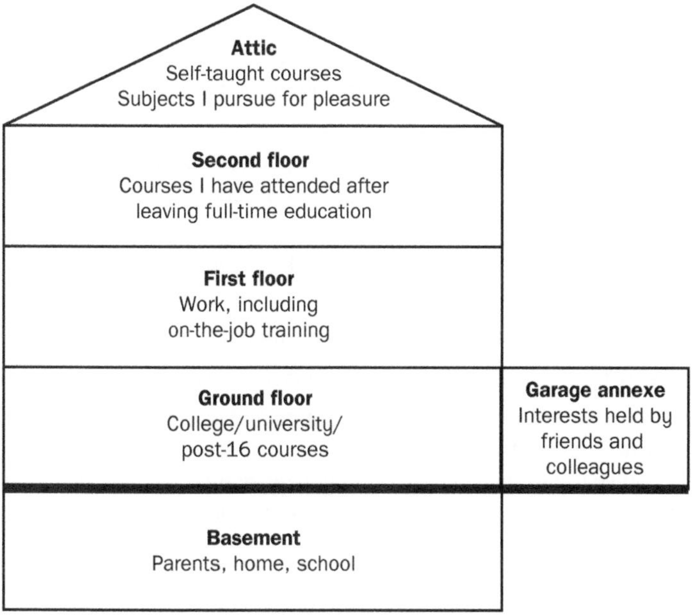

Attic
Self-taught courses
Subjects I pursue for pleasure

Second floor
Courses I have attended after
leaving full-time education

First floor
Work, including
on-the-job training

Ground floor
College/university/
post-16 courses

Garage annexe
Interests held by
friends and
colleagues

Basement
Parents, home, school

Like most exercises in this book, this works better if you have a conversation with someone while you are doing the exercise, or as soon as you have completed it.

1. Begin with the **basement** of your house, the firm foundations provided by your home and school. The following questions will help:

    ● What did you learn from your parents? What was your favourite subject at school?

    ● What projects or activities engaged you outside the classroom?

    ● What was the first thing you wanted to read when you put aside your textbooks? What was that about?

    ● When were you so enthusiastic about a subject at school or college that you went off and found more to read in your own time?

2. Complete the list for the **ground**, **first** and **second floors**. Think of knowledge areas which do not yet appear in your CV – including the things you forgot you know about. Here are some prompts:

    ● Think about the training courses you attended that you got most out of. Include (a) courses you chose to put yourself on and (b) courses you were sent on which turned out to be more interesting than you expected. What was the subject covered? What did you learn?

    ● What subjects led you to turning points in your life (that night school in Photoshop that made you change degree course, for example)?

    ● What job have you enjoyed most in terms of learning opportunities?

    ● What subjects have you enjoyed training others in?

    ● Where in your career were you hungry to extend your learning?

3. Now think about your leisure activities and interests. This is your **attic**, the part of your brain where you store all that old junk you've forgotten you have, stuff you never thought you would find a use for. What areas of knowledge are hidden in those dusty trunks? Some prompts again:

    ● Where have you taught yourself something or learned something just for your own amusement?

- When do you find yourself reading, talking or thinking about a subject and others have to shut you up? When do you find yourself so engrossed in an article or a book that the time passes unnoticed?

- Given a free choice, what subjects would you choose to talk about over a relaxed meal?

- Think of a time when you have enjoyed learning about someone else's favourite subject or hobby. What was the subject?

- Which internet pages do you have bookmarked at home?

- If you could teach a workshop on any subject in the world, to any audience, and given unlimited preparation time, what would that subject be?

- If you could learn about any subject in the world, from any teacher, what would that subject be?

- If you were accidentally locked into a large bookshop for the weekend, in which section would you camp out? Once you got bored, where would you go next? And next? Write down the headings that would appear on the bookshelves.

- When your Sunday newspaper arrives, fat with different sections, which part do you turn to first? Which part second?

- If you received a bequest from an aged relative that would fund a return to full-time education, what would you study?

- If you won the lottery and didn't have to work, you'd spend a few months indulging yourself, but eventually you would get bored. What would you do to fill the time?

4. Last but not least, the **garage**. It's in an annexe at the side because it's about vicarious interests, living life through the eyes and minds of other people. Think about close friends whose interests you share. My very dear friend Peter Maybank has a long-held interest in the First World War. I've joined him on battlefield trips to both Verdun and the Somme, and I realised through this experience how important the enthusiastic knowledge of others can be in shaping my own.

5. Look at your complete house. What have you missed out? It'll probably be things you consider 'trivial', such as cooking, home-making or family history. If you enjoy it, include it.

It's important to remember what you are *really* interested in, and to remember all the things that you have chosen to know about. This tells you a great deal in terms of motivation and subject interests, and can lead you on to potential areas of work (moving from personal subjects in which you are interested into fields of work). This step is important because it's about recovering parts of your past which you undervalue, and interests that will give you energy and enthusiasm in the future.

'The most successful people are those who do all year long what they would otherwise do in their summer vacation.' **Mark Twain**

'Knowing about' and 'passionate about': the things that won't leave us alone

The attic of the House of Knowledge potentially reveals more about us than any other part of the building. This is where we store away the special projects, the things that call to us from time to time and just won't go away. When work feels like this we have our strongest sense of 'flow'. I had the chance to work with the Liverpool-based photographer Colin McPherson some time back and asked him in passing 'do you still enjoy taking photographs when you're not taking them for a living?' 'Oh yes', he said, and showed me a card with one photograph on it, part of his long-term project photographing the last working salmon net fishermen on the east coast of Scotland (see www.colinmcpherson.com).

'Must do' list

- ✓ Look at your completed House of Knowledge. What activities in your past filled you with energy? Where is that energy today?
- ✓ Sit with someone else while they explore their own House of Knowledge, and your partner's ideas will probably jog your memory.
- ✓ If you've caught yourself saying 'ah, I *really* used to enjoy ...', then look at why you dropped the activity or interest. Is there a 'yes, but' in there somewhere?

The personality dimension

'If you are all wrapped up in yourself, you are overdressed.'
Kate Halverson

This chapter helps you to:

- See how personality and work are connected
- Gain insights into your personality and working style
- Understand how you might face tests as part of a selection process
- Discover your different intelligences

Personality type

Personality type is broadly connected with career choice – but the word *broadly* should be emphasised. If you're a people person you will almost certainly choose an occupation that allows you to work with others, but this could be in a very wide range of work sectors. Equally, quiet people can work for organisations which are full of outgoing people. So, given the wide range of sectors you might work in with any personality, it's perhaps best to focus on areas of comfort and discomfort.

Your personality in the workplace

Work role. If the majority of the tasks you undertake are a good match to your temperament, work generally fits well.

For example, if you love the opportunity to perform detailed work and that's exactly what you're hired to do, the working day may be well balanced. If you find yourself constantly outside your comfort zone that's a fair indication that your personality doesn't suit your work.

Where your **values** are matched in work, you receive more than a short-term buzz. There is a sense that you are doing something important or meaningful, and your small part of the world is improved by the fact that you're doing it. Alternatively, if you feel there is something missing, it may be that your role is hollow: productive on the outside, but empty at its core.

Using the right **skills** can be related to personality. Doing things well and enjoying what you do may feed a sense of self-esteem. A mismatch between your motivated skills (see Chapter 6) and your work role can easily make you feel underappreciated.

Your personality provides strong clues about the kind of **team** you would work best in. Look at past team experiences to work out what your natural role is in any team. (Leader? Diplomat? Go-getter?)

Personality also links strongly with the kind of **boss** you will work best with. How do you feel about being micromanaged? How important is it to have a boss who trusts you to get on with the job and supports you even if you make the odd mistake?

Do you respond best to a small **organisation** which offers variety and challenge or where you need to be self-reliant, or are you happier in the more defined structure of a larger organisation? Do you feel constrained by too small an organisation, or by being an anonymous cog in a large concern? Perhaps you have struck the wrong balance between growth and security, between variety and structure.

Career drivers also have strong links to personality (see page 64 for your career hot buttons). Compare your main drivers to what your job requires of you. Look at past roles as well – how is your work performance changed by being in a role which more closely matches your hot buttons?

Working conditions can affect mood and commitment in some personality types. How far is your motivation affected by the following: location, travel, the kind of building you work in, what you can see from your office window, where you spend your lunch hour?

Self-esteem is often linked to **personal growth**, including the ability to keep learning. Does your job keep stretching you? What have you learned in the past 12 months? Who sets your learning agenda? For some personality types, growth is linked to **advancement**. Is your present role a useful stepping stone to the future? Do you have a clear plan for the next five years? Do you need one? How would a recruiter see your present role: as a dead end, a side alley or a building block in your career?

People often seek different kinds of **pace** and **challenge** at work. Do you prefer to be constantly facing new problems, or do you need time to deal with the work you're given and to process new ideas? Does rapid change fill you with energy, or do you find it threatening? Does your organisation make things happen quickly enough for you? Are you being pushed at a speed which is faster than your natural or comfortable rate? How do you feel about leaving things half completed?

Discovering the best you there is

Whenever TV deals with career change, it emphasises the 'fake it until you make it' school of thinking. It's a real misrepresentation. People who make job offers are good at screening out all but the most accomplished fakes, and what's the point of getting a job which is a poor match for your strengths? A better principle in career development is for you to stop pretending to be someone else, and start celebrating the best version of *you* – what you are like on a good day, firing on all cylinders. That's the impression to leave in an interview room, and also the picture to hold on to when planning a career change.

Personal barriers, and creative ways to overcome them

Some barriers are external; most arise from the way you see things.

Lack of confidence. The key to getting an ideal job lies as much in your confidence as in your skills or the state of the labour market. Seek out positive feedback and record it somewhere so you can retrieve it when you feel low. Resist every temptation to put yourself down.

Being held back by your CV. You would be surprised to realise how many very senior people feel uncomfortable once they have prepared their CV. They feel that an employer will 'see through it'. They are worried about all those positive claims, and feel they are exaggerating. The reality is that employers, just like you, are good at latching on to negative pieces of information. So, don't give them the opportunity to do so. In your CV and at interview you should be the best possible version of you that you can be.

Fear of making mistakes. The world's greatest inventions are the result of mistakes. Mistakes are simply feedback on our performance. Winners make far more mistakes than losers – they get more feedback as they continue to try out more possibilities. The more timid mind stops after one mistake. Thomas Edison failed to invent the light bulb several thousand times before coming up with a version that worked. IBM chief Thomas Watson once said 'the way to succeed is to double your failure rate'.

Fear of rejection. Statistically you will be rejected more times than you are accepted. This is a fact of life, not a reflection of what you have to offer. The positive career changer looks at every interview, every discussion, as a learning opportunity. The most important question is 'what did I learn from this?' If you find yourself thinking 'all I learned was that people don't want me', then look again.

I don't know if I want the job. Research, and find out. Compare your 'I wish' list to the employer's 'We want' list. If it seems right, throw yourself at the opportunity with enthusiasm. If there are difficult decisions to make about moving house, or whatever, don't worry about them until the job offer is actually in your hand.

No achievements. Everybody has achievements, but some people choose not to recognise them. It's all relative. It is part of human nature to have goals and to overcome obstacles. The point is to recognise your achievements and to celebrate them, rather than assume they are of little worth and of no interest to others. In some cultures the idea of the 'tall poppy' means that people actively avoid being seen as distinctive or having particular achievements. If being ignored suits your career plan, it's a sound principle.

No clear direction. Not a problem, but a continuing opportunity. It simply means you have not yet finished exploring. Remember, though, that an employer is not interested in hearing about your areas of uncertainty. Do not use the job search process as a way of seeking answers to the questions you hold most deeply – all you will do is increase an employer's perceived risk.

Image. Find as many ways as you can to improve your own self-image (see the paragraph on lack of confidence above), but also learn to see how the world sees you. Ask your friends how they and others perceive you; most people find this feedback rather surprising.

Fear of boasting. Some people feel embarrassed describing their own strengths and successes. Boasting is when you come to the conclusion that you have something better than everyone else, and ram it down their throats. Discovering your true skills, talents and attributes is about learning to be at peace with the way you are.

Self-criticism can be helpful and is sometimes painful, but should be a short-term burst of activity, not a way of life. The human brain is finely attuned to living out negative messages, and we all gravitate towards our dominant thoughts. If you keep telling yourself 'I'll never be a manager' you will subconsciously use every ounce of energy to make sure that it becomes a self-fulfilling truth.

The shock of the new. It takes courage to make dramatic career changes, and courage to throw yourself into an entirely new job. Try to remember times in your past when you made similar leaps. How long, in fact, was your adjustment period? We are actually quite good at adjusting to new conditions. Even the most demanding and strange environment can become familiar and routine within a matter of months.

The expectation of others. Don't let other people live your career for you. Everyone does it: parents, teachers, friends and colleagues. They paint a picture of the future and you feel obliged to live it out. They often do so on scant information. You need two kinds of people to make these decisions properly: (a) skilled professionals who can help you to identify where your career is going, and (b) a core team of supporters who can positively encourage you to make it happen.

Lack of information. I talk to a great many people who try to imagine what new fields of work will be like. Imagination can be a helpful step in reaching a goal, but in an age full of information we can take solid steps towards finding out a great deal more. Talk to people who are currently doing the job. Find out what a job feels like from the inside.

Be careful what you ask for. One peculiarity of the brain is that we attract what we fear. If you see a small child carrying a glass of water and then say 'be careful you don't spill that', what happens? The child's focus goes from carrying to spilling. The drink is spilled. If you concentrate on the things you fear, you unconsciously put energy into a negative outcome. It sounds corny, but there really is power in positive thinking.

No goals. Set goals. Start with small goals, and stick to them. Plan your week ahead: apply for a course, read a book, get an appointment with someone who works in marketing, increase your typing speed.

Protect your ideas about your future. New ideas need 'greenhousing'; when we have new ideas sometimes the worst thing we can do is to share them with the wrong kind of people and have them dismissed or trashed. Cultivate ideas quietly and share them with positive-minded people.

Watch for **drains and radiators.** Some people around you are *drains*, who absorb your energy; others are *radiators*, who push energy out. Radiators will say 'go for it'. Drains say 'that will never work'. Drains tell you to be 'realistic', which usually means doing next to nothing in the hope that something else will come along.

Watch your **energy levels.** When you begin exploring you're full of enthusiasm. Watch out for the point where it flags – it will happen, often when you reach the first obstacle or start to lose confidence. Plan *now* to talk to someone positive at that critical time. Set short-term goals, and ask others to help you stick to them.

It's a dog eat dog world. David Sarnoff once said 'competition brings out the best in products and the worst in people'. Don't make the mistake of thinking you're in competition with everyone else. You're not. You're up against the requirements of a particular job and the needs of a particular employer. Co-operation is far more productive than competition. Pass on the lessons you learn about your own career explorations, and help others on their way. Beginning a network based on co-operation is one secret of a successful career.

Dealing with barriers

Look at the barriers identified above, and also the constraints you listed using Exercise 2.2 (page 28). Ask what your working life would be if you assumed a completely different mindset for each barrier you face. To take a fresh look is to see things as if you had just landed on the planet, or as if you were an inquisitive child: 'What does this do? Why do you do this?' It breaks you out of your habitual ways of thinking. Look at what normally energises you in life. If you obtain your energy from contact with others, then look at ways of finding your own company more enjoyable and productive. Just as you should get out of your normal physical environment from time to time, it helps to step outside your own personality.

Being 'realistic'

Let's look again at 'realistic', the most dangerous word in the career changer's vocabulary.

Listen to everyday career conversations going on around you in coffee shops. Someone asks the question 'what are you looking for?' and the answer often begins, 'Well, in an ideal world ...'. As the thought develops, watch the body language as the voice becomes more downbeat. Whether voiced or not, a presence stalks: that word 'realistic'. On the one hand, that interesting 'ideal' world where work would feel like fun. On the other a rather less exciting option, a compromise that looks and feels like trading down.

Applied too early in the process, so-called 'realistic' thinking can stop you at the first hurdle. Advice which says 'just dream the dream' or 'you can be anything you want to be' doesn't cut it, even in a buoyant market. The reason the word *realistic* is dangerous is because it is rarely about what is real. It's usually second-hand information, someone else's picture of the way the world works. This doesn't mean that your next move should be made without any reference to the real world of employers and hiring decisions. It's vital that you understand yourself, and how the world will react to you.

This advice is *not* encouraging people to try to shift into a fantasy world that doesn't exist. All work is a compromise between what you want out of life and what your employer wants out of you. Good career coaching finds the right balance between inspiration and what is actually out there. An inspired career coach will be able to bring out the best in you *and* tell you how the market will react – to your CV, your interview performance, your 'pitch'.

Many great ideas for career change are trampled by other people's 'yes, buts', or by the jaundiced, narrow perspective of people who really do see the glass as half empty every time. What's real is this. If you get half a dozen seasoned recruitment consultants telling you that even with the best CV rewrite in the world you will never break into sector X, that's data. Everything else is just experiment. In short, keep pushing, keep finding out, and keep looking.

From imagination to reality

Captain Jean-Luc Picard, second-generation *Star Trek* captain played by the inimitable Patrick Stewart, executed commands with three simple words: *make it so*. There comes a point where we have to make our ideas work. From 'what if' move on to 'how could I make this work … ?'

Think in terms of pilot schemes and experiments. In businesses these provide effective safety valves for introducing new ideas. We can apply the same thinking to our own careers by finding opportunities to try things out. One way is to extend yourself by going on courses, studying in your own time. Another is to take up some form of voluntary activity outside work in order to experiment with your career longings. Short-term or temporary employment can sometimes help to provide a useful 'laboratory' for your career plans. Sometimes the best prompt for everyday experiment is: 'don't think, just leap'.

Thinking in different colours

Expand your range of thinking styles. Edward de Bono offers us **six thinking hats** which work well in the context of career planning.

De Bono's six thinking hats applied to career transition

White hat	The information collector. What more facts do I need? Who else could I talk to?
Red hat	Emotions, feelings, intuition. What do I really feel about this? How far do I let these feelings affect my behaviour and my decision making? What gets in the way of change?
Black hat	Judgement, caution, conformity, truth. Will it work? Is it safe? How big is the risk? (Warning: Black-hat thinking can easily become 'yes, but' thinking and suppress new ideas.)
Green hat	Seeking alternatives, exploring, extending the art of the possible. How can I look at this differently? How can I generate new ideas for my career?
Yellow hat	Advantages, positive benefits. What would be the advantages? Why would it be good for me? How could I make it work?
Blue hat	The hat you use for thinking about thinking. The blue hat controls all the other hats; for example, it tells me 'isn't it time I used some yellow-hat thinking, agenda setting here?'

Adapted from: Edward de Bono, *Six Thinking Hats* (Penguin Books, 2000).

Inventing your future

It takes bravery to give the time to think laterally and flexibly about the way your life is going. It takes even greater courage to tell other people about your discovery. It takes maximum courage to begin to put your discoveries into action. Those with higher self-esteem find it easy to adopt and explore new ideas, because those new ideas are not threatening their core selves. But don't make the mistake of trying to do it alone. Ask yourself this question: *did you buy this book in order to avoid a conversation?* In order to avoid picking up the phone and finding out?

Getting a handle on your personality

'To the man who only has a hammer in the toolkit, every problem looks like a nail.' **Abraham Maslow**

Try the Exercise 8.1 opposite to gain some broad indicators about your personality. Put a score on each scale, avoiding the mid-point. Note: there are no 'right' answers. Think about the way you see yourself, the way others see you, and the way you react under pressure. Increased self-awareness will provide good clues about your best fit in terms of people and organisational culture.

After completing the chart, ask someone who knows you well to judge how far you have produced an accurate self-portrait. Use this information to increase your level of awareness of the way your personality operates in work.

Personality testing

There are a number of standard tests available. These vary from ability tests including numerical and verbal reasoning tests to personality tests. The Myers–Briggs Type Indicator

Exercise 8.1 – Personality Overview

How would you describe yourself?

Confident ─────────────────────── Cautious

Head in the clouds ─────────────── Practical

Abstract ─────────────────────── Concrete

Logical ─────────────────────── Intuitive

Emotional ─────────────────────── Analytical

Optimistic ─────────────────────── Pessimistic

Open to change ─────────────── Reluctant to change

Self-reliant ─────────────── Need the approval of others

Emotionally vulnerable ─────────────── Self-assured

Follower ─────────────────────── Leader

Solo artist ─────────────────────── Team player

Steady ─────────────────────── Flexible

What energises you?

People ─────────────────────── Solitude

Activity ─────────────────────── Calm

Thinking ─────────────────────── Doing

Schedules ─────────────────────── Improvisation

Groups or teams ─────────────── One-to-one

(MBTI) is used widely in staff development, but has its critics because it is based on Jungian type theory. More recent tests (for example 16PF5) are constructed around what psychologists describe as the 'big five' traits. Tests of this nature should be conducted by a qualified practitioner.

> **Personality tests – what candidates should expect from an assessment process**
>
> *When going through a selection process you may be asked to take a psychometric test of some kind. I couldn't think of anyone better than my colleague Peter Fennah, Chartered Psychologist, to explain the process.*
>
> You will be asked to complete a personality questionnaire, perhaps towards the end of a day's assessment if you are attending an assessment centre. You will complete it under exam conditions and there will be a couple of example questions to complete to ensure you fill the form in correctly (pay attention here if you know you get easily distracted). Often employers will ask you to complete the personality questionnaire and ability tests (such as numerical and verbal reasoning) online before meeting you. If this happens, ensure you are relaxed, distraction-free and able to complete the questionnaire. Ideally this should be in one sitting – if you have to stop part way through or your internet connection breaks, your answers are likely to have been saved up until this point, so you shouldn't lose more than a few answers and can pick it up again from where you left off.
>
> The test publishers who produce these questionnaires, such as Wave, 16PF5, OPQ32 and HPI, can vary questions, so don't expect the same order of questions, or indeed the same ones, if your friend has been asked to

do the same questionnaire. Just answer the questions as honestly as you can.

The reason you may be asked to complete a personality questionnaire as part of the recruitment process is to determine your likely fit for the role, team, pressure of performing the role and operating within the culture of the organisation. At this point you may be thinking of how to skew your answers to what you think they want to hear. There are three risks to this. First, psychologists designing robust personality questionnaires put in a number of devices to check the consistency of your answers as well as comparing your responses to those of a comparable population group (who don't have pressure to fake their answers). This allows us to spot exaggerated responses which we will then probe further. Being 'found out' in this way can be uncomfortable and unhealthy for your career. Second, if you are a poor fit for some parts of the role but your performance on the other elements of the assessment process is good, the employer would normally want to talk about effective coping strategies to help you perform to your best in the role. If you have skewed your answers then this conversation won't arise. Third, no one is a perfect match. Every person will shape the role around their strengths so it is better to be authentic and work with what you have got and make a good success of it. If you really are a wrong match then it is far better for both you and the employer to know this early. Another role may be available that would suit you better.

Good practice means that employers should provide you with feedback on your psychometric results. This may in part be through an online or physical report, but ideally you should also have around 30 minutes with a trained professional who will explore your key results with you in order to determine that they have an accurate interpretation of your report. Psychometric tools are not perfect and there can be a lot of legitimate reasons for different results to emerge, therefore if there are any surprises in the results it is good to explore these. This is why trained professionals play a key role in the feedback and assessment process.

Peter Fennah is a Chartered & Registered Occupational Psychologist and accredited executive coach. He focuses upon developing agile leadership and aiding those in career transition. Visit www.careersynergy.com.

Exercise 8.2 – Discovering your strongest areas of intelligence

Professor Howard Gardner argues that intelligence is not a single faculty that can be accurately measured, for example by an IQ test. He believes we have several separate but related intellectual capacities, each of which deserves to be called an intelligence.

The following inventory helps you to discover your strongest intelligences, and matches them to your preferred style for developing ideas or managing problems.

Completing the Seven Intelligences Inventory

Please note: this inventory is not a psychometric test. The results are not intended to limit your occupational choices or to indicate a personality 'type'. Its aim is to add to your self-awareness and suggest further areas of exploration in terms of the kinds of working activities you find most stimulating.

Under each of the seven headings is a list of characteristics. Tick any sentence that describes what you are like most of the time. There are no right or wrong answers – if in doubt, put a tick. Then give yourself a score between 1 and 5 after reading the longer description of each intelligence.

Add up your total score out of 15 for each category, and transfer your scores to the final panel. At the end of the inventory write down your three strongest intelligences.

Linguistic intelligence

		Tick
1	I enjoy language and word games	
2	I enjoy crosswords or other word games	
3	I like telling stories or jokes	
4	I enjoy reading for pleasure	
5	I enjoy choosing the right word	
6	I like listening to spoken word programmes	
7	I enjoy intelligent debates	
8	I hear words in my head before I speak or write	
9	I can often remember exactly what was said to me	
10	I rehearse things verbally in my head	

Total number of ticks/10	**Score**	⇨⇨⇨ ☐

Linguistic people enjoy reading and writing, love word games, and are responsive to the spoken or written word, and the richness of language. They often have a good memory for names. They possess a wide vocabulary and speak and/or write fluently.

Give yourself a score between 1 and 5 in terms of how well this paragraph describes you

Not me at all	Spot on	
1 2 3 4 5	**Score**	⇨⇨⇨ ☐

Linguistic intelligence	**Total combined score/15**	⇨⇨⇨ ☐

Logical–mathematical intelligence

		Tick
1	I am good at mental arithmetic	
2	I enjoy games or puzzles which require logical thinking	
3	I enjoyed maths and/or science in school	
4	I enjoy practical experiments	
5	I enjoy strategy games like chess	
6	I like things to be clear and well organised	
7	I think things through logically	
8	I am interested in new developments in science	
9	I like to have prioritised lists	
10	I believe that most things have rational explanations	

Total number of ticks/10   **Score**   ⇨⇨⇨ ☐

Logical–mathematical people respond well to patterns and structures, and prefer to do things in a sequential order. They organise experiments to test theories, and enjoy opportunities to solve problems. They reason things out logically and clearly. *Give yourself a score between 1 and 5 in terms of how well this paragraph describes you*

Not me at all   Spot on

   1   2   3   4   5   **Score**   ⇨⇨⇨ ☐

Logical–mathematical intelligence	**Total combined score/15**	⇨⇨⇨ ☐

Visual–spatial intelligence

		Tick
1	I can interpret plans or diagrams easily	
2	I quickly understand symbols on signs, instrument panels and equipment	
3	I enjoy cartoons	

4	I like to draw, sketch or doodle	
5	I enjoy photography	
6	I have a good sense of direction	
7	I prefer books with illustrations and diagrams	
8	I am good at giving road directions	
9	I am good at reading maps	
10	I feel strongly about the layout and 'look' of a document	

Total number of ticks/10	**Score**	⇨⇨⇨ ☐

Visual–spatial people tend to think in images and pictures. They enjoy visual puzzles and mazes, and tend to organise ideas visually in their heads, drawing maps or networks to connect ideas.

Give yourself a score between 1 and 5 in terms of how well this paragraph describes you

Not me at all	Spot on	
1 2 3 4 5	**Score**	⇨⇨⇨ ☐
Visual–spatial intelligence	**Total combined score/15**	⇨⇨⇨ ☐

Bodily–kinaesthetic intelligence

		Tick
1	I would rather drive than be a passenger	
2	I prefer it when my hands are occupied with something practical	
3	I find it difficult to sit still and relax for long periods	
4	I am well co-ordinated physically	
5	I am good at building or repairing things	
6	I enjoy hobbies which have a physical result like carpentry, wood carving, knitting, model building, gardening	
7	I enjoy physical sport or exercise	

8	I like to spend my free time outdoors	
9	I enjoy human touch and use expressive body language	
10	I would rather play than watch	

Total number of ticks/10   **Score**   ⇨⇨⇨ ☐

Bodily–kinaesthetic people like to interact with the world physically. They have an ability to control their bodies and handle objects skilfully. They respond best to work that is physically active, 'hands-on' and practical. They often enjoy sports and the outdoor life.

Give yourself a score between 1 and 5 in terms of how well this paragraph describes you

Not me at all   Spot on

   1   2   3   4   5   **Score**   ⇨⇨⇨ ☐

Bodily–kinaesthetic intelligence	**Total combined score/15**	⇨⇨⇨ ☐

Musical intelligence

		Tick
1	I have a good 'ear' for music	
2	I can hold a note	
3	I sing or play a musical instrument	
4	I often remember tunes in my head	
5	I would rather listen to music on the radio than discussions	
6	I can follow a musical score	
7	I have a good sense of rhythm	
8	Music speaks to me emotionally	
9	I am very aware of an 'off' note or an instrument which is out of tune	
10	I enjoy rhymes, poetry and limericks	

| Total number of ticks/10 | **Score** | ⇨⇨⇨ ☐ |

Musical people respond well to sound, music and rhythm. They often have a talent to interpret or produce music. They will often find it helpful or soothing to listen to music while studying or reading. Music will often 'speak' to them in terms of colours, emotions or themes, even when there are no lyrics.

Give yourself a score between 1 and 5 in terms of how well this paragraph describes you

Not me at all				Spot on		
1	2	3	4	5	**Score**	⇨⇨⇨ ☐

| Musical intelligence | **Total combined score/15** | ⇨⇨⇨ ☐ |

Interpersonal intelligence

		Tick
1	I would rather be in company than on my own	
2	I'm a good listener	
3	I prefer group sports like football or badminton to solo sports like swimming or running	
4	I generally talk about my problems with my friends	
5	I enjoy parties and other social events	
6	If I learn a skill I am happy to teach it to someone else	
7	I quickly tune in to the moods of other people	
8	I can express an idea best by talking about it	
9	I have a number of close friendships	
10	I am often called on to manage teams or organise social activities	

| Total number of ticks/10 | **Score** | ⇨⇨⇨ ☐ |

Interpersonal people are interested in others around them, are good listeners and communicators. They prefer to be in company, and like to share with others. They are naturally inclined towards teaching, caring or nurturing roles.

Give yourself a score between 1 and 5 in terms of how well this paragraph describes you

Not me at all				Spot on		
1	2	3	4	5	**Score**	⇨⇨⇨ ☐

Interpersonal intelligence	**Total combined score/15**	⇨⇨⇨ ☐

Intrapersonal intelligence

		Tick
1	I enjoy my own company	
2	Learning and personal development are important to me	
3	I have some strong opinions	
4	Spending time alone reflecting is important to me	
5	I have a strong sense of intuition	
6	I enjoy a quiet space in order to meditate and reflect	
7	I keep a journal that records my thoughts and feelings	
8	I have a strong sense of independence	
9	I normally solve my own problems	
10	I would probably enjoy being my own boss	
Total number of ticks/10	**Score**	⇨⇨⇨ ☐

Intrapersonal people value time spent alone and are very aware of their own personality, strengths and weaknesses. They tend to solve problems alone. They are often highly independent and self-motivated. They value the inner self, personal development and spirituality. They may be entrepreneurs or interested in becoming self-employed.

Give yourself a score between 1 and 5 in terms of how well this paragraph describes you

Not me at all	Spot on		

1 2 3 4 5	**Score**	⇨⇨⇨ ☐
Intrapersonal intelligence	**Total combined score/15**	⇨⇨⇨ ☐

Primary intelligence	Your total
1. Linguistic intelligence Using and loving language, whether written or spoken	
2. Logical–mathematical intelligence Using or interpreting numbers, data, facts, sequences, scientific research	
3. Visual–spatial intelligence Seeing things in pictures or images, map-reading, making 3D models	
4. Bodily–kinaesthetic intelligence (sometimes known as 'physical intelligence') – the ability to control one's body and handle objects skilfully	
5. Musical intelligence Having an 'ear' for music, a talent to interpret or produce music	
6. Interpersonal intelligence Communicating with and responding to other people	
7. Intrapersonal intelligence Valuing personal growth, independence, reflection, meditation – the inner world	

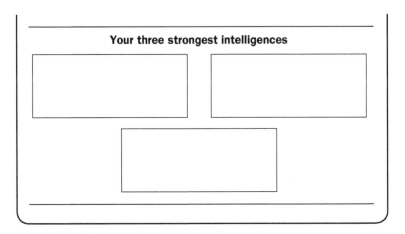

Interpreting your primary intelligences

What do the results mean? First of all, they should make you look again at the way you respond to people whose intelligences are very different from your own. (It can be very difficult, for example, for visual–spatial people to understand what those with high linguistic intelligence are explaining in such a long-winded way. They will say 'just draw me a diagram!')

How can the results help your career choice? It will be rare that you will see a direct correlation between one strong intelligence and one occupation, for example, 'I should be a mathematician!' Your intelligences combine with your preferred areas of knowledge, your motivational skills, your upbringing and your personality.

Here are some pointers in relation to strong scores. In every case what you may be spotting is an opportunity to expand your natural intelligences.

- **Linguistic intelligence.** Does your work give you opportunities to express yourself clearly in writing or in speech? Where can your organisation improve its communication? How can you adapt messages so that they are better perceived by those who have strong intelligences in other areas?

- **Logical–mathematical intelligence.** Your preferences lie with numbers, statistics, data or scientific investigation. How far is this intelligence being stretched? Do you have difficulty communicating what you see in numbers to others?

- **Visual–spatial intelligence.** Where in your job is this intelligence used? Can you learn how to use software to design slides and presentations? Can you make signs or posters?

- **Bodily–kinaesthetic intelligence.** What happens if your work is entirely intellectual and desk-bound? Can you translate your work into another context (for example, move from management training to outward-bound leadership training)?

- **Musical intelligence.** Can your musical intelligence be used in any way other than a career in music, for example, in sounds, jingles, rhymes (perhaps in advertising copy or rhymes to help people to learn and remember things – 'an apple a day …')?

- **Interpersonal intelligence.** Your skills in 'handling' people and relationships are much in demand in the modern workplace. Which aspects of interpersonal intelligence are strongest for you, and which need nurturing?

- **Intrapersonal intelligence.** Do you take your inner world seriously enough, and apply reflection to your work? Some managers consciously set aside thinking time when they can reflect. Don't always take work with you on the train. Sit and think. Advice to this group might be 'don't do something, just sit there …'.

'Must do' list

Questions to help you to reflect on your personality and working style:

- ✓ What brings you to life? When or where do you become *energised*? What has a deadening effect on you?
- ✓ How far do you understand your personality? Can you identify work environments where you will be effective *and* comfortable?
- ✓ What barriers to career success have been caused by problems you have in reading people? How can you develop your emotional intelligence?
- ✓ How far might your next career step require you to work on self-awareness, resilience or improved interpersonal skills?
- ✓ How well can you anticipate what a psychometric test will reveal about you?
- ✓ What preparation do you need to do to be ready to answer questions about how you operate under pressure, or your strengths and weaknesses?

Matching yourself to work you will enjoy

'Find a job you like and you add five days to every week.'
H. Jackson Browne

This chapter helps you to:

- Understand why it's difficult to choose a career path
- Find out about kinds of work you know nothing about at present
- Identify subjects and work sectors for investigation
- Use lateral thinking to help you to identify new areas of work
- Draw all your discoveries together in a Master Plan

Choices, choices

Think of the billions of people who have ever lived on this planet. According to the *New York Times* in January 2010, approximately 9% of them are alive today – there are more of us, and we're living longer. This 9% slice of human history has more life choices and more work choices available to it than any previous generation. Even three generations ago, the average European worker probably had about five to ten obvious occupations to choose from. Today we have tens of thousands. What's more, since this is such a new phenomenon, we don't have the mental toolkit to help us choose.

More than a few people wonder *what would be my dream job?* This question, of course, relies heavily on the idea that there might be a single, 'right' path for each of us, and some people believe that a simple career test will reveal the answer. We live in a society that believes it has choices about everything, so there is a real pressure to find the 'perfect' job, which will solve every one of life's problems. You may also face pressure from friends and family to 'find something better'.

This book will show you that having a job you love needn't be about waiting for your dream job to come along. The answer is usually about finding work which is a healthy match to who you are.

Sectors, and choosing them more carefully

Workers today have much broader choices than any previous generation. How do we deal with these choices? First of all, we need to learn to draw maps of what is out there, which means understanding fields of work. One sensible way of looking at jobs is to categorise them into groups and subgroups. Imagine an office block full of filing cabinets. Every type of job in the world you can imagine, from Aardvark Handler to Zebra Painter, has its own file. To make sense of all these files, you would want to group related jobs together in one place. This is what we mean by fields of work or, as we describe them here, *sectors*. Some sectors are huge, such as health. Within that large 'job family' are several smaller sectors, including nursing. But even if you choose nursing, you will soon have to decide on a main focus, and also on the likely workplace.

Discovering what enlivens, and what dampens

The main reason you are unhappy in your work may be about the people you work with. It may be environmental: you don't like your place of work or the journey that takes you there. These can all alter (change of boss, relocation) without your role changing at all. You may be out of tune with the organisation – particularly if you don't share its values (see Chapter 10).

Would you enjoy your role anywhere (in another organisation, or in a different sector)? You might, for example, enjoy training staff in people skills but have no interest in training in technical skills. Some people are happy in their role no matter which sector they work in. Someone who enjoys networking computers, for example, probably doesn't mind doing the job in a factory, hospital or office building. Yet many are dissatisfied in their careers because they haven't yet found a work sector which feels interesting.

Resources

In the past we had to rely on careers libraries, but today a wealth of in-depth information is two or three mouse clicks away. Read the careers pages of general newspapers: note that sections on graduate careers often contain career tips and company information useful to the full range of job seekers. Research organisations thoroughly, noting the titles of jobs you see mentioned. Check out online video interviews (for example, www.careersbox.co.uk) where people talk about their jobs. Websites such as www.glassdoor.com can be a good starting point for learning the downside of a job, but do check out assumptions by looking at a range of opinions, some of which should be from your own personal investigations.

Why sectors are powerful

Sector choice can be a powerful route to an inspired career, influencing a range of factors:

- the kind of people you work with and the things that matter to those people
- the skills you will be using, and the skills valued by the organisation
- the main purpose of the organisation
- the main focus of your working activity
- the values underlying the work which is performed
- the likely speed of change in the job, and how much learning you have to do.

Sectors and funnels

Society likes to put information and ideas into compartments, beginning at school. You didn't have classes titled *Thinking*, *Speaking*, *Imagination* or *Wisdom* (you might have done if renaissance ideas about education had continued). In the Victorian age, educators reclassified what was taught into narrower boxes (and at the same time invented new subjects, including English and Physics). We choose between the arts and sciences, with very little cross-over between the two.

The subjects you learn in the classroom prompt further courses of study. They also *seem* to suggest career paths. If you have academic strengths in one area, a certain number of obvious careers come to mind: ('I'm good at science, so I should be a scientist'). The problem here is that some of these suggest broad possibilities (for example, 'finance', 'law', 'business', 'computers'). Knowing that there is a wide range of well-paid jobs out there which fit under these very general headings, we continue our studies with optimism, even if the direction is vague.

Some early indications are rather more negative. If you're good at languages, for example, you'll think about being a translator, teaching, or possibly working in export/import. Beyond that you may run out of ideas. If you're a child good at music, art or drama, well-meaning relatives will doubtless remind you of the fact that artists in these fields often struggle to make a living. Options close down quickly, and soon you're drifting towards 'sensible' subjects and jobs, even though these routes are less exciting.

It's all driven by two very lazy bits of thinking. The first is viewing the world in terms of occupational titles. When an uncle who pats his six-year-old niece on the head and asks 'what do you want to do when you grow up?' the question clearly requires a job title as an answer. We're expected to choose the right label very early without knowing anything much about work. Later in life, in social situations, you're asked 'What do you do?' – again, seeking a job title. We'd get very different results asking questions about what people enjoy, and what their ideal mix of tasks would look like (see the jigsaw job exercise in Chapter 5).

This early game of career snakes and ladders describes much of what goes on when we choose subjects at school. It's easy to make the assumption that taking the right subjects will move you in the right direction, and to believe that study and work are very closely linked. This promise of 'educational funnelling' is the basis of early career thinking. We really do give young people a sense that when they narrow down their choices, for example at A-level, they are becoming more focused in career terms. Every year we turn out thousands of newly qualified people who have no idea how to make their qualifications relevant to employers (see Chapter 17). Few degree subjects outside science and technology are *directly* related to the jobs that graduates will actually perform.

Your secondary education narrowed your studies down to no more than about a dozen subjects, but there are literally thousands of sectors of knowledge and work out there. Anyone working with school or university leavers needs to explore this thinking carefully: there are few people practising 'pure' geography, history or mathematics in the world, and there are many top-level generalists.

Sectors and motivation

It's easy to choose a sector that seems 'safe'. At times of crisis you will be attracted by sectors where you can operate inside protective boundaries – your comfort zone. It's common among career changers to hear people say 'I would really like to work in a sector which inspires me, but I will find it much easier to get a job in the sector I have been working in for the last 20 years'.

Talk to people who love the work sector they have found themselves in. You will hear in their voices enthusiasm, love of detail, a willingness to share what they know with others, and a wish to encourage others to follow the path they have taken. Once you find a sector that gives you the same 'buzz', you will approach both your job search and the work you do with a far more positive spirit. The spin-offs, both for yourself and for any organisation which employs you, are important:

- You will be more enthusiastic at interviews – and employers love enthusiasm.
- You will retain what you learn and enthusiastically pass it on to colleagues.
- Your love of your work will communicate itself to clients and increase their loyalty.
- You will find it far easier to fit into an organisation where others share your passion.
- Efficiency and productivity will come naturally to you.
- You will be forever interested in new ideas, new connections and increasing your learning.

Sector problem 1: Not knowing what's out there

Choosing from unknown careers is like trying to plan a journey using a road atlas full of blank pages. Sector discovery helps to draw the missing maps.

If you can't find a sector that suits you then you may have to find a new angle. Work is changing so rapidly that new disciplines are being created all the time. Maybe you'll dream up an entirely new sector. Before Galileo there really wasn't a field you could describe as experimental physics. The word 'scientist' wasn't invented until the 1830s. Before Freud there wasn't a sector called psychoanalysis. In view of the range of jobs now associated with Google, social media and online sales, it's worth remembering what business guru Kevin Kelly said in 2009 – at that point the web had only been around for 5000 days. Something that has transformed society has only been around, in human terms, for a heartbeat. If it was a human being it wouldn't be old enough to vote.

'The best way to predict the future is to invent it.' **Alan Kay**

Sector problem 2: Starting with the wrong idea

A huge amount of the information we hold about sectors of work comes secondhand. We rely on out-of-date information from family, colleagues and friends. The problem is that most of this information is filtered and interpreted by someone else, and probably out of date. It doesn't give you an overview of the job.

The second problem is that what we see is weighted. When people describe jobs to you they attach value tags (safe/ risky, dull/exciting, boring/cutting edge, fixed/changing). Sometimes this information is entirely accurate, providing you with really important clues about what work is actually like. At least 50% of the time, however, it's out of date, subjective or just plain wrong.

The first principle is to start with your own impulse, not with someone else's idea of what a job is like. Find out for yourself. Don't rely on the slanted, possibly jaded views of retired professionals, recruiters or friends.

And remember that *the* great question to someone doing any job is 'what do you do most of the time?'

Sector problem 3: Choosing too narrow a range

The problem with looking at sectors is that they are just ideas in boxes. They can provide a very helpful filter in terms of identifying jobs that would suit you. For example, you may have a very clear idea that your work needs to be in education, or at least in learning and development. However, choosing by sector can also be restrictive. You may choose sectors that are obvious and safe, and miss opportunities elsewhere. You may miss new, growing or changing sectors that can provide pathways you haven't discovered yet.

You may be in danger of a blinkered, over-optimistic reliance on sectors – the idea that choosing the right field will solve your problems. Let's say your interest is in forestry. You like working outdoors in the wild woods. You go through the training which adds to your depth of background knowledge about forestry and conservation. You get a job. You find yourself dealing with peripheral problems such as record keeping, litter or car parks. You find that less and less of your knowledge and enthusiasm is being tapped, and you are increasingly learning about regulations, funding and government initiatives: possible career crisis. You find yourself saying 'I came into forestry because I love conservation and wildlife, but I've become a bureaucrat'. I hear the same story almost every week from people in teaching, personnel, nursing, travel, university lecturing and ministry, across a wide range of sectors. 'I was attracted by the box called nursing', they say, 'and I liked what it said on the label: caring for people, being there for patients and relatives. What am I now? A form filler.'

You can only begin to really know what's out there by being fascinated by what's out there. One characteristic about people who have made huge, brave career changes is that they became excited about what they didn't know, and started to do something about the gap in their knowledge. Chapter 10, designed to help you if you sense that you want to do something completely different, will also point to the importance of active exploration.

Sector problem 4: How do I know if I'll like it?

This is my colleague Gill Best's favourite question. It gives away a secret game plan: keep everything at the ideas stage and pretend that *the only way to find out about a job is to take it and see if it works out.* It's worth reading that last sentence again, as it is in fact one of the nation's favourite career strategies, the great high-risk experiment of taking a job because it looks OK, and hoping for the best.

You'll never know enough about a new sector or role until you find out by using the right approach and the right questions well before you go anywhere near a job interview. This means active investigation, not turning the idea over in your mind until you generate the right answer, or trying to undertake career exploration just by reading web pages. You can't know if you will like it, but you have to learn ways of finding out.

Sector problem 5: Moving on from subjects to sectors to choices

A common place where my clients get stuck is that they identify subject areas that interest and inspire them, but they can't make a connection between a subject of interest (for example, history) and a sector of work. They succumb too quickly to 'either/or' thinking: sectors are for work or pleasure. You will hear some career coaches say things like 'maybe you should follow this interest in your spare time'. Even more worrying is the idea 'if I do what I love for a living then I might get sick of it ... better to have an ordinary job and do what I love in my own time'. All this can be a great way of keeping work separate from 'life', in other words, a new excuse for avoiding enjoyable and interesting work.

If you can't see how you can move from subjects you love to potential sectors of work, you need to do some work on ways of making connections.

Where do I begin? Identifying sectors that will interest and inspire you

Begin with yourself. Look back at your House of Knowledge on page 91. What subjects, topics and themes energise you? What do you love learning or talking about? What do you want to know more about?

Exercise 9.1 – Prompts to get you thinking about sectors

Use this tried and tested prompting sequence to identify possible sectors of work:

Stage 1: Remembering

1. Dream jobs you had as a child. What sectors do they suggest?
2. The most enjoyable subjects you've studied.
3. Sectors where you have had some work experience.
4. Sectors which appeal to you when they are portrayed in documentaries or articles.
5. Jobs done by friends or family which you find fascinating.
6. Advertised posts that attracted you, even if you never applied for them.

Stage 2: Three great days at work

7. Think about a time when you had a great day at work. The sort of day where everything went well and you went home energised.

Write down what you were doing, what you enjoyed and what you achieved.

8. Do the same thing for two other memorable days.

Stage 3: Imagining

9. What jobs have you ever imagined doing?

10. If you could try someone else's job for a day, what would it be?

11. If you could do any job in the world for a week and still receive your normal salary, what jobs would you try?

12. Who are your role models or champions, and what sectors are they in?

13. If you won £10 million and you didn't need to work, what activity would you happily do for nothing?

Exercise 9.2 – Work themes

Starting from the inside means putting together a starting recipe for the kind of job that will work for you. One simple index of whether the job will work well for you is to think about the big themes that characterise work.

Give each work theme a score reflecting your level of interest, from 5 (high interest) to 3 (moderate interest) to 0 (no interest at all).

Creativity	Your ideal work is mainly about working imaginatively with ideas or designs; for example, the arts, performing, creative writing, visual design, lateral thinking, business creativity, adapting ideas, coming up with new ideas, challenging assumptions.
Score:	

Hands on Score:	Your preference is working hands on, engaging with the physical world; for example, building, shaping, cooking, craft, DIY, working with animals, plants, machines, vehicles, sports, physical fitness, physiotherapy, or working outdoors.
Influence Score:	Your ideal work is mainly about working through other people and will involve: leadership, management, changing organisations, setting up a new business or department, inventing, reorganising, shaping teams, driving others, influencing, persuading, motivating, selling, getting results.
Information Score:	Your ideal work is mainly about working with information; for example, analysing, cataloguing, gathering, planning, managing projects, researching, tracking down information, working with numbers or accounts, making the most of computers.
Systems Score:	You are most attracted to working with systems; for example, processes, quality control, continuous improvement, legal processes, procedures, book-keeping, record keeping, database management, health and safety.
People Score:	Your preference is for working with people; for example, training, teaching, coaching, mentoring, developing, caring, nursing, nurturing, healing.

Look at your top three work themes. How is your career a unique interaction between these themes? How can you make sure that your work feeds all three? For example, if your top three work themes in order are Creativity, People and Hands On, you'll want to ensure that your work allows you a high degree of creativity generated by teams of people, with the chance to invent new rules from time to time, but you'll be happiest working where you achieve results that you can see and feel. Remember, your work theme combination is a combination unique to you, because it also draws upon your knowledge, values and experience.

Try out your work theme combination as a working recipe for your ideal job. Add information about your skills to the mix. Combine this information to the Master Sheet at Exercise 9.4 (page 142).

If I could do anything at all ...

If you're discussing career choices with a friend, a common question is 'what would you do if you could do anything?' or 'if you could do any job in the world for a month, what would it be?' Another variation, which I prefer, is 'what would you do if all jobs paid the same?' The interesting thing is that having taken status and money out of the picture, you can focus very simply on that key question: *what would I be doing most of the time?*

Another common prompt is 'what would you do if you won the lottery?' People who have won millions on the National Lottery seem to follow an interesting pattern. After playing with the money for a year or two, buying houses, holidays and cars, they tend to get bored and look for something to do. Now that money is not the reason for working, what they choose to do is somehow even more authentic. This might mean investing in a business or starting a charitable foundation, or it might be taking up a simple trade. One lottery winner went back to his job as a staff trainer for McDonald's restaurants. So the real question is 'If you won the lottery, what would you do two years later when you were bored and could do anything you wanted?'

Pushing sector alternatives

The ability to push for alternatives is a powerful thinking skill for all aspects of life. The natural tendency of the mind is to move towards certainty and security. We often shun alternatives. A training colleague used to have a phrase for this: 'Don't confuse me with facts, my mind is made up.'

Most career changers love tests, boxes and checklists because their mind is saying 'I feed the data in here, and the answer pops out *here*'. We all love that idea of a magic button, which is why formal testing is so hit and miss in career work. It's so easy to sit back passively and wait for a computer or test to tell us the job we should do next. Most dangerous of all, in my estimation, are computer programs that sample your interests and aspirations and then give you a list of job titles. First, this kind of test cannot identify what really motivates and interests you. Second, no careers test can keep track of the huge range of jobs that are available in the world of work. Tests should only ever be used as a way of seeking possibilities for exploration, and never as a way of narrowing choices.

We feel that our thinking should follow a logical sequence:

This might look a little like scientific investigation, but science is a rather slippery model for thinking. In the twentieth century, scientists learned that there are few certainties and an infinite number of strange possibilities. Light appears to behave as both a particle and a wave. Heisenberg's uncertainty principle means that we can no longer say where something is and what it is doing at the same time. Quantum theory blurs notions of common sense and logic, while relativity challenges any secure notions we have about space and time.

'Problems cannot be solved at the same level of awareness that created them.' **Albert Einstein**

On first impression, having too many alternatives seems a recipe for indecision and vagueness. One of the great tools to business creativity is the process of brainstorming, but this is often misused because the process is cut off halfway through. Brainstorming is a good way of generating a large number of ideas in a free-flowing, non-critical environment. The effect is rather like a shotgun blast: broad and inaccurate. What any brainstorming session needs (and this will apply to your own creative thinking applied to the career process) is a secondary tool to help you to prioritise, test ideas, group ideas together and focus on the next step (see de Bono's six thinking hats on page 105).

Confidence

Notice that moment of hesitation before you write down the name of a sector. Look at what's going on in your head. *I'll never get into this sector. I don't have the training. I don't know enough.* In those moments remember this: US President Abraham Lincoln carried with him everywhere a newspaper clipping stating that he was a great leader. John Lennon's school report read 'certainly on the road to failure'. We all need a little more encouragement.

Switching sectors: the practicalities

Building on a formula first developed by Richard Nelson Bolles, here is an overview of the graduated difficulties of career change:

1. It is relatively straightforward to change occupations and remain within the same sector. For example, you may remain in secondary school education but become an administrator rather than a teacher.
2. It is relatively straightforward to switch sectors but remain in the same occupation. You may want to remain an accountant, and switch from manufacturing to the hotel trade.
3. The hardest shift is to change both occupation and sector at the same time. Don't believe those negative voices that tell you this is impossible. You just need better research, and a better strategy for finding out what's really out there. Sometimes it's worth thinking about a stepping-stone approach: change one element now, and another in, say, 12 months' time, when you have gained some relevant experience.

'What work I have done I have done because it has been play. If it had been work I shouldn't have done it.' **Mark Twain**

Lisa Johnson's story

Lisa Johnson enjoyed her job worked as marketing and sales executive for a company supplying quality cakes. She was really busy and enjoyed the variety of the role, even the challenge of working with supermarket buyers.

Lisa had suffered from eczema for most of her adult life. She found she was unable to use 95% of shop-bought toiletries and skincare products, and the 5% that didn't make her eczema worse were out of her price range.

When her baby daughter developed similar symptoms Lisa decided to investigate complementary therapies. After retraining as an aromatherapist she began to develop effective skincare products based entirely on natural ingredients. She started her own business in aromatherapy massage and making bespoke organic aromatherapy products. She initially kept up her day job as well, but now runs LJ's Natural Solutions (www.lj-natural.com) – what she describes as 'my own little empire from my kitchen table, working hard at something I totally believe in … your skin is the largest organ in your body and I want to help everyone treat theirs with respect.'

Lisa's story shows how you can begin with a subject of interest that matters to you personally and turn it, step by step, into a viable career path.

One-step-at-a-time career breakthrough

Many career and self-help books are written around the idea that we all have a hidden, 'real' self, and if we can unlock this secret then the answer to the question 'what should I do with my life?' will become crystal clear. The popular press reinforces the idea that deep down we all have a single dream job, and what we long for is an overnight transformation. That's why newspapers love stories of 'accountant becomes skydiver' or 'commando becomes nanny'.

In fact, such transformations are relatively rare. It's far more common that people progress by gradual steps and 'try on' different careers. Many of us do this quite naturally in our first ten years of work, when it's relatively easy to change direction and experiment. We often write off this period of our life as uncertain 'drifting'.

The idea that we are more likely to make incremental than dramatic career changes was explored in depth in Herminia

Ibarra's book *Working Identity* (2003). A new twist has been added recently in the application of 'chaos theory' to careers work (see www.brightandassociates.com.au). *The Chaos Theory of Careers* (2011) by Robert Pryor and Jim Bright suggests that we often look back at career decisions and rationalise them, but at the time they were in fact largely unplanned, improvised responses to a complex and unpredictable world.

Making a huge leap in your career is not straightforward. This is particularly true if this involves a change of field (for example, moving from marketing to photography) or a major change of lifestyle (for example, from financial director to author). It's a risky process because it's about moving from known to unknown. And others will be only too keen to tell you how risky your idea is.

If you want to achieve a career breakthrough it's vital that you commit some time to exploring your sectors of interest. If some of the following exercises make you feel uncomfortable or seem unconventional, then it means they're working. Sector exploration is about putting aside the rulebook and discovering new ways of thinking.

Exercise 9.3 – Moving from subjects to sectors

Step 1: Listing the subjects that interest you

1. Begin with the subjects you are interested in. Use the House of Knowledge exercise on page 91 to identify all of the subjects you have ever been interested in. Write them down.

2. Pick your top 20 subjects. Do this by asking yourself the question 'Which subjects am I most interested in?' At this stage don't think about work, just think about the subjects you would like to know more about.

3. Transfer your top subjects on to 20 cards; use cards about the same size as a playing card.

4. Review your cards by discarding anything that is essentially a repetition of something else. Combine any duplicated or very similar sectors. You may have *Product Design* and *Design* – perhaps they would be better as one card.

5. Add cards to get a total of 20. Think again: 'What would I like to know more about/study/think about/spend time discussing …?'

Step 2: Refocusing on sectors

6. Review your top 20 cards, splitting them into two columns:

Primary sectors Sectors I would like some contact with through work during the next 12 months	**Other sectors** Sectors which I found interesting, but don't need to be part of my work during the next 12 months

7. Look at the cards you have placed in the Primary sectors column, and choose your top ten.

8. Look at your top ten carefully. Redefine any sectors that are too vague: 'Management' or 'Administration' or 'Company Director' – these are roles that can be exercised in virtually any occupational sector.

9. You have now arrived at your top ten sectors for further investigation.

10. Check: are your sectors too big? If so, they will not be helpful to you. People tend to select too wide a sector, assuming that this will lead to a wider range of opportunities. In fact, what it leads to is a vagueness that quickly communicates itself to recruiters. If necessary, convert sectors into sub-sectors. For example, if your sector is Marketing, ask yourself whether there are any particular sectors where you would like to work as a marketing professional. Are you more interested in marketing products or services? Do your interests lie in advertising, direct mail, brand development or at a strategic level? Are you more interested in marketing one kind of product or service than another?

Step 3: Sector combining

11. Look at the connections between sectors. Move your cards round on a table or notice board to see what happens when you combine them. Try grouping your sectors in different ways.

12. Take three of your chosen sectors and put them in a row. Then take three more and put them in a column. Draw a 3 × 3 grid of nine squares between the two. In each of your nine blank squares write down any new sectors or sub-sectors that come to mind. An example is shown below.

	Physical fitness	**Translating**	**Export/import**
Creative writing	Writing self-help books to encourage fitness	Translating novels	Writing export guides
Safety management	Organising safety in physical fitness programmes	Specialist translation of safety management material	Exporting best practice in safety
Ecotourism	Environmentally friendly mountain biking	Translating commercial tourism ideas into ecotourism	Importing ecotourism models from other cultures

Step 4: Putting ideas into action

13. Now begins a key step: research. Investigate the key information about these sectors (entry routes, qualifications and training you need, measures for success, prospects). Talk to people actually working in these sectors to find out what the job is really like.

14. Once you have researched your top five or six sectors, come back to this exercise. You will probably find that sector exploration leads you to redefine and adapt your working list. Don't think of your sectors list as definitive or fixed; think of it as a work in progress.

Exercise 9.4 – Master Sheet

The Master Sheet (overleaf) brings together the results of various exercises on to one sheet so you can see, at a glance, the key ingredients in your ideal career. Every time you look at it you may see new ideas and connections. Review it frequently (try keeping a copy on the fridge door). Share it with trusted friends and colleagues.

You can download a blank copy of this Master Sheet from www. johnleescareers.com.

The various boxes on the Master Sheet relate to different exercises in this book – see the page numbers provided. The last box in the bottom right-hand corner is where you record ideas for sectors you are going to explore. Your goal is to come up with five target fields to investigate, and then begin your enquiries. Pick up the phone and talk to someone who is easy to approach.

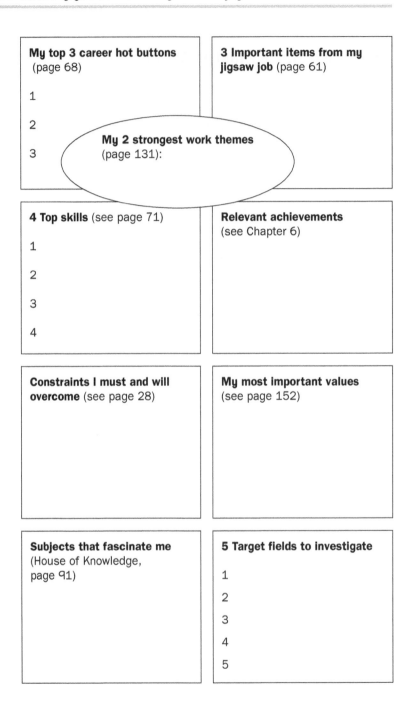

My top 3 career hot buttons
(page 68)

1

2

3

3 Important items from my jigsaw job (page 61)

My 2 strongest work themes
(page 131):

4 Top skills (see page 71)

1

2

3

4

Relevant achievements
(see Chapter 6)

Constraints I must and will overcome (see page 28)

My most important values
(see page 152)

Subjects that fascinate me
(House of Knowledge,
page 91)

5 Target fields to investigate

1

2

3

4

5

A step-by-step guide to exploring new sectors

- Begin by looking at the subjects you have really been interested in, including outside work.
- Look back at your working life. What sectors have you found most satisfying? Why?
- Draw up a prioritised list of sectors that appeal to you. Set out a plan to investigate more about them.
- Write down your top three work themes. If you combine those three together, what ideas do you come up with?
- Talk to people in jobs. Find out how they got them. Use information interviews (see Chapter 13) to help.
- Look for sector ideas in unexpected places which say something about you: your bookshelves, your photograph albums, articles you have clipped from newspapers.
- Become a future watcher. Read articles about how the world of work is changing. See how many new sectors and new job titles you can discover.
- Don't be put off if you can't find sectors which interest you – it just means that you need a new way of looking.
- When you've decided what you find exciting, tell people. Ask for their help.
- Don't allow 'yes, but' thinking to prevent further investigation of a sector that interests you.
- Research career ideas energetically and thoroughly. Investigate them as if you were finding out for somebody else.

10

How do I change career?

'Your imagination is your preview of life's coming attractions.' **Albert Einstein**

This chapter helps you to:

- Rethink the way you choose your career
- Explore sector combinations
- Map out sectors you would like to actively research
- Take the first steps towards a total change of career

'I think I need a complete change of career'

Let's tackle head-on the whole 'change of career' idea. There is a strong case that we have only one career, built up through a range of experiences which include work, learning, personal development, interests and activity outside work. In fact, you will do better at interview if you talk in these terms rather than apologising for 'changing career' or 'switching paths' or any other loaded language which implies that (a) there's only one, conventional way of having a career, and (b) you have no idea where you're going next.

So how do you begin if you want to add more colour, more variety to your single, integrated career path? Here's an interesting fact about the world of careers advice. People prefer to buy careers books with the words 'interview' or 'CV' or 'job search' in the title. However, when it comes to asking for help, most enquirers begin with a statement like 'I would like to find out what else I could do' or 'I have a feeling I want to do something completely different' – questions about direction of travel rather than means of transport.

People ask for help partly because of the huge ranges of choices available in life, as explored in the last chapter. Making a career change is much tougher than making a job change. It's a journey into the unfamiliar that will require new information, new ways of thinking, a strong CV and well-planned interview answers. Deciding to change career increases risk: small risks of rejection, and big risks that it will all go wrong. So, confidence and learning how to make progress without burning all of your boats are both critically important.

Many areas already touched on by this book will help you if you would like to try a very different career path. You have already looked at your constraints, examined your personality, skill set and knowledge base, and looked at the activities in life and sectors that give you a sense of fulfilment. You may already have a half-formed idea, matched by a sense of longing. That's where you begin. This chapter will take you forward so you start looking at – and acting on – completely new options.

How do we decide on a career path?

When I have a first session with a client, I want to know a few basic things: past, present and future. What has motivated this person in the past, both within work and outside it? What was the best job? The best organisation? Then the focus shifts to the present: what's going on right now that makes the client ready to make a change. And so to 'what next?' People usually begin by stating that they have no idea about what they want to do next, but they usually do. I think it was the US careers specialist Richard Knowdell who stated that everyone in the world knows exactly what job they should be doing. The problem, he says, is that half of the people haven't yet found the words to describe what they're looking for, while the other half knows exactly what they should be doing but is too frightened to say it.

The most demanding question you'll ever face if you see a career coach is not 'what are you going to do next?' or even 'how are you going to get it', but *how are you going to decide?'* Most people secretly believe that the answer will just come along if they take a test, read a book, or just sit at home long enough with the curtains closed and think really, really hard.

Let's backtrack slightly. How do we choose our career paths? As Chapter 9 revealed, we are initially funnelled into sectors of work by academic choices. It's worth looking at the influences which typically shape career choice:

Influences that affect the way we choose career paths

- **Parental expectations** – occupational groups tend to repeat themselves in families.
- **Parental aspirations** – pushing young people towards careers that match what parents believe to be the right kind of work.
- **Academic subjects** – what you choose to study may seem like the key to your future.
- **Money and status** – academic high-achievers are often pushed towards high-pay, high-status occupations such as law, finance or medicine.
- **Peer pressure** – doing something cool; avoiding things that look boring.

- **Advice from your first boss** – the opinion of your first ever boss is often highly influential.
- **Personal values and beliefs** – the kind of work that seems worthwhile.
- **Media influence** – the jobs we see done on TV or in films or on YouTube.
- **Teachers and lecturers** – because of the effect of educational 'funnelling'.
- **High visibility** – jobs you see around you a great deal of the time.
- **Careers advisers** – particularly influential while you are also making study choices.
- **Work-related tests** – ranging from *bona fide* personality or interest inventories to something you found on the internet.
- **Personal inclination** – your strong (or vague) sense of what might work, what you are 'supposed' to be doing or what you feel called to in life.

We understand jobs that touch our lives. If you're a child and spend a lot of time in hospital, for example, the chances are that you may want to be a nurse or a doctor. In a recent TV programme about a remote island in the Indian Ocean that lacked even a school or post office, a young boy was asked what he wanted to do when he grew up. *Fishing*, he said, naming the one job he could see available to adult males. Even in our developed society, we are exposed to only a fraction of the jobs available. Do you know what a systems analyst does, or a risk assessor, an order picker, or a voice coach? In our modern economy, new types of jobs are created every day. Most will be invisible to us, and we have to rely on hunches, insider information or assumptions to choose between them. Some jobs are more visible than others. You know what a surgeon, a barrister or a fire-fighter does. Or, you *think* you do, but how much of your perception is based on TV roles rather than the way people really do their jobs?

The influence of the media on career choice cannot be underestimated. TV, in particular, samples the world of work in a very slanted way. Some jobs are never off the screen (medics, lawyers, teachers, police officers, CSIs, chefs), others shown rarely (when did you see TV fiction include an offshore rigger, 3D designer, personal shopper, car valeter, book-keeper, or even a career coach?). Some occupations in the same sector are given very different weighting: TV loves architects but tends to ignore surveyors.

TV shows you a limited picture, but also a distorted one. When you see a police officer on TV, either in fiction or in a documentary, what is shown? Normally an officer chasing, apprehending or cautioning a member of the public. If you talk to actual police officers you discover that even those on the 'beat' spend most of their time checking emails or completing paperwork. TV prefers the more exciting moments: the airline pilot avoiding a crash, the lawyer bringing in a surprise witness or the ambulance crew saving a patient's life.

In fact, TV shapes the way we see jobs more than anything else. We work on the assumption that viewers can tell the difference between television and reality. Worryingly, more than a few can't. The actor Johnny Briggs played the factory owner Mike Baldwin in *Coronation Street* for 30 years. Every week the soap star received a handful of genuine job applications seeking work in his fictional factory. Even more worryingly, about once a week someone applied for the job of assistant manager.

Deciding what or who?

The trouble with most of the careers advice we receive as young people is that it revolves around the question 'What do you want to do when you grow up?' We are supposed to look thoughtful, and then come up with a job title: 'Er ... a ... chartered accountant!'

A more authentic decision might be about what kind of person you hope to be. So, many people, particularly those taking a more spiritual view of life choices, say that the most important thing to consider is who you are, not what you do. Others will say that it's self-indulgent to focus on the individual, and more practical to focus on the work that is actually available.

The answer, I believe, is like so many of the most important truths in life, a matter of holding conflicting ideas in your mind at the same time, as the **Three Career Circles** diagram below makes clear:

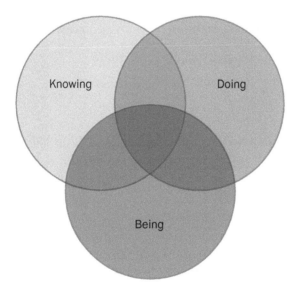

The first step to a complete career change takes very little time at all. Draw a larger version of the Three Career Circles for yourself, and within each circle write in the key words that capture what's important for you, right now, using the paragraphs overleaf if you need a nudge.

Knowing

Chapter 7 revealed the way *what you choose to know about* provides powerful clues about the kind of work that will seem meaningful. So, if you are considering a complete change of career it's worth thinking carefully about the kind of topics you would like to read or talk about while you are at work. Second, review all the things you know about so you have a clear idea of the underpinning knowledge you may need to demonstrate for handling competency-based interviews (see Chapter 14).

Understanding the knowledge angle of work is also an insight into your motivation, both now and in the future, because it treats each job as a learning curve. Most roles are interesting in their first few weeks or months, but whether a job is intrinsically interesting in the long run is often about how much you will continue to learn and grow.

'We are what we repeatedly do.' **Aristotle**

Doing

Aristotle was writing about developing virtuous habits, but his words remind us of another powerful notion: *what we choose to do most of the time matters.* The activities that take up most of our waking hours have a strong influence on our effectiveness, the outcomes our work generates, and the way people see us. Remember that word 'occupation'? A job is what 'occupies' our time and attention.

Skills are powerful reinforcers of self-esteem and are the best way of making our values tangible in the world by getting things done. Skills need refreshing and updating, but more than anything else they need to be used. Using only part of your skill set, or using skills you really don't value very much, can lead to long-term demotivation and cynicism.

Refer to Chapter 6 to refresh and build on your understanding of what you do regularly and well in terms of behaviours, skills and competences.

Being (and valuing)

How you exercise the skills you have is very dependent on your attitude and values, two factors which are strongly linked to personality. To perform a task well, accurately, with care, taking into account the needs of other people, to be able to meet deadlines, to be cheerful or resourceful under pressure, these are all aspects of personality that you should revisit through the various opportunities offered in this book, notably in Chapter 8.

The question of 'being' is not just about the personality you were born with, but also a big clue about values. During life we also build up a sense of what is important to us. Some of those things are clearly demonstrated through the things we choose to learn about under the 'know' heading, but others are deeper still. Think about the causes or charities you support (whether with time, money or sympathy). What issues energise you? What makes you angry?

Values: the bigger picture

We all take our values to work with us. Your values are expressed in work through the tasks and outcomes you find interesting and meaningful. Sometimes this is on a macroscale: you're interested in what your organisation contributes to the world. For others, values are expressed in relationships at work and the way colleagues are treated. Ultimately, you will be more motivated in work situations where the organisation and your colleagues share most of your values.

Values, in the simplest terms, are words which describe principles that you want to live out. Values often describe positive behaviours, for example, 'doing the right thing', 'treating others as you'd like to be treated'. Sometimes it is easier for us to recognise our values when we are confronted with behaviours we don't want to see, for example: 'not reneging on your promises', 'not having to lie to customers'. You might find more clues by looking at the basement of your House of Knowledge on page 91 – values often begin at home.

Exercise 10.1 – Discovering your values

Values provoke strong feelings, and we often have a sense of what is important or true for us. This can be especially noticeable when you are faced with doing something that conflicts with your values.

I'm indebted to my colleague Gill Best for co-authoring this exercise, which is new to this edition. Start a notebook page to write down the answers to the following questions. Use the following question sequence to identify your values. Share the results of this with someone you trust and who is interested in your development.

People you admire

1. Think of people you admire. Who are your **role models?** Who do you respect most?

2. What is it about these people you admire? (Think of *how* they live and work, not just what they've achieved).

3. Write down **one or two words** which sum up each person, using the grid below. (Some words to start you thinking: *modest, risk-taking, self-sacrificing, entrepreneurial, caring, creative, brave, honest, challenging, encouraging, ethical, reliable, consistent.*)

	Words to describe HOW they live and work
Family members	
Bosses	
Work colleagues	
Friends	
Coaches/mentors/teachers	
Famous people	

Looking at the list of people and qualities you have recorded, write down your answers to the following question:

4. What *qualities* and *attitudes* do you admire most in other people?

People you don't admire

5. So far you've looked at your heroes. You might want to think about people whose behaviour you find unattractive. What *qualities* and *attitudes* in others do you dislike? (Some words to start you thinking: *judgemental, intolerant, lazy, arrogant.*) List these qualities, and then in the bottom line record how you wish people would behave.

Behaviours and attitudes I don't admire	
How I wish my least favourite people would behave	

Your personal values

6. How do you want to behave at work, given the choice? Record examples.

7. How do you want your working life to be remembered after you've retired? Again, write down some examples.

Look at *all* the positive values you have recorded above. Highlight the five or six words that matter to you most. Now you have a working list of your **values**. Prioritise your list. This list will help you to identify if a job or an employer matches or conflicts with your values.

If you want to go deeper to explore what part values have played in your life, use questions 8–14 below. Record examples wherever possible.

Changing and conflicted values (listing examples)

8. What values did you have when you began your working career?

9. How have they changed?

10. What experiences may have caused your values to change?

Values at work

11. Where have your values been affirmed at work?

12. If you've had a day when you felt you made a difference at work, what values did you put into practice?

13. Where have your values been challenged or questioned?

14. Where have you had to work in a way which didn't fit your values (for example, you were asked to work in a way which felt unethical)?

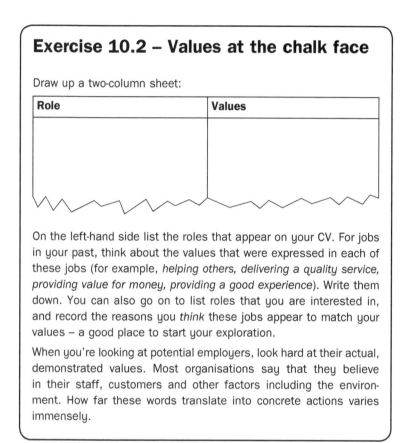

Exercise 10.2 – Values at the chalk face

Draw up a two-column sheet:

Role	Values

On the left-hand side list the roles that appear on your CV. For jobs in your past, think about the values that were expressed in each of these jobs (for example, *helping others, delivering a quality service, providing value for money, providing a good experience*). Write them down. You can also go on to list roles that you are interested in, and record the reasons you *think* these jobs appear to match your values – a good place to start your exploration.

When you're looking at potential employers, look hard at their actual, demonstrated values. Most organisations say that they believe in their staff, customers and other factors including the environment. How far these words translate into concrete actions varies immensely.

Career change: starting from the inside out

What's calling you?

'Job: what you do to support your vocation.' **Anonymous**

Do you sense that you might be looking for a *vocation* rather than just than a job? The word comes from the Latin *vocare*, 'to call'. In popular usage a 'vocation' feels different from an occupation. Sometimes it's used to describe a job, either professional or voluntary, that makes an important contribution to society. It also describes an occupation for which a person is specifically gifted. Not only have we redefined what we mean by 'career' in the past 50 years, we have redefined what we mean by 'vocation', too. Some feel a 'vocation' towards working with animals, being a chef, making handmade furniture, or serving in the armed forces. Others might talk in these terms about their commitment to being an artist.

A vocation is, however, something we feel 'called' to do; we feel a sense of commitment stronger than ordinary levels of motivation, and a sense of 'rightness' in our choice. It's not just a strong career impulse, not just this year's big idea. To choose a vocation often implies turning your back on conventional career satisfiers such as money and status, and it is a pathway which may take years to explore and resolve.

One interesting assumption is that following a calling means putting aside work satisfaction: the work is about duty, not about personal choices. This is probably something worth questioning. A vocation may provide someone with a strong sense of purpose and may involve some self-sacrifice; however, a vocation can also be something which is fulfilling and a good experience. 'Good experience' isn't the same as 'fun', but shouldn't be a million miles from it. Those living out vocations will admit that they are not 100% committed to their calling all of the time. The difference is they keep to the path, trying to be authentic to that original calling, and to live out long-term life choices even when things are difficult.

Peter Sinclair, originator of the 'After Sunday' movement, is fond of reminding people that one of the clear signs of vocation is that you should look happy, at least some of the time. There are an awful lot of glum-looking people in teaching, nursing, clergy and charity jobs. Living a vocation may fill a useful social purpose, but if it makes you miserable it's probably a poor long-term match. Being of service to other people can sometimes start with doing things you find fulfilling.

Feeling called to a particular role often provides a strong sense of fit – you've found the place which is authentically *you*. Former Archbishop of Canterbury Rowan Williams wrote 'vocation is … what's left when all the games have stopped'. Your calling may draw you towards the best version of yourself.

Perhaps the biggest feature of vocation is that it's *not just about you*. Most vocational choices that lead to the commitment of decades rather than weeks or months arise out of faith, strongly held personal values, and a sense of service. So, three benchmarks might help if you think you're considering a vocation rather than a job:

1. Your gifts will be recognised by others as well as by you.
2. You understand, and commit to, a long game which may include fallow years.
3. What you will be doing will be, one way or another, a life lived for others.

Career change: starting from the outside in

Are you sure you don't know what you want to do? Begin, as suggested above, with the question *what work would you do if all jobs paid the same?* Then try on the question *which jobs would you like to try out just for a week?*

Look again at the sector choices prompted by Chapter 9, particularly from the work themes discussion (page 131). Explore:

- Sectors of work you know well.
- Sectors and sub-sectors that have intersected with your job.
- Sectors you have had some contact with during your career.
- Sectors you know something about through your personal interests, friends or commitments.

At this stage, try not to allow 'yes, but' thinking to get in the way. You don't have to make a decision at this stage – all you are doing is generating ideas. Here are some other tried and tested prompts to get you to generate job ideas:

- Think of people you know who are doing interesting jobs. What's interesting about them?
- What jobs have you applied for in the past but didn't get?
- What jobs have you seen advertised that caught your attention for 30 seconds, even if you did nothing about them?

Go back to your House of Knowledge (page 91). The clues are all there in the topics that have called you, year after year. Somewhere in a box, in your loft or under the stairs, there's a box with the evidence: those projects that keep coming out every two or three years. Look, too, at the things you have chosen to study over the years. Refer back to Exercise 9.3 on page 138 to look at the way you can move from subjects that interest you generally in life to sectors of work. Try Exercises 10.3 and 10.4 at the end of this chapter to use lateral thinking about 'what next?'

Don't get hung up on another job myth: that if you try to turn a hobby into a living you will fall out of love with it. Plenty of people are busy being paid to do things which they would happily do for nothing in their own time. Starting with subjects means starting with enthusiasm and energy. The things that fill us with happiness, no matter how trivial, are clues about activities which feed you. Sometimes it's even more important to find the things that will feed the tired soul – the kind of mid-life realignment that often matters a great deal.

Career change: just do it

As this chapter has rehearsed, the question is not how you are going to find a new career, but how you are going to decide. Thinking things through matters. Reimagining the possibilities of your career makes all the difference.

The next big question is *what are you going to do about it?* The second half of this book provides several prompts to activity, but let's nail down one plain fact. If you want to put off career change forever (or at least until it's too late) then keep on reflecting, analysing and mulling over. Keep on thinking that you have to make the perfect decision before you act. That will happily put change off forever.

However, if you don't want to be spending your last inactive years saying 'I wish', then do something. There is research (summarised in Richard Wiseman's 2009 book *59 Seconds*) suggesting that you're more likely to reach goals if you have a short-term, step-by-step plan, and if you do something about step one.

Finding out and following your enthusiasm costs very little. You don't need to have a perfect target job to start the process of discovery, just a sense of curiosity. And here's a big clue: your breakthrough probably has a 5% likelihood of happening as a result of reading or thinking, and a 95% likelihood of occurring as a result of a person. Someone you already know, possibly. Or, even more likely, someone you meet in the next two or three months as a result of your active enquiries. So what's the first step? A conversation. Start with people you know, even if they seem very disconnected from the world you want to enter. Find opportunities to talk to people who love what they do for a living. Experiment with information interviews (see Chapter 13), and act on the career change checklist given at the end of this chapter.

Pass it on

With luck and a little application you'll move towards a job you love doing. Once you've found what you're looking for, share your insights. An important part of career discovery is being able to share our discoveries and improve the working lives of those around us.

First of all you discover your talents – the solo instrument you play. As exploration continues you start to hear the other instruments people are playing. Soon you understand your role in the orchestra. The final step is to help others to begin to hear the music.

Exercise 10.3 – The Field Generator

The **Field Generator**, described below, helps you to generate new ideas for work sectors. You begin with things that interest you, and then follow a thought process to help you to generate ideas – new fields for you to wander into and explore.

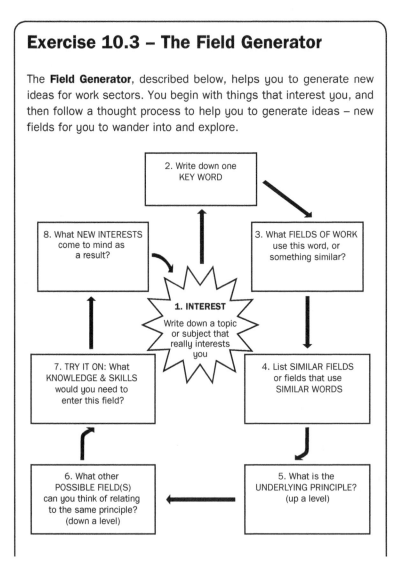

2. Write down one KEY WORD

8. What NEW INTERESTS come to mind as a result?

3. What FIELDS OF WORK use this word, or something similar?

1. INTEREST
Write down a topic or subject that really interests you

7. TRY IT ON: What KNOWLEDGE & SKILLS would you need to enter this field?

4. List SIMILAR FIELDS or fields that use SIMILAR WORDS

6. What other POSSIBLE FIELD(S) can you think of relating to the same principle? (down a level)

5. What is the UNDERLYING PRINCIPLE? (up a level)

If you are short of sector ideas, go back to the House of Knowledge exercise on page 91. Use a highlighter pen to mark your preferred interests. Now use this information in the Field Generator.

'The brain is a wonderful organ. It starts working the moment you get up in the morning and does not stop until you get to work.' **Robert Frost**

How to use the Field Generator

Step 1	Make copies of the Field Generator diagram, and try this exercise out using as many interests as you can. This exercise works best with someone else working with you, prompting and asking questions.
	Make sure you have completed the House of Knowledge exercise on page 91. Pick five or six of your strongest interests.
	Write one of your interests in **Box 1**; for example, boats, sailing and the sea.
Step 2	In **Box 2** write down a key word from your area of interest; for example, sailing.
Step 3	Look at your key word and in **Box 3** write down three sectors of work where this word appears; for example, sailing instruction, sailing boat design, sailing restoration.
Step 4	Now that you have expanded your sector a little, think of fields of work that use similar words, and write them in **Box 4**; for example, ship building, naval architecture, merchant navy, navigation. Make a note in the margin of any new fields that you hadn't thought of before that may be connected in some way with your interest; for example, outward-bound training, water safety.
Step 5	This is where you have a chance to use a technique which in idea-building terms is called 'going up a level'.
	Look at your fields in Box 4. Is there any overriding category that describes them? If you were to find these ideas together in one drawer, what label would you put on the front of the drawer? (For example, nursing and

	osteopathy can be placed within the general category of 'medicine' or 'physiology'.) This may take a while to work out, or you may think of several alternatives. The answer will be unique to you. In this case you might come up with weather, racing, healthy competition, low technology, getting away from it all, being captain of my own boat …
	What is the underlying 'big idea'? Write down your final answer in **Box 5**; for example, healthy competition might be your preferred underlying principle here.
Step 6	In Box 5 we moved up a level to the underlying principle. In **Box 6** we come down a level at a different point.
	In this case you might come up with something totally unconnected to sailing arising from 'healthy competition'; for example, sports coaching, teaching kids about diet and exercise, teaching fund-raising skills to charity staff, or selling ethical financial products. Write down any ideas that appeal to you, making sure you don't try to exclude them at this stage by misguided thinking about what is 'practical'. You may discover sectors or new interests here that could one day become part of your House of Knowledge.
Step 7	Underline one of the fields or ideas generated in Box 6, and write it in **Box 7**. It's probably best to begin with one that has surprised you most (for example, in this case you might have come up with teaching fund-raising skills to charity staff).
	Write down what you feel to be the key skills and knowledge that you would need to work in this sector. Begin by putting down what you already know, and add more by putting yourself mentally into the shoes of someone working in this area. The only way to build up an accurate picture is to find out. Ask someone already working in this sector, or do some desk research.
	If this step was productive and interesting, go back to Box 6 and do the same again with any other interesting sectors.

Step 8	**Box 8** allows you to record any new areas of interest that the exercise might have brought up; for example, coaching. Take a new copy of the Field Generator and put this new interest in Box 1, and begin again.

A completed Field Generator is shown below.

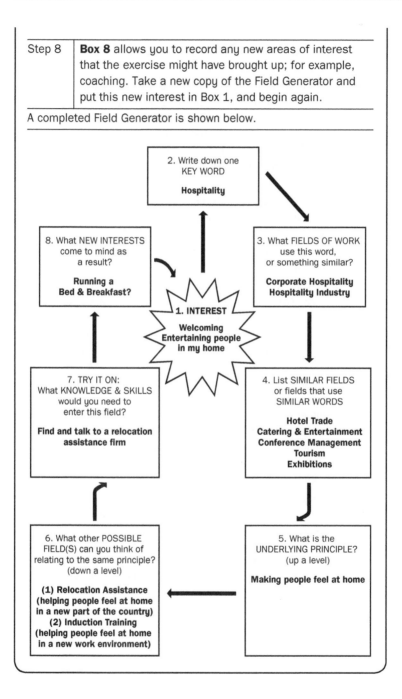

2. Write down one KEY WORD

Hospitality

8. What NEW INTERESTS come to mind as a result?

Running a Bed & Breakfast?

3. What FIELDS OF WORK use this word, or something similar?

Corporate Hospitality Hospitality Industry

1. INTEREST

Welcoming Entertaining people in my home

7. TRY IT ON: What KNOWLEDGE & SKILLS would you need to enter this field?

Find and talk to a relocation assistance firm

4. List SIMILAR FIELDS or fields that use SIMILAR WORDS

Hotel Trade Catering & Entertainment Conference Management Tourism Exhibitions

6. What other POSSIBLE FIELD(S) can you think of relating to the same principle? (down a level)

(1) Relocation Assistance (helping people feel at home in a new part of the country) (2) Induction Training (helping people feel at home in a new work environment)

5. What is the UNDERLYING PRINCIPLE? (up a level)

Making people feel at home

Exercise 10.4 – Discontinuous thinking

This process is great for times when you are completely stuck for ideas, and works well alongside the Field Generator. Discontinuous thinking is about provoking your mind into making new connective pathways. It's the driving force behind Edward de Bono's concept of provocative thinking, and also one of the characteristics of Roger von Oech's delightfully off-the-wall classic *A Whack on the Side of the Head*.

There are few rules with this kind of exercise. One of the principles behind it is that you think about something else entirely, and then allow some kind of connection or comparison between your thought process and your main problem. Here are some ideas that might work particularly well with sectors:

1. *Try a provocative statement that sounds deliberately illogical or nonsensical*. For example, 'a sector which is about persuading and influencing but avoids people'. This might take you into ways of translating your interpersonal skills into text-based or alternative contexts, for example, writing to influence, finding great words for websites, writing other people's speeches, designing models for negotiation and conflict management that can be communicated by distance learning. Another one might be 'building houses that nobody will live in'. You might apply your construction skills to buildings used for housing animals or equipment; you might start building models rather than sketching things out in words; you might create 'virtual' libraries, supermarkets or conference centres on the internet.

2. *Try turning your sector upside down*. For example, you may be interested in child development because you are interested in the way young people grow. Turning that upside down might lead you to thinking about the effects of ageing. This may be a sector which interests you in itself, or it may help you to refocus on your chosen sector, for example, by looking at the effects of head injury in young people.

'Must do' list

Your checklist for beginning a career change today:

Knowing	1. Review what you enjoy knowing about (try the **House of Knowledge** on page 91). 2. Review your preferred **work themes** (page 131). 3. Look seriously at the things you have chosen to learn about in the past. 4. Use the **Field Generator** (page 160) to translate ideas into potential sectors for investigation.
Doing	5. Review your skills using Chapter 6. 6. Consider using the **JLA Skill Cards** to identify your motivated skills (see page 89).
Being	7. Look at the values and preferences expressed in your **jigsaw job** (page 61). 8. List your top three **career hot buttons** (page 64). 9. Review your personality by looking at Chapter 8. 10. Complete the **values** exercises in this chapter (pages 152 and 155).
Next steps	Now *stop* reflecting and move into action steps, namely: 11. Put together the above information on your **Master Sheet** (page 142). 12. Show your results to friends and colleagues. Ask for ideas and connections. 13. Talk to people about what you think you might be looking for – use the two-breath message on page 209. 14. Write down five potential target fields. They don't need to be perfect. 15. Use the REVEAL method on page 215 to generate meetings with interesting people.

11

Job searching creatively and effectively

'An idea is nothing more nor less than a new combination of old evidence.' **James Webb Young**

This chapter helps you to:

- Avoid first-time job searcher mistakes
- Debunk job-hunting myths
- Anticipate employer risk aversion
- Discover the hidden job market

Why do we keep making the same mistakes?

No matter what electronic tools and advice are available, we keep making the same mistakes when we try to change jobs. It all looks deceptively simple, yet employers complain every day that candidates haven't undertaken basic preparation. Even in a tight market, they fire out indifferent CVs and talk themselves out of the job in the first minutes of an interview. People generally feel that job searching is about as straightforward as making an online purchase, and generally just feel their way forward instinctively rather than learning from others who have done it before them. As a result they make early, repeated and sometimes career-tilting mistakes.

First-timer mistakes in job hunting

Anyone can be a novice in the job search game – you might be 16 and leaving school or, after 25 years of automatic promotions within one organisation, you might face your first competitive interview in your 40s. No matter how old you are, you'll probably make the same rookie mistakes.

It pays to be very aware of the mistakes that people make in the first two or three months of job searching. The biggest error is generally pitching yourself at large targets too soon; for example, registering with employment agencies when you don't know what you're looking for, or emailing out a vague, untested CV to all your contacts. Applying for jobs where you're unlikely to fit leads to early knockbacks, which dents interview confidence and causes you to start tinkering with your CV and downgrading your ambitions.

At workshops I will often list the behaviours and strategies which *extend* your job search time. How many of these dead-end strategies are you currently adopting?

- Relying on the internet to find jobs.
- Pursuing only advertised positions (when you are easily up against hundreds of others).
- Applying for jobs you don't really want 'just for the experience' (and yet getting knocked back by rejection).
- Chasing jobs in declining sectors (rather than seeking out the sectors and organisations that are going against the tide).
- 'Lowering your sights' when things go wrong.
- Using up all your best contacts in the first three weeks and then complaining because you don't know anybody.
- Sending out a CV which communicates lack of fit when you want to change career.
- Hiding behind computer screens – approaching potential contacts by email rather than by phone.

So what works? Here are the activities likely to *shorten* a job search:

- Shaping and road testing your CV thoroughly before you send it to important contacts.
- Carefully rehearsing what you want to say about yourself.
- Reaching out through social media to generate conversations, ideally face to face (see Chapter 12).
- Networking of any kind – even just talking to friends and neighbours about job ideas can make all the difference (see Chapter 13).
- Telling people what you're looking for, keeping it focused and simple, or offering a summary message (see 'two-breath message' on page 209).
- Conducting information interviews (see Chapter 13) so you get under the skin of target sectors and really understand what they are looking for.
- Using your best contacts at the right time – only approaching senior people who are great door openers when you are clear how they can help, and you can give them three or four clear reasons why they should recommend you.

Smarter searching

Don't spend the first three months of searching recovering from basic mistakes. Practise talking about yourself – particularly weak points – before others turn the spotlight on you. This will make you more focused and less nervous in the first round of interviews.

Even a first-class job search strategy and the smartest CV don't guarantee an immediate job offer – often it takes time to find your way. However, even if you are fairly marketable it pays to do some planning before you throw yourself at the market. For a structured, step-by-step approach to job seeking see my book *Just The Job!* The basics are covered by the 'six steps' model on the opposite page.

Six steps to a smarter job search

1. **Work out your story.** Learn how to communicate why you are on the market at the moment, but also your career story as a whole – if you don't make sense of your skills and experience, an employer won't.
2. **Set out your stall.** Make a list of projects completed, tasks attained, achievements you're proud of, skills and supporting evidence, know-how, supporting qualifications and training. Catalogue your best material and use the highlights as the main features whenever you summarise what you do.
3. **Focus on target jobs.** Take advice and hunt the internet to find out the names and specifications of the kinds of job you'll be chasing.
4. **Deal with problem material.** Make sure your CV covers gaps in your history, your experience, or your qualifications – explain why you should still be considered.
5. **Market test.** Find people with hiring experience to give your CV a cold read, and practise your interview performance thoroughly before you get into a selection process.
6. **Go for it!** Use a multi-strategy job search (see below) to discover, reach out, and get yourself in front of decision makers.

Reducing the time you spend hunting has a major impact on your motivation levels. If things don't work for a while you can probably weather that and keep your confidence levels intact. If you're job hunting for months on end your confidence in your abilities will start to lag, which will impact on the energy you convey in any conversation.

Beginning a creative job search

Most people rely on one or two channels to find a job, usually preferring activities which require the least energy – job boards where you can upload your CV at the press of a button, or advertised positions. This is rather like deciding that whatever your health problem is, that you are only going to treat it by taking an aspirin. Today's job market is complicated, with lots of distractions and dead ends. As this chapter will reveal, employers are shifting their recruitment behaviours and using methods which cost little, give good returns, and rely on personal or web-based networks to deliver talent to their door. To succeed, you need to operate using all channels, *not just the channels you prefer*. The better you get at job searching the more you will prioritise channels according to their rate of return.

For now, let's examine what it might mean to use a creative, flexible, multi-strategy job search. That means you do *all* of the following, but you will prioritise activities in the bottom third of the list:

- Register with appropriate job boards.
- Monitor job boards operated by employers and agencies.
- Make applications in response to vacancies advertised in a range of media.
- Scrutinise all job ads, whether paper or electronic, to identify likely employers and useful agencies, and approach them directly.
- Maintain a strong online presence through appropriate use of social media.
- Join online discussion groups and forums.
- Talk to recruitment consultants who regularly advertise jobs in your sector.
- Make other, speculative approaches to recruitment consultants who you believe may be able to help you, or those you have been recommended to contact.

- Approach companies in your chosen fields on a speculative basis with a strong covering letter matching four or five of your key areas of experience to the employer's needs.
- Undertake temporary or project work which increases your visibility to decision makers.
- Encourage an employer to create a new job where one does not already exist.
- Follow up recommendations to talk to people and organisations, but do your homework first to make the most of opportunities.
- Conduct information interviews (see page 214) to deepen your understanding of sectors and improve your contacts.
- Ask for meetings with decision makers and people who are at the heart of great networks.
- Undertake personal networking to increase your visibility.

As the above list shows, the multi-channel approach doesn't ignore online activity, but ensures it takes up no more room in your portfolio of activities than it deserves. The key to a successful job search is to combine methods effectively and by doing so, increase their power. Review your activity and ask yourself why you are avoiding certain activities. Get it right, and you will consciously target the hidden job market and anticipate employer risk thinking, and you will be choosing a different strategy from the majority of job seekers.

Myth cracking

When I moved from training recruiters to career coaching I was surprised to discover that the facts about how people get jobs are not well known. We create urban myths, believe that all recruitment processes are open and fair, and feel that we should play a numbers game by applying for as many jobs as possible.

If you've been waiting for the moment when you felt you got your money's worth from this book, this may be it. Let's debunk some job-hunting myths – those pictures of the labour market inherited from friends and family.

Most jobs are found on the internet. Although job boards may help, the internet is not the magic tool it seems. The web can be a great source of information, but statistically it is one of the least effective job search methods. However, managing your social media presence can open doors very effectively (see Chapter 12 for more about online searching and social media).

You need to rely on published vacancies. This is still relatively true in some sectors (notably charities and the public sector), but in today's market only a small proportion of jobs are advertised in print, and online listings are often suspect (see Chapter 12). Advertised positions are 'candidate magnets' – they can easily attract hundreds of applications, making it very hard to stick out from the crowd. In addition, someone may already be the preferred candidate even before the job is advertised.

It's who you know, not what you know. Making connections will increase your chance of being seen, but job offers arise from old boy networks less often than you might imagine. What employers do is to draw on expertise which is recognisable and close by, so they tend to favour people who are already in their network rather than strangers. The key issue therefore is not who you know now, but *who you get to know in the next few months.*

It's easier to get a job when you have one already. Employers are highly influenced by recent experience and the ability to bring skills online quickly, so a track record of recent work can help. However, in the past five to ten years employers have got used to seeing candidates who are between jobs. If you've been out of a role for a while it pays to keep your skills up to date, for example by volunteering.

Qualifications count. Employers often have only a vague sense of how the huge range of qualifications available translate into employable skills. Apply what you can do to the needs of the job. If you are less qualified than your peers, emphasise the intellectual standards you have achieved through your work experience.

Employers only see people who have done the job before. This is often fairly true in a tight market, but three things may get you into an interview if you are a career shifter – enthusiastic interest in the sector, real knowledge of the job, and the ability to show how your skills and experience can add value, even if your experience doesn't obviously match.

You'll have to retrain if you want to change career. Believing that you will have to stop working and spend serious money to retrain is the most common reason for avoiding even thinking about career change. Unless you are moving into something highly specialised with prescribed entry qualifications, you can probably make progress entering a new sector and then learning the ropes until you can fit into the right role. Mistrust absolutes: even if you are told that you can't work in an industry without a key qualification, seek out people who have discovered backdoor routes.

Apply for as many jobs as you can. Playing the job search lottery has one major consequence you haven't factored in – *disappointment.* It knocks you back every time you get a rejection, or no response. Applying for roles where you are unlikely to be shortlisted wastes an employer's time and sets you up for repeated failure. Save your energy – make well-researched applications for roles where you're a credible addition to a shortlist.

Get that CV out there! How much time do you think a busy manager will give to a speculative CV where there is no obvious connection to the company's needs? Five seconds? Speculative letters and CVs can give you access to the hidden job market, but only if they are extremely well targeted and followed up by personal contact.

You have to sell yourself. Overselling can easily sound false or a symptom of desperation. Don't try to fake it or present yourself as a superhero, but present the best version of yourself, with clear supporting evidence.

Only pushy people network well. Networking works for everyone as long as they do it openly, honestly and in a style that suits them. See below for more on networking for softies.

A job's a job. Think of the money. Good jobs are hard to find. OK, red card. Go back to Chapter 1. Do not pass Go. Do not collect £200.

How employers prefer to find new staff

Here's another section that in itself probably justifies the cover price of this book.

In 2012 the UK Commission for Employment and Skills asked employers which methods they used to fill vacancies. Paid-for services include employment agencies and published advertising. Free public resources include Jobcentre Plus and government schemes, but there are a number of other private sector channels which cost employers little (word of mouth, local newspapers, company website, internal notices, free websites, job fairs, social media and speculative enquiries). The findings are summarised in the graph opposite.

The survey differentiated between free and paid channels, and between private and public sector resources. It found that employers made more of 'private free channels than of channels and services which they have to pay for', and two-thirds of employers 'combine private paid services with other recruitment channels'. Fifteen per cent of recruiting employers surveyed used only word of mouth or personal recommendation. Word of mouth was more commonly used by smaller establishments and new businesses.

The report continues: 'Personal connections play an important role in recruitment, with word of mouth/personal recommendations from family, friends or colleagues being the single most common channel that employers use to find candidates to fill vacant posts.' The indications are that the proportion of employers using word of mouth to recruit increased between 2010 and 2012.

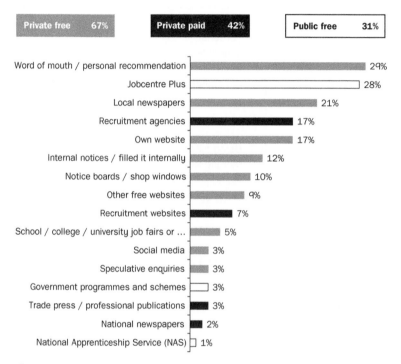

(Reproduced with permission from Shury, J., Vivian, D., Gore, K. and Huckle, C. (2012) *UK Commission's Employer Perspectives Survey 2012.* UKCES Evidence Report No. 64. UK Commission for Employment and Skills, Wath-upon-Dearne. page 30.)

Employer safety habits

When it comes to finding and filling jobs, employers and job seekers use totally opposite strategies, and see risk very differently, as follows:

How employers and candidates see risk differently

Perceived risk level for candidates	Employer method of attracting candidates to a vacancy	Perceived risk level for employers
High Medium Low	1. Personal connections 2. Word-of-mouth recommendations 3. Using external recruiters 4. Finding people using social media 5. Unsolicited approaches from candidates 6. Advertising the job on the company website or externally 7. Advertising the job externally	Low Medium High

We will look at each employer strategy in detail below.

1. Employers draw on personal connections

Organisations like to hire people they already know pretty well, so often make internal appointments. If they can't find what they are looking for internally they find others close by who feel 'almost family'. Their likely work performance feels like a known quantity. For a senior role this might be through a networking contact. At a more junior level your visibility may relate to work you did as a temp or an intern.

Some candidates feel this is 'old school tie' networking, and unfair, but the simple fact is that organisations see reduced risk in speaking to known contacts rather than strangers.

2. Employers seek word-of-mouth recommendations

If an employer doesn't already know someone that might fit the role, they don't rush to the market. They ask around: 'who do we know …?'

This explains why some people are invited on to a shortlist of one. It's all about being recommended, not about being the best candidate. It's not about who you know *now*, it's about who you get to know in the next six months. Look around you. Who admires what you do and would be happy to recommend you to others? Have you enlisted help from these people as career coaches, dummy interviewers, idea factories? Look more closely at family, friends, local contacts – anyone is good at sharing information. Life has its natural match-makers and fixers, and they love to be known for their contacts and good judgement.

3. Employers use external recruiters

Where an organisation works with a professional recruitment consultancy that really understands it, this can be a highly effective method. However, employers have become attuned in the past decade to finding low-cost solutions. Knowing this, you shouldn't be surprised to discover that in today's market recruiters don't get to handle a lot of jobs, particularly if those roles are not very senior.

See the material later in this chapter on working with recruitment consultants.

4. Employers seek recommendations and candidates via social media

If an organisation can't find the right person through personal networks, it may reach out via social media. The knowledge that a vacancy is being created tends to filter out informally. Sometimes recruiters will approach you directly because your LinkedIn profile records relevant skills or organisation names. At other times social media can alert you to the fact that an organisation is interested in meeting the right people.

Informal networks like this often alert candidates who are currently in full-time employment and not job hunting, which appeals to employers because they are interested in talking to people whose skills are current.

A friend may see a tweet and may mention it to you over coffee. You might reach out via LinkedIn, make a speculative phone call, or go through a formal recruitment process. Informal and formal, electronic and human – all becomes blurred. However, what an employer is really doing is seeking staff on a 'friend of a friend' basis: 'who do we know who knows someone worth talking to?' Recommendations now come in many packages, some as small as a tweet.

How do you get to be a known quantity identified in different networks? Shine. Get to be good at your job and let others know it. Keep a record of your achievements. Write articles or circulate good ideas. Talk with energy to customers, suppliers and partner organisations.

5. Employers receive unsolicited approaches from candidates

Sending unsolicited applications to employers often means that candidates press 'send' and hope for the best. If an employer has spent time informally broadcasting a vacancy, incoming expressions of interest are welcome. If an employer is anticipating work problems, they sometimes like to meet candidates who might fit at some stage in the future.

It won't work if an employer always uses a prescribed application process. It won't work if your CV makes no connection to an employer's needs, if your experience looks irrelevant, or if the tone of your approach is wrong. It does *not* mean emailing CVs on a 'spray and pray' basis. Try to make personal contact before you pitch in with an email.

6. Employers advertise the job on the company's website

If an organisation puts a vacancy on its own website it's speaking to multiple audiences. The first is internal candidates. The second is that cloud of potential hires surrounding every major employer regularly checking them out online. The third category is people who are well-connected enough to be directed towards roles through tip-offs and recommendations. Apply carefully, showing how you match as many of the job's key requirements as possible.

7. Employers advertise roles externally

By the time an organisation decides to formally advertise a vacancy (in print or online, paid or unpaid), the risk factor increases substantially, simply because the floodgates will now open. Job advertisements in a tight labour market are widely recognised as *candidate magnets* – all kinds of people apply, including many who are totally unsuitable.

When applications flood in it's easy to remain an undifferentiated, 'vanilla' candidate. Your chances of being shortlisted are low, even if your skills are excellent, and yet many people put most time and effort into advertised roles. It's fairly passive: you fill in a form or submit a CV and then pat yourself on the back for a good day's work.

Someone relatively junior may be shortlisting, probably into three piles: 'No', 'Possible' and 'Yes'. In a competitive market 'Possible' gets rejected alongside 'No', so you need to work hard to get that initial 'Yes'. Your covering letter needs to point to half dozen or so pieces of evidence showing you're a good match. Remember that reading a CV is a dull chore for HR professionals, and a frustrating distraction for line managers. Make it count (see my book *Knockout CV*, and also Appendix 1 at the end of this book).

Making good use of recruitment consultants

Recruitment consultancies find candidates to fill jobs for employers. Agencies range from high-street operations placing temps to executive search consultancies, or 'headhunters'. Although recruitment consultants keep candidate databases, they are largely vacancy driven and so have a good feel for the market. They are most interested in you if you fit a vacancy that needs filling immediately. Poor agencies simply distribute unsolicited CVs, overpromise and underdeliver.

The main advantage of recruitment consultants is their closeness to decision makers: they can persuade employers to see you quickly. Do your homework – find out which consultants *regularly* place staff in your chosen sector, and try to establish contact with up to 12–15 agencies. You will also be asked to register, usually online. That's fine, but recruitment consultants are strongly people oriented, so establish a relationship. You do this best by meeting face to face. Find the names of the individual consultants handling the roles you're interested in. Send a speculative email with your CV. Phone a couple of days later and ask for the opportunity to meet the consultant. Recruitment consultants like to be valued for their industry knowledge, and often agree to meet if they feel they can learn something about the organisations you've worked in.

Recruitment consultants can sometimes give good career advice but their primary role is to find the right person to fit the job, so they can often provide sound feedback about how an employer is likely to react to your CV. Less professional agencies don't always know as much as they should about the requirements of the job, and they frequently stereotype candidates, ignoring those who have not performed a similar role elsewhere.

A good recruitment consultant will also tell you what you are worth in the marketplace, and what hurdles you will have to jump if you want to change sector. Many recruitment consultants have strong views about CV construction, so the best question to ask isn't 'what do you think of my CV?' but *what does my CV say to you?* Listen to the story coming back at you. If you recognise and like what you hear, your CV is working.

Working with executive recruiters

No-nonsense tips about how candidates should establish and build a good relationship with recruitment consultancies.

1. Focus on being exceptionally good at your job and making a positive impact. Good headhunters will then find you – but make yourself visible to them so that they can.

2. Identify recruiters who specialise in your industry/ function and build a relationship before you're in job search mode by using your network to gain introductions and being helpful and considered when you're asked for recommendations; then prioritise who you want to stay in touch with. Don't forget you are divulging confidential information about you and potentially your employer, so do your homework

around the recruitment company's reputation, expertise, values and ethics. Do they feel a good match?

3. Strategically target a single consultant within a firm. This individual will facilitate connections to colleagues who might be pertinent to you. It is not necessary to contact multiple individuals within the same firm.

4. In terms of cold-calling a headhunter, email is still preferable to a phone call as a first introduction in spite of the heavy volumes headhunters receive, since it gives a quick impression of you and allows the headhunter to circulate your credentials among their colleagues and enter them into their global databases. The headhunter immediately will look for what is unusual or uniquely differentiating in your résumé, including qualitative information such as the size of the jobs you have held, organisations for which you have worked, the number of people you have managed, and results/profits for which you have been accountable.

5. The email accompanying your CV should give a quick snapshot of your career drivers: title, geography, compensation and the types of opportunities you are interested in. If you do send a cut-and-paste email to a variety of headhunters, make sure it's personalised and all the typeface is in the same size and font!

6. Avoid 'spamming' headhunters with multiple unsolicited emails each week or phoning them several times in a day, as these efforts may backfire.

7. Be transparent without being overly self-promotional during any phone or in-person meeting with a representative from a search firm. Do not make claims that will not stand up to rigorous background and

reference checking – the headhunter's duty of care to their clients necessitates a reasonably thorough investigation of candidates, and they will quickly discover anything that is fabricated or exaggerated.

8. Assess opportunities proffered by headhunters realistically. Do not feign interest in a job that you are not intending to follow through on simply to get facetime with a recruiter – it will waste their time and not position you as a serious candidate.

9. When meeting the recruitment consultant, always have in the back of your mind that first impressions count: be prepared, be punctual, be smart, don't be afraid to 'use' the headhunter – ask for honest feedback on interview performance.

10. Once you've had a positive meeting or telephone call, ask the headhunter for their preferred method of staying in touch – phone or email – and how often.

11. Demonstrate that you 'know how the system works' by offering to help with open assignments, and enhance your reputation with the headhunter by referring friends and colleagues that you hold in high regard (assuming they're at the right level and in a relevant sector) to them.

12. Be open with the headhunter about which firms you are trying to establish a relationship with – ask if there is any one they would personally recommend. Share openly and honestly how the rest of your job search is going.

Joëlle Warren, Executive Chairman,
Warren Partners

The hidden job market

'Insanity is doing the same thing over and over and expecting a
different result.' **Eva May Brown**

Let's get straight to the point. You think that most of your job searching is going to be about chasing advertised positions, probably discovered online. Think again. A substantial proportion of jobs are not advertised. If you only ever respond to job advertisements, you'll never know about them. This is the hidden job market. Many job hunters are unaware of it; most don't know how to break into it.

If you want to slow down your job search and limit your options (maybe somebody is paying you to fail?), then act on the negative job myths set out above and limit your job search to advertised positions. You'll miss out on most newly created jobs, all positions filled by word of mouth, and most jobs with small, energetic companies. You'll miss out on all those companies that are just on the edge of thinking about creating a new job. You'll never have a chance to be recommended by a friend or colleague.

The UK Commission's Employer Perspectives Survey 2012 shows how employers are increasingly relying on word of mouth to find talent. Whether they will do so as the market improves is open to question. Early indicators would appear to suggest that most employers are keen to harness a range of free and cost-effective methods, including social media. The reality is that not only is word-of-mouth recruitment low cost, it also feeds an employer's sense of risk avoidance.

We've looked at employer preferences. Any attempt to research which channels job seekers actually use to identify jobs is problematic – as explained above, in the age of instant communication channels overlap hugely. However, Jobcentre data taken from a decade ago shows that even among those candidates registered with the employment service about a third of men and just over a quarter of women found a job by hearing directly from someone who worked at the organisation. There is little research undertaken internationally on the ways people find work, but those surveys available also suggest that, across the board, about a third of workers find jobs through word-of-mouth connections, and men generally find this easier than women. Sometimes, the personal connections are undertaken by sheer instinct, at other times candidates learn new interpersonal skills to get them in front of people with the right influence (see Chapter 13).

The hidden job market seems confusing and complicated, because so much goes on under the radar. People hear about organisations that are interested in talking to candidates – through conversations over coffee, Twitter, news feeds, from other candidates. Communication channels blur and overlap. There are as many urban myths about the unadvertised market as there are jobsites. However, it's important to remember that this 'one third' rule represents a baseline. As soon as you go up the scale in terms of more skilled, professional, managerial roles – or jobs in highly competitive sectors such as media and publishing – the proportion of those who find work through personal connections rises. In some sectors it may well be that 90% of roles are never advertised.

'Open', unhidden jobs may not be as open as they look. Someone may already be considered a good fit for a role, and may even have been promised it informally. There may be an internal candidate who everyone but you knows is in line for the job. Even advertised positions can have a hidden dimension: talented candidates are told that a job is about to be advertised and are invited to apply, so they are already on the shortlist. This happens more often than you think. Sometimes, employers have a preferred candidate already but go to the market to find benchmarks for comparison. Therefore jobs are filled every day without the market having any sense that a vacancy ever existed. This feature of the marketplace can take a lot of stress out of job hunting. If you meet an organisation and they like you, a job may be created around you. If an employer finds you through personal connections and recommendations (see above) you can easily end up in a shortlist of one.

Job seeking: the ADEPT model

Here's a model which summarises the whole process of moving on into a new role:

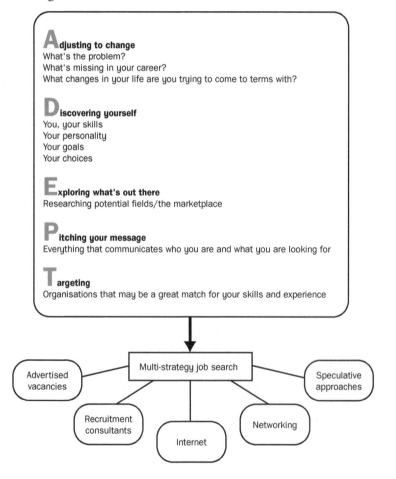

Adjusting to change
What's the problem?
What's missing in your career?
What changes in your life are you trying to come to terms with?

Discovering yourself
You, your skills
Your personality
Your goals
Your choices

Exploring what's out there
Researching potential fields/the marketplace

Pitching your message
Everything that communicates who you are and what you are looking for

Targeting
Organisations that may be a great match for your skills and experience

Multi-strategy job search

Advertised vacancies

Speculative approaches

Recruitment consultants

Internet

Networking

- **A – Adjusting to change.** The first stage covers much of the work of this book: your mindset, constraints, and understanding what gets in the way of finding a job you love. Look at what you are putting in the way of your own progress, and then look hard at what you need to start to make change happen. How are you going to overcome difficulties talking about your past, or difficulties making change happen in a tight market?

  This phase is about getting your mindset right, and starting to work on yourself, and also with others. Plan now to deal with setbacks and rejection, and recruit supportive friends to help keep your spirits up during the process.

- **D – Discovering yourself.** Catalogue your skills, strengths and personal qualities. These will become the ingredients of your marketing message. You don't need to be overanalytical, just get a really strong sense of what you are good at, where you have achieved something, and what you have to offer a new employer. Work through the relevant exercises in this book and learn to talk about yourself.

- **E – Exploring what's out there.** Before long you'll be itching to get to grips with something even more tangible, so the exploring stage means finding out what's really out there. Put research before job search: follow your curiosity and get information from real people holding down real jobs, not second-hand information. Become hungry for new discoveries and connections. Your research should be focused on conversations, not the internet, to ensure that you learn quickly and get yourself remembered in the process.

- **P – Pitching your message.** Now is the time to decide on the message you're going to communicate, in your CV, at interview, and in every conversation you have about career change. To do this you need to know (a) what you are selling and (b) who you are selling to. Next you need a quick summary in under two minutes that captures your background, what you have to offer, and what you're looking for. Test your message out for impact by rehearsing it with anyone with hiring experience, then try it out on people you are comfortable talking to. Once you feel it is working reasonably well you can pitch it at useful contacts and then decision makers.

Look at the two-breath message on page 209 in Chapter 13, and rehearse short, positive presentation statements to back up your main pitch.

- **T – Targeting.** Set targets for your job search. Decide how many people you are going to talk to each week and how many organisations you will approach, and keep a log to make sure your activity levels are maintained. Use a multi-strategy job search (as outlined on page 170) – ensuring that you include all the elements of the mix, particularly direct, speculative approaches to companies who are not advertising, and both face-to-face and online networking.

'Must do' list

- ✓ Base your job search on reality, not urban myths.
- ✓ Avoid the mistakes many people make in the first few months of job searching.
- ✓ Avoid rookie mistakes.
- ✓ Take account of employer risk aversion in your job search strategy.
- ✓ Focus on the hidden job market.
- ✓ Use every job-seeking strategy in the box. Combining them improves their effectiveness and shortens your job search.
- ✓ Start your networking today – think of two friends you can approach.

12

Online presence and searching

> 'Live in fragments no longer. Only connect ...'
> **E.M. Forster**, *Howards End*

This chapter looks at:

- The value, and necessity, of having an online presence
- How to use social media as part of an active networking plan
- The classic errors people make online
- Adding an electronic dimension to your job search

Why the internet probably won't save your career

In the twenty-first century, job seekers make the same mistakes career changers made in the 1980s and 1990s. We're still essentially passive, waiting for the right opportunity to come along, waiting for the phone to ring, waiting for someone else to take control of our career. In the past, passive behaviour was about putting your future in the hands of agencies, your boss, HR, and firing off lots of application forms. Now we sit at our desks and pray to St Google.

In earlier recessions redundant workers stayed home in case the phone rang. Now, you can be anywhere you can pick up a phone signal, but still a large proportion of job seekers give most attention to one activity: searching online. Why do so many people believe this is the quickest and best way to find a job?

Modern technology appears to have all the answers. Jobsites issue a barrage of statistics about how many people find a job using the internet, and point to an increasing trend of people using mobile devices for this purpose. Second, sitting in front of a screen looking at job boards *feels* productive. Even more importantly, it *looks like work*.

Research published by Evenbase in 2013 claimed that the job seeker's preferred searching method was looking at online job boards or company websites. Interestingly, the same research also showed that the preferred method for employers (large and small) was personal networks, with social and business networks also featuring. This very evident contradiction underlines the arguments set out in Chapter 11 – even in the internet era employers are still heavily dependent on people connections.

Some years ago I helped out at a job workshop in the San Francisco Bay area. It was salutary to see that even in a relatively buoyant, hi-tech economy there were career changers expressing the same worries and facing the same problems as the jobless all over the world: 'there are no jobs out there', 'I don't do well at interviews', and 'it's who you know, not what you know'. I learned a good rule from outplacement specialists operating in California at that time: use your PC outside working hours only. During the day, use shoe leather. The reason is simple. The web is fantastic for research, but poor for communication. A tweet is forgotten in seconds, an email in minutes, a phone call forgotten in about half an hour, but a good face-to-face meeting (followed up by a thank-you note) can be remembered for six months or more. As Americans say, do the math.

Sometimes the first step in a creative career process, as Chapter 11 made clear, is to go against your instincts.

Nothing new there. Talk to anyone who has made a career breakthrough and they will tell you that at some stage they had to adopt new ways of thinking, and new behaviours. Otherwise, all we do is seek repeated negative experiences: 'I know this doesn't work but I might just try it again a few hundred times to be sure.'

In a tough market an average job search strategy gives you below-average results. This means looking long and hard at online activity, partly so you don't over-rely on job boards, but also so you make the most of social media to maintain your visibility.

Use job boards as a back-up system, not the main event

It makes sense to ensure that you are registered with job boards that (a) handle enough traffic so that jobs relevant to you come up every week or (b) specialise in your field. Upload a good-quality electronic CV, and make sure that you use the key words that a database will be searching for. You will also find that you can use electronic job boards in unconventional ways – to identify recruitment agencies that regularly handle vacancies in your sector, for example, or search by location to find organisations on your doorstep. In general, job boards work best for workers with sought-after job titles in their work history, or with skills easily communicated through key words (for example, computer programmers).

They are best used as part of a multi-strategy approach. Use job boards to work out salary levels, to spot employers and to identify recruitment consultants you can telephone. Appendix 3 contains a list of websites useful for online job hunting and career development.

You will also find it useful to look at employer job boards, where you may come across jobs you don't see advertised elsewhere.

How using social media can give you an edge

While some are happy to follow and update Twitter all day, others fail to see the point, or just see an embarrassing over-supply of trivial information. There are two main reasons you may discover that social media can make a difference.

The first reason is connected to visibility. How are people going to find you and recommend you? If they do find you online, will they like what they see? If you're looking for a job as a senior manager and all that can be found about you via Google is something about your weekend hobby or your last holiday, how does this help you to get a job or win customers?

The second reason is all about people. Making a big life change is about relationships: finding stuff out, talking to people who can give you ideas and encouragement, making connections. Yes, your relationship needs to be with people, not with Google, but the best way to find and contact the right people now is to use online networks: creating your own, building on other people's connections, joining in online communities. So use the full range of tools available to you. Not to do so is to be the equivalent of the 1980s' job seeker who refused to use the phone to follow up on opportunities – if you limit the tools you use, you will still get a result, but it will take much longer.

Using social media to underpin your job search

In the past, job seekers were advised to have their own web page, but this probably only makes sense if you are offering some kind of product or service. However, you do need some kind of professional shop window somewhere on the web setting out who you are and what you do. LinkedIn is an ideal tool for this purpose as it's widely used, easy to manage, and gives you a great deal of freedom about how you present information.

Look at your online profile with a critical eye. Is your main focus of work clear, at a glance? Have you said the right things about your background and experience? Get someone to look at your online information, and ask them to summarise what they see. Users of LinkedIn have two ways of getting strapline messages across. The first is your job title, or a summary phrase that captures the kind of work you do. Look at this as carefully as you would examine the first sentence of your CV – does it help the busy user to understand what kind of work you do? Second, you will have some kind of 'status bar', which is essentially a quick update of what you are doing. Sometimes this is linked to your Twitter account.

In the UK it's generally unacceptable to attach a photograph to a CV. Opposite rules apply – if you don't include a photograph you look as if you don't know what you're doing or your profile page is incomplete. There are some really bad photographs on LinkedIn where you can't see someone's face properly. It's only a thumbnail image, so your face needs to fill the frame, and you should look professional but approachable.

Don't confuse business with letting your hair down. If you want to look like a serious, committed candidate don't fill online space with updates on your cat, your love life or favourite recipes. Use a separate account on Twitter or Facebook to do that.

Tips for making the most of electronic media

- Keep abreast of developments – join relevant online discussion groups and forums, and be seen to be asking questions and making contributions.
- Make connections – as soon as you have about 30 or so people visibly connected to you for professional

reasons, that shows you are serious about using the web for work purposes.

- Think about how people are going to find you using the web. Try Googling yourself and see how long it takes to find yourself. You will discover that having an article, a review or similar online usually does the trick – as long as your email address is then available.
- Think in terms of attracting interest rather than just chasing jobs. Becoming a content producer instead of just a consumer attracts job opportunities to your doorstep – for example, launch a blog that showcases your expertise and interests. Review books or events, contribute to online discussions, recommend people and organisations.
- Check your voicemail regularly. It's worrying how often key messages are left unheard.
- Use the tools your contacts and colleagues are using – whether it's Facebook, LinkedIn, Twitter or other channels, work out the cultural norm for the people you are trying to reach.
- Some people don't want to use social media because it gives away sensitive personal information. Never put your CV randomly online where anyone can find it, and never submit information that could be used for identity theft (your home address, date of birth, details of family members, etc.). Some security advisers recommend that you should create your own social network profile before someone else does so using your name.
- That said, don't get too precious about privacy. The principle of the web is open access to information. If you don't have an electronic footprint you make yourself difficult to track down – and people give up very quickly.

- Keep good electronic records of contacts. Beyond 40 or so connections your memory will fail. Record personal 'hooks', factors that you have in common, which help in future conversations.
- Keep on top of your inbox. Even a hint that you don't regularly pick up your emails or use the web as a research tool will indicate to most employers that you're past your sell-by date. Pick up and respond to emails at least once a day – what's the point of being out there making an impression if you can't reap the side benefits?

Look for people, not jobs

If you want to make a difficult career change (and difficult could simply be about the state of the market) then focus on the one activity that is likely to make the biggest difference: *contact with other people*. You'll often hear the suggestion 'it's not what you know, but who you know', and as Chapter 13 will reveal, that idea is often used as a great excuse not to find anyone to get to know. Career change is about who you choose to get to know. The great advantage of social media is that you can make more contacts and at greater speed than you could have done in the past. If you use the right tools your contacts will update themselves so you have no difficulty keeping in touch in the future.

However you look for a job, you are more likely to find something through conversations with other people than any other method. Apply this principle to electronic job search. Although your ultimate aim is to get face-to-face meetings, you have to find some means of initial contact. Fortunately, most of the people you need to reach can be contacted online. However, you need to learn how to approach them. An email out of the blue is likely to be ignored, so how do you use electronic communication to reach decision makers?

Focus on an organisation that interests you (try using the **connections game** suggested on page 222). Look for named individuals – decision makers with real needs. This usually means someone who does not work in HR. Once you know who you're interested in, see if that person has a blog or Twitter account you can follow; find out what interests them. Try to become part of the same online communities as the people you want to work with, ask questions (about the sector, not about jobs) and post useful information.

Once you know something about a decision maker, you are in a much better position to make a direct approach. Before you do so, ask yourself the most important question: 'Is there any method I can use which is better than email?' Ask around: who do you know who works in your target organisation, or has worked there in some capacity, including a consultant or supplier? Word of mouth referral will always get you in the door quickest. Having a strong enough message may mean that you are able to make a direct approach by telephone.

Use LinkedIn to spot people who are connected to someone in or near your target organisation. If you find someone you know who has a connection, pick up the phone and ask for an introduction. If that really isn't possible, make your own direct approach by email. When you do so, remember the principles of any job search letter: keep it short and focused, and spell out just two or three reasons why that person might want to see you. You're after a face-to-face meeting at this stage, not a job offer.

How do I manage my online presence when I am unemployed?

People are often unsure about the best thing to write if you're looking for a job. You might be employed and wanting to make a change (you probably don't want your current employer to know you're looking), or you're not working and you don't want to sound desperate about it.

Avoid statements that hint at desperation, for example, 'would appreciate any help you can give me', 'been looking for some time now' or 'will consider anything'. You wouldn't put that in a CV, so don't make it part of your LinkedIn profile. Keep things updated: don't leave your LinkedIn page dormant with no updates for several months, or people will assume you have found a position or lost interest. Most advisers will tell you to update something every couple of days because this triggers online alerts.

Don't use LinkedIn to broadcast the fact that you are out of work. You waste the opportunities it presents by using your status bar to say that you are seeking work or still unemployed. Quirky phrases like 'looking for next great opportunity!' or the rather twee 'in the enviable position of being available to assist a new employer' sound like mild desperation. Your message is your expertise, not your availability for interviews. A phrase such as 'Qualified procurement specialist' is great; condensing experience and credibility into three words works fine. You may, however, get away with a clear, focused and unemotional statement, for example, 'seeking full-time employment as an HR Manager in the East Midlands area'. Questions of tone are difficult to get right – ask the opinion of someone you trust to give you objective advice *before* you publish.

It's sometimes hard to think of updates when all you can really say is 'I am still here and still looking'. You can talk about the fact that you are 'researching organisations', 'talking to interesting people', 'actively networking' or 'eager to broaden my range of contacts'. A key sub-message is the fact that you are doing something for yourself rather than waiting for the market to come to you. This is why it rarely works simply to send your CV to a colleague and say 'would you kindly email this to everyone you think might be interested?' To do so has already passed the buck in terms of relationship building and turned you back into a passive career changer.

Use your online profile to make yourself stand out. If you are in a job, update your status bar with news of current projects, areas of research, things you want to know more about. In some sectors this will be enough to attract enquiries, possibly even approaches from recruiters, although you can't rely on this until you have extended your visibility. Don't forget that you can always send direct messages to online contacts, but don't confuse private requests for help with online 'broadcasts' which everyone can see.

Make regular updates to your status. Think about ways of keeping your message varied and interesting. Demonstrate enthusiasm, for example: 'Reading everything I can get my hands on about healthcare reform ...' or 'Just watching a fascinating presentation on green building construction'. Show not just your interest, but the fact that you are up to date. Mention conferences you have attended (or conference summaries if you can't get there in person), books you have read, sites or people who have inspired you. Bookmark interesting pages so you can send out recommendations on a drip-feed basis – one a day, for example, rather than a whole burst in one evening.

LinkedIn: Top 12 tips for job searchers

1. Think of your LinkedIn profile as a next step towards intimacy with someone who has just read your formal CV ... consistent but more informative so that a reader can feel they know you a little better or more personally from considering it.
2. If LinkedIn is a high street, then your profile is like an individual shop from which you are selling

expertise and experience services under your personal brand. Use your first name and surname as simply as possible and in the same format as on your CV, business card, email address and signatures. Variations confuse.

3. Promote your business pitch succinctly next to your name and make it as unique as possible. Mine reads 'Careers Expert, Marketer, Networking Dynamo, Opportunity Catalyst' and at the time of writing this was the only one out of about 250 million people, compared to over 260,000 people who describe themselves simply as 'Career Coach'.

4. Upload a pleasant, friendly, approachable, smart and professional looking photo of yourself. Colour or black and white is fine but do not use holiday snaps, arty poses, cartoons, symbols, company logos or avatars.

5. Link the Update box to your Twitter account and use it occasionally to share your views, opinions, business quotes or authoritative articles – perhaps from the selection that LinkedIn suggests daily at the top of your home page. Used well, a quick update makes you look more expert – but be careful: you will also look silly if you do it badly, or too often.

6. Edit the URL that LinkedIn allocates to you so that it mirrors your name and personal brand. Then copy this detail on your business card, email signature and CV to encourage people to visit your profile.

7. The Summary section of your profile allows you to craft, test and communicate a powerful elevator pitch. Use the Specialties sub-section to list your areas of expertise and interest for search engines.

8. Write a brief description of your responsibilities and achievements at each position in your career path

and, if possible, secure a strong recommendation or two for each role.

9. Join and follow the alumni groups for everywhere you have studied, as well as the largest and most relevant LinkedIn groups in every industry or professional sector that you wish to explore. Monitor these daily for jobs and influential contacts, and participate in group discussions to feed your expertise and interview prowess.

10. Select the 'Companies' search bar and 'Follow' your target employers for news and contacts.

11. Using the 'Jobs' search bar, enter an ideal job title or company to identify relevant vacancies.

12. Click the 'People' search bar and type in your ideal job title, organisation and location. This reveals people already doing it and allows you to search their profiles to see how they got there. Then use your LinkedIn contacts to find someone you know to introduce you to them so that you can ask for an information interview using the REVEAL method detailed in Chapter 13 to gain access to the elusive hidden job market.

Julian Childs, career coach and business advisor
(www.linkedin.com/in/julianchilds)

Think about who will be following you

In order to follow you, someone needs to be able to find you. Having a page set up on one of the social networking sites is usually the easiest way, and because someone needs to know they have found the right person, make sure you include up-to-date information about your location, specialisms and work history. Many commentators recommend that you build a strong personal brand, which isn't just about content but also about connections – your page should show that you are in touch with the right organisations, discussion groups and professional bodies. It takes no more than an hour or so to research which online forums are right for you. This not only helps when people are checking up on you, but also makes you visible to people searching for qualified candidates.

While putting the right kind of information online can help, anything negative will slow you down like a dead weight. Don't say anything online, even in emails, that might be copied or forwarded outside your control, which conveys a negative message about your previous employer, former colleagues, how you have been treated, unhelpful recruiters, or how and why you have been rejected. You never know who is checking out your online presence and history.

Similarly, take great care about the amount of information you really want to be spread across the web. If you want to live on the wild side, make sure that your on-screen confessions, conversations and photographs are visible only to trusted friends. Many employers and recruiters use the internet for background checking. If you insist on putting embarrassing photographs of yourself in a state of undress or inebriation, you might as well bring them with you to the job interview – it's called *public domain* for a reason.

Twitter – can you get a job in 140 characters?

If you believe the hype, Twitter is the new job tool. There are, certainly, great jobsites broadcasting through Twitter. Its main uses are, however, still research and a means of following and connecting directly with key staff at organisations you want to work for.

If you are going to use Twitter as a job search tool, set up an account specially for the purpose. Before you follow anyone on Twitter, it's important that you have a completed profile that shows, at a glance, who you are. This means a short biography, some well-chosen statements about your expertise, your approximate location, and a link to a site that recruiters can go to for more information (a blog or your LinkedIn profile).

Some social media experts argue that to get jobs on Twitter you need to have thousands of followers, but if you already have that kind of presence you can pretty much do anything you want. For most people it's about having a co-ordinated way of reaching out through all forms of social media, and simple ways for people to find out about you and get in touch. However, don't overlook the simplicity of tweeting 'just got laid off, looking for a job in HR', because that alone may be enough to get you some offers of help. Don't get locked into electronic correspondence – try to turn those offers into direct (private, offline) messages and then actual conversations. Whatever you do on Twitter, present a succinct, understandable picture of who you are and what you do: keep it clear and simple. Be consistent in your use of Twitter – become known for what you say and the way you use Twitter, and stick to it.

> **@matthias_feist: Top ten tips for using Twitter when #jobhunting**
>
> In September 2014 Matthias Feist set himself the challenge of summing up his advice in ten tweets, using the hashtag #10tweets, reprinted below. His tips work on the assumption that you know basic twitter functions and terms, such as 'hashtag', 'mention' and 'retweet/RT'. There are many tutorials available on the net. Find and share ...

1. Create Twitter profile connected to #LinkedIn. Use same picture and mission statement throughout. Put Twitter name on your CV. #10tweets
2. Follow target #employers, their followers, #job tweets, relevant bloggers and experts. Following others brings followers. #10tweets
3. Use #LinkedIn to update Twitter once a day. Never push all updates via LinkedIn, only #work relevant ones. #10tweets
4. Tweet a lot, say about 5 times daily to keep a flow. Many still use email alerts for #socialmedia sites – so don't flood them. #10tweets
5. Only tweet what you think is relevant to your audiences. Use #hashtags picked up in relevant discussions. #10tweets
6. Thank others publicly for mentions & RTs. Adding value to their #professional lives will be good PR for you and them. #10tweets
7. Don't worry about producing own content at first, focus on sharing & adding value. 1st own tweets always suck a bit. Relax. #10tweets
8. Find your own voice: Write like you're in a #job engaging with peers: talk about topics relevant to #employers in twitter chats. #10tweets
9. Offline world rules online world: go #networking and meet the people you tweet. Also, live-tweet from events. Follow speakers. #10tweets
10. Check interviewers' tweets in advance, quote or refer to them if appropriate. Include your twitter name on your CV for them. #10tweets

Matthias Feist, head of careers and business relations at Regent's University London and Chair of PlaceNet, the Placements in Industry Network.

'To do' list: online job search and job applications

1. Be proactive. Every month new employers switch to online recruiting, so don't leave online applications out of the mix. But don't use online job search instead of other methods, or as an excuse for not speaking to real people.
2. Remember the range of resources online: vacancy listings, CV databases, internet-based career centres, self-assessment tools useful in career search, search engines to help you to find companies and organisations, trade associations and professional bodies, as well as news and information services.
3. Check sites regularly and learn how to use the relevant search criteria. Use job board aggregators like Indeed or Twitter job search to expand your reach. Be careful with sites which charge to show you job ads – the adverts can sometimes be found on other job boards or company sites simply by searching on Google.
4. Don't define your search too early, too soon. Use broad categories at first, then use search tools to refine the listings. Don't just search on your old job title – jobs have different names in different organisations.
5. Electronic job applications, like conventional applications, need a brief covering letter. Format this as neatly as a printed letter, and cover the essentials: what the job is, why you are applying for it, what you have to offer.
6. Compose a CV in plain-text form in a word-processing package. Ignore all text effects except for capital letters. Do not use tabs or columns. Once you have a clear layout you can copy and paste your CV on to a jobsite.
7. Make your electronic CV concise: be exact, be interesting and communicate your strengths. Do not clutter your online CV with unnecessary detail – think about

someone searching for key words rather than a whole CV.

8. Set up more than one CV – think about the different kinds of employer that may be hunting for you online.

9. Renew your uploaded CV every month or so. If you do this, the database will usually treat your document as a new CV and put it to the top of the electronic pile.

10. Plan an electronic campaign using a range of social media tools, but have at least one 'base' where people can find your online profile easily. In the business world LinkedIn probably works best for this purpose.

13

Networking and information interviews

'The greatest obstacle to discovery is not ignorance – it is the illusion of knowledge.' **Daniel J. Boorstin**

Not networking

Chapter 11 investigated the hidden job market, showing how it has grown and job searching has become more complicated. When I begin to work with a new client I often ask them which job search method they think is most likely to bag them a job offer. While some are stuck in online application mode, even at this stage many already sense they are probably more likely to get a result through conversations and connections. They are, however, reluctant to do anything that looks or feels like networking.

Nearly all job searchers, whether graduates or executives, hate the idea of networking. They say it feels uncomfortable, it's 'pushy', or 'it exploits people and loses you friends'. Some are even more honest: 'it makes me look – and feel – desperate'. We should respect these suspicions. Anyone who suggests networking without addressing those issues is trying to get you to buy a jacket that doesn't fit, isn't your colour, and is something you'll never wear after you take it home.

I mentioned above the conversations that I have with people at the beginning of a programme. I also ask them to review their job search when they have accepted a job offer. My question is 'what would you do differently next time?' The answer, from clients at all levels, is usually 'I would start talking to people earlier'. So often it is the connection or phone call that comes out of the blue that makes all the difference, and savvy job seekers know that this apparently random event is the result of communication and relationships.

Networking is something we all do unconsciously. If you move to a new town and want to find a good child minder, dentist or plumber, you ask around without worrying what that looks or sounds like. Networking has been done a huge disservice by people and organisations who exploit human networks for commercial advantage. You know who they are: those people who want to sell you things you don't really want, and use friendship or family connections to make you feel guilty enough to buy something.

Networking books will tell you about 'working the room' and giving your business card to as many people as you can. That's another huge misunderstanding. Anyone who thinks that networking is about exploiting people has misunderstood the whole concept. True networking is about a fair exchange of helpful information and ideas.

Networking for softies

How can we tap the power of the network economy to assist our career development and job search? First, it's vital to recognise that networking is *not* about getting a job. It's about expanding your range. It's about creating new possibilities. It's about learning more about other jobs, other fields. It's about identifying key people and decision makers.

It's about *what you put in*. The process was once described in the 1950s by US careers writer Bernard Haldane as a 'chain of helpfulness'. It begins not with the question 'who do I know that I can exploit?', but with 'who do I know that can tell me something interesting?' It may even begin 'who do I know that I can help?' Personal webs are connections of people. This doesn't mean trashing friendships for the sake of a quick fix. Networks are *social* networks – they work best when we take a genuine interest in others. The best personal webs are a pool of freely shared knowledge; everyone puts something in, everyone has a chance to take different things out. Begin with what you can add – this 'what do I know that would be helpful to others?' It can be something quite ordinary or modest, such as useful web pages, book recommendations, telling people about cheap travel deals or free resources. A chain of helpfulness begins with what you are prepared to give, not what you want to take.

Be kind to yourself, and network like a true softie. Never put yourself in the situation where you are ringing someone and saying 'you don't know me, but ...'. Start with people you know really well – who are they? – the people you can ring up *without having to compose an opening statement in your head*. In difficult calls the telephone feels heavy as lead – for this kind of call it should feel feather-light. The kind of people you can take out for coffee and say 'this is going to come out all wrong, but can I try this out with you?' Ask them to help you with something and arrange an actual meeting – learn the habit of speaking to people face to face because it will make all the difference in the long run. Ask them about anything you like, but learn the skills of *asking rather than telling*: find out about the work they do, how they got into it, what overlaps exist between their world and yours. Thank your friend for their time, but don't say goodbye until you've asked the number one all-time breakthrough networking question:

Who else should I be talking to?

Don't call it networking. Networking specialist Stuart Lindenfield calls it '101 cappuccinos'. It's just one interesting conversation after another. In order to get close to jobs you have to reach decision makers, and that means speaking to a number of other people along the way.

Networking isn't about the total number of people you know, but the connections between them. If four people are connected, that's 12 relationships. If you simply add one more person to the group, you get 20 relationships. As your personal web goes beyond ten, the number of possible interactions explodes. This shows the difference between mailing lists and interest groups. A mailing list may be 1000 separate, unconnected people. An interest group as small as 1000 can overturn national policy.

Your two-breath message

Learn to compose a short, two-breath message. Something that sums up who you are and where you want to get to. Two sentences which sound something like this:

> *'I want to do a job that allows me to do A and B and C*
> *... in an organisation that's doing X and Y and Z.'*

Items A, B and C are your motivated skills – the things you do best. X, Y and Z describe the key ingredients in the mix as far as your next employer is concerned. You might be talking about what the organisation actually produces or the services it provides. You might also talk about the style (hi-tech, customer-focused, etc.) or culture of the organisation (private, public, blue-chip, privately owned, etc.).

Networking contacts respond well to this kind of message because it's succinct, memorable and enthusiastic. People respond to it very differently compared to the alternatives, mentioning job titles, or asking for help to identify job opportunities. The two-breath message might remind you of the TV show *Ready Steady Cook*: you dump the ingredients in front of someone and ask for a good recipe. What people say in response to this quick summary are things like 'you know, you really should talk to my friend Rashid ...' or 'have you thought about talking to Acme Industries ...' or, best of all, 'that sounds to me like ...' – they identify a sector or field you haven't yet fallen across. This statement will help you in any situation where someone asks what you're looking for. You only get a few seconds of their attention, so leave them with a message they will remember.

Degrees of separation

The theory of **six degrees of separation** was popularised by the US playwright John Guare. The idea is that you can reach anyone in the world in six jumps – or fewer. Person A leads you to B, and so on. You can often begin by talking to someone who has only the vaguest connection to your target individual.

Here's an example. I regularly ask audiences 'who's met someone who has been into space?' Twice in my life I came close to famous astronauts without even trying (Yuri Gagarin was Manchester's guest of honour when I was in my pram, and some 40 years later Neil Armstrong spoke at a venue ten minutes' walk from my office). Even though the first manned space flight was Gagarin's flight in April 1961, fewer than 600 people have been up there. Yet, in my average audience, one person in 50 or so has talked to someone who has been in space. The first time I asked, a woman in the second row put her hand up, and told me that for her personally, her astronaut encounter was a life-changing conversation. Even the most extraordinary people are not that far away.

With large audiences I make sure that everyone in the room has a conversation with a stranger. It begins with a question: 'what are you looking for?' It's sad that out of 300 people half a dozen will sneak out at this point, claiming an urgent appointment. Sad because those 140-plus conversations are always useful, sometimes amazing. Later someone from the audience will find me and say 'you know, I had a conversation today which may have changed my life'. The fact that it happens every time means that it just happens – you just need to keep asking.

Following the maze

It's easy to feel sceptical about networking. People ask 'does it work?', 'how long does it take?', and 'is there something else I can do instead?' To answer the last question first – yes, there is always an alternative to talking to real people. It's called an average, dull, low-octane job search. As for questions one and two, talk to people who have been made redundant in the last two or three years and have gone on to find interesting work. Many will tell you that the new opportunity emerged from a breakthrough conversation. However, it's hard to predict which conversation is going to get you that result. It's like working your way through a maze. The treasure could be there at the first turn, around the next corner, or deep in the maze. You have to trust and keep searching, knowing that you are working your way towards the centre. The more turns you take, the closer you get. Networking is like that: the more you do, the clearer the process becomes, and you see what the end result might look like.

Be assured: things will happen along the way. For example, you will fall over jobs. You may not want the jobs that are mentioned, but alert others in your network to your discoveries – it's a really good way of putting something back into the system. Second, simply because you are talking to people who share your values and interests, you are going to meet very interesting people, some of whom will become friends. Keep things mutual. Find out what you have in common with contacts, and spot what you can do in return. Once you get someone to talk to you, focus on the things they can help with rather than things they find difficult, and thank people for whatever assistance they provide, even if it's just encouragement.

Pick up tips from people who are great networkers, focusing on the things you find difficult. Gael Lindenfield and Stuart Lindenfield, authors of *Confident Networking for Career Success and Satisfaction* (Piatkus, 2010) advise: 'Plan assertive answers to questions that might floor you. For example, if you are in 'transition', and are worried about being asked what you are doing now, confidently state what you are (even if you're thinking of a career change) and say what you are evaluating and exploring. Rehearse your key lines. Confidence is built on experience. But, like an actor you can fake that experience! Scripting and editing some of your 'lines' will enable you to be more brief and articulate – especially important if the person you are meeting is a high level contact and you have little time to make an impact.'

Three predictions

Here are three calculated predictions. The first is the fact that you already know at least one person who can really help you. When we begin networking we scan the far horizon for contacts, people we know only vaguely. First you need to take baby steps. Who do you know who is close by? There's a simple test: you're looking for the kind of person you could pick up the phone and talk to without having to plan what you're going to say.

The second prediction is that you will probably find a job through someone you know already, or someone you meet in the next three months. Play the game backwards. Imagine it is six months down the line and you have found your unusual and absorbing job, and think about how you got it.

The third prediction draws on the exciting work of Geneva-based careers expert Daniel Porot, who says that the best results come from the third level of networking. The first level covers the people you know well. The second level describes people you know vaguely and the people you get introduced to. The third level is composed of people you don't know at all right now. Why does the third level work? Possibly because it puts you in front of people who have no assumptions about you. Not only that, but by the time you get to the rich territory of the third level you've got pretty good at the process.

Managing your personal web

It's possible to build up a personal web of between 60 and 100 useful, curious and interesting people within about three months. Here are some principles that will help:

- Learn how to conduct information interviews (see below).
- Start the easy way. Begin with people you know, asking them the question 'Who do you know who works in ...?'
- Build slowly and methodically. Put time aside each week. Keep good records of who you have spoken to and who you're trying to contact.
- Practise the skill of approaching people and conducting a meeting. It may take half a dozen attempts to get it right, so start with people who you already know well.
- Get people to introduce you to other people. Don't make cold calls.

- Keep a printout to hand of all the people you're trying to reach at the moment (not just networking connections but employers and recruiters). When somebody returns your call you need to be clear who they are.
- Ask yourself 'what can I add to this network?' and 'how can I be helpful'? Be remembered as a source of information, a person who brings others together.

Information interviews

Asking rather than telling

A job interview is about persuading someone to move you closer to a job offer. An information interview (also known as an *informational* interview) is very different. It's primarily about discovery, but also about many other things: learning, deciding if you like a job or sector, matching yourself, picking up vital information and the language used within an organisation. Finally, and possibly most important of all, it's about improving your visibility in the hidden job market (see Chapter 11). An information interview helps you to spot the roles and fields which are a great match for your skills and experience, and then helps you to identify target organisations. You may also find that you fall over jobs before they become vacancies.

The idea is simple: find someone who knows about a field or occupation, and ask to see them for a short face-to-face interview. You're not trying to push yourself forward or subversively obtain a job interview. In the conversation you'll do far more talking than listening. You will ask a series of key questions about entry to the field, rewards and pitfalls. Along the way you'll say something about why you're interested, and you'll gather the names of other people to talk to.

The REVEAL method of conducting information interviews

Information interviewing is a powerful technique pioneered by both Richard Nelson Bolles in *What Color Is Your Parachute?* and Daniel Porot in his PIE method. I am indebted to both of them for kick-starting my thinking and encouraging me to design and market test a method that works well in the UK.

REVEAL conversations are meetings you are going to arrange with key individuals who will love to talk about their industry sector. You will add to your personal knowledge, increase your network and learn how jobs 'feel' from the inside. The principle is *research before job search*. You are not making a once-and-for-all career decision or trying to get a subversive job interview. You are simply finding out vital pieces of information to move your career transition forward:

- What kinds of roles exist?
- What organisations are out there?
- Would I find the job interesting?
- How do people get into this field or occupation?
- How can I match myself better if a role comes up in the future?

Information interviews are not directly about job searching. Think about how you would react if someone contacted you at work and asked for a meeting. If the caller said 'I'd appreciate your help in identifying jobs in your organisation', you'd feel pretty uncomfortable. You don't know the caller, so why should you recommend this person for a post? The conversation would probably end there.

Think about what your contact can actually deliver. If the request is about you and your sector knowledge, it's fairly easy to comply without too much preparation: most people are happy talking about themselves and the job they do, and usually prepared to give you information and contacts if the meeting goes well. Don't ask questions that are even tangentially about job search ('I'd like your advice on my CV' or 'I'd appreciate an early tip-off if any jobs are advertised'). If the interview goes well, this will probably be offered anyway.

What do REVEAL interviews achieve?

- You get to wear smart business clothes and go to workplaces, which maintains your confidence levels in a job search.
- You meet people in real jobs by moving from desk research to field research. You will learn about entry routes, sector trends and organisational cultures.
- You see jobs from the inside, which helps you to choose a career path.
- The depth of your research shows your commitment to work in a particular sector.
- You are often talking to decision makers, so you get on their radar as a credible candidate.
- You pick up insider language which allows you to convince people you really understand the sectors and organisations you're targeting.
- You learn how organisations describe top performing candidates.
- You begin to learn how to talk about your experience if you're changing sectors.
- Since you're tracking down people who are passionate about a field of work that calls you strongly, you will end up with interesting new contacts and friends.
- You leave people with a positive impression of you, and enough information to recommend you to others. People remember you, and make connections on your behalf.

- You fall over jobs. It's true. Ironically, the indirect route which is not focused on job search often turns out to be the number one strategy for getting at the hidden job market.

REVEAL: how to get meetings

Think of the toughest way of doing it. It's possible to work your way through the Yellow Pages or to turn up at the reception and demand a meeting, but it's an uphill struggle. If you approach an organisation as a stranger, the first question in the contact's mind is 'what am I being sold?' (followed swiftly by 'is this someone asking for a job?'). If you think of information interviews as hard-nosed networking, you've found the perfect excuse not to start.

Begin with people you know

Get this step right and you never have to make a terrifying phone call. Begin with people who you can approach without any hesitation – practise on family, friends and colleagues while you build confidence. Can't think of anyone? Use Exercise 13.1 on page 221, making sure you don't exclude friends and family. Often we never ask those near and dear to us who it is they know. Even people who never think about networking usually have about 100 people within their immediate contact circle. You can begin with relaxed questions about how they got into the careers they are in, but don't forget to ask two things even at this stage: (a) 'who do you know who works in ... ?' and (b) 'any ideas about who I should be talking to next?'

At this stage, what you're after is the names of **three initial contacts** who can help with your main career questions.

However, knowing a name is not enough. It looks like your only option is cold calling, but you know how hard it is to begin a conversation 'You don't know me, but …'.

Avoid cold calling

At the beginning of every conversation say something like this: 'What I am hoping to do is to get to speak to six or seven people who can give me some real insights.' That way, when you get to the end of the conversation and say 'that was really helpful. Who else should I be talking to?' your colleague will probably already have thought of a name. Next move on to questions about sectors, about entry routes, about potential growth areas.

The mistake at this stage is simply to walk away with a list of names. If you do, you're back to cold calling. That means you have to ring someone and start by saying 'You don't know me, but …'. It takes a huge amount of confidence to get past that difficult moment. So, you need introductions, not just names. Before you head for the door, say: 'I hate ringing people cold. Would you be kind enough to telephone ahead for me, just to say who I am and what the conversation will be about?' That way the person you want to reach expects your call and knows what it's about. Try it. When you phone your next contact to make an appointment, all you need do is mention the person who recommended you to call. This should be a good enough memory prompt ('Sure – Bill called me about you'). Look for personal connections between one contact and the next ('Bill tells me you're a keen fell walker …'). Next, offer a quick reminder about why you want a discussion. Ask for a face-to-face meeting. Some contacts may try to get you to settle for a phone call. Be honest: say that you learn much more by visiting people in their own organisations. Say that you'd like to ask a short number of key questions. Ask for 11 minutes of the person's time. 'Five minutes' or '15 minutes' is too vague.

Conducting a REVEAL interview

When you get to the meeting

When you get a face-to-face meeting, you're ready to use each step of the REVEAL method, as set out below.

The REVEAL method of information interviewing

Stages of REVEAL	Notes
Recap	'I am here because ...'
	Remind the listener of who introduced you, why you asked for the meeting and what you want to get out of it. It always helps to say that you have been recommended to speak to your contact.
	Make it clear that you will be asking for referrals at the end of the conversation. You might say at the outset that your plan is to talk to a dozen people who know what's going on in a particular sector. At the end of the interview you can then happily ask for further contacts.
Explore	'I'm here to find out as much as I can about ...'
	Your opening underlines your main purpose – to explore and ask questions. You might start with an easy-to-answer opener like 'how did you get into this line of work?' You can move on to more in-depth questions about the sector being explored, such as 'what do you find most interesting/challenging about working in this sector?' This part of the conversation will probably contain most questions.
Vision	Now your focus shifts. You're after two kinds of perspective. The first is a vision of what's ahead: 'What changes can you see in this sector in the next two years?' This should give you some useful data on anticipated changes, and may also flag up further research you need to do on the sector, and other organisations you should be talking to.

	Your second vision question will give you a clear picture of individuals who are seen as good recruits: 'What kind of people are doing well in this changing sector?' This reveals the ideal skills profile of successful candidates – useful information to store away for the first time you match yourself against a role competitively.
Entry routes	'How do people normally get into this line of work?' Probe the conventional *and* unconventional ways of getting work in this sector. There are usually non-standard routes into most careers.
Action	'What should I do to find out more?' 'If you were in my shoes, where would you look next?' Draw your interview close to its conclusion by seeking ideas for organisations and sub-sectors to research.
Links	'Who else should I be talking to?' Your closing statement is also about connections, but focuses specifically on people: 'Thanks very much for your time today. As I mentioned before, I'm keen to talk to a number of people in this field. Who else should I be talking to? Can you please recommend two or three other people who can give me an equally useful perspective?' This is an issue you have flagged up earlier in the process. Show how appreciative you are, otherwise your request sounds a little like 'is there anyone I can talk to more useful than you?' If no names are forthcoming, probe for: • names of organisations • names of network conveners, for example, branch chairs of trade associations • (if nothing else is forthcoming) the names of good recruitment consultants dealing with this field. There is one more step. Ask your contact to phone or email the recommended contact. You might say 'I hate ringing people cold, could you do me a favour and let them know why I'd like to speak to them?' Do this and you constantly avoid having to begin a conversation 'you don't know me, but … '.

The first few times you use the method it's probably wise to stick to this structure (although find a way of wording the questions which works for you; don't use the script parrot-fashion). Later on you can develop your own questions.

What if I am invited to consider a job?

Don't let the meeting become a job interview – that's a breach of trust. If a specific position enters the discussion, say you'd like to go away and prepare for a proper interview. Offer a time when you are free within the next few days. Ask for full details of the job and prepare thoroughly, even if you are in a shortlist of one. That way you come back fully prepared, matching your selling points to the key requirements of the job.

Exercise 13.1 – Who can you reach?

Networking for softies means that you start with people you already know, but it's useful to have some sense of where you want your conversations to take you. Start with the questions you want answering. What sectors do you want to know about? What organisations would you like to reach? What jobs do you want to find out more about?

Put each of these networking targets down on a large piece of paper. Draw a circle around each topic. Then draw connecting circles to outline people, organisations and sectors that have some overlap with your networking targets. The first circles you draw describe the people you eventually hope to reach, step by step. The secondary circles give you big clues about intermediate steps.

Exercise 13.2 – Play the connections game

Decide what record-keeping system you are going to use so that you can build your network methodically. Keep a note of the name and contact number of people you are trying to reach. A spreadsheet works well for this purpose, with a printout ready at hand so you can respond quickly to incoming phone calls. Set a diary reminder of any action or follow-up you have agreed.

One spreadsheet should be a target sheet and you can use it to play a game against yourself. On this sheet include the names of organisations you would like to approach. You can use spreadsheet columns to record contact information, but give each organisation a score from 0 to 10. Zero means you know nothing about the organisation about from its name and main products. A mid-range score means you know a lot about how the organisation operates, its style and culture, and the kind of roles they regularly fill. A score of 8–10 means you have lots of contacts inside the organisation, you have met people there, and you are close to at least one decision maker capable of making you a job offer.

Having given each organisation a score out of 10, your next task is to create a new column titled 'Next Step'. What do you need to do in terms of research to increase your score from 1 to 5? How can you reach out to people via LinkedIn or your personal network to improve that score so it's 7 or above? Constantly improving your scores means that you keep finding ways to build connections and get closer to people until you're a known quantity. (Information interviews will help – see earlier in this chapter.)

'Must do' list: ground rules for information interviews

- ✓ Use the REVEAL structure. Be confident.
- ✓ Don't exceed the time limit unless it is at the other person's insistence. Don't ask to be shown round the building or site, but warmly accept the offer if it is made.

- ✓ Don't offer your CV unprompted. A CV requires time and is a complicated thing to comment on. Send it afterwards if it's requested.
- ✓ Don't ask about specific job openings because that undermines everything you've said about the purpose of the meeting.
- ✓ Be prepared for the question 'and what about you?' This is a good chance to try out your two-breath message (see page 209).
- ✓ Don't neglect to ask for three names. It's very easy to walk out of a meeting missing one of the main reasons for the interview.
- ✓ Keep a record of each interview, who you have seen and all connections made.
- ✓ Send a thank-you email when you get home. Don't attach a CV, which is a conversation closer, but perhaps include three to five bullet points reminding someone what you're looking for.
- ✓ Send a thank-you card a week or so afterwards: it's an unexpected gesture, and you will be remembered. Recipients are often touched by the gesture and keep your card for a long time. Put your name and email address somewhere discreetly on the card. Say how the meeting was useful to you and what has happened as a result of it.
- ✓ Remember that some people will say no to a meeting. Think carefully about whether this is because of how you asked, or simply because the contact was too busy. Approached the right way through an intermediate contact, about four out of five requests lead to information interviews.
- ✓ At any stage, if all else fails, fall back on your last ditch question: *who else should I be talking to?*

14

Job interviews: tipping the odds in your favour

'Find out what you like doing best and get someone to pay you for doing it.' **Katherine Whitehorn**

This chapter helps you to:

- Rethink interview preparation and performance
- Understand the interviewer's mindset
- Deal with interview anxiety
- Improve the way you get evidence across
- Spot buying signals and move towards a job offer

How we only pretend to prepare for interviews

Many candidates don't take their interview performance seriously. They leave too much to chance (hoping that certain questions will come up) and improvisation ('winging it' rather than pre-packaging answers). They plan for their *ideal* performance (the kind of interview they would give if asked questions by a friendly coach or colleague) not the actual event where they will be nervous and under pressure.

Even in a tight market candidates don't prepare very much. They plan answers, but they don't plan the exact words they will use to get across difficult messages. They skim-read the job description and don't really work at anticipating questions. They don't take opportunities to rehearse the most important statements, like a short summary in response to the classic openers 'why are you interested in this job' and 'tell us about yourself'.

Everything you do, from the moment you enter the interview room, should be about reassuring the interviewer you can do the job, you will fit in, and hiring you won't look like an odd or embarrassing decision. For question-by-question preparation, turn to my books *The Interview Expert* and *Job Interviews: Top Answers to Tough Questions*. This chapter provides an overview of the worst of what an interview can put you through, and the best that you can draw out of yourself.

Nerves

Don't beat yourself up for being nervous at interview. Anxiety, if directed the right way, can be strangely enjoyable – and useful, if adrenaline gives sparkle to your answers. Use the energy coming out of anxiety to your advantage, allowing it to make you more responsive. Make sure that fear doesn't prevent you really anticipating what will be said in the interview room.

The real downside of nerves is not being able to think of an answer even though you have dozens of examples in your CV. Evidence is no use to you unless it's pre-rehearsed, fine-tuned, and available to you when you need it. My colleague Kate Howlett describes the well-prepared candidate as someone who imagines themselves with a large selection of coloured boxes within reach, each containing a good story. Taking interview nerves seriously means doing the work of the interview well before you go into the room, learning short bursts of information and thoroughly planning your answers to the questions which are most demanding.

Alternative ways of seeing the interview process

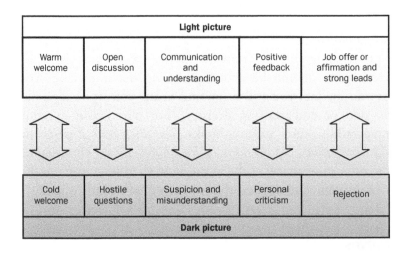

Light picture				
Warm welcome	Open discussion	Communication and understanding	Positive feedback	Job offer or affirmation and strong leads
Cold welcome	Hostile questions	Suspicion and misunderstanding	Personal criticism	Rejection
Dark picture				

The prospect of hanging, said the writer Samuel Johnson, concentrates the mind wonderfully. Interviews can do the same thing. Your mindset shapes the whole experience. If you see an interview as a nightmare situation, that will influence your behaviour. What happens if you tell yourself how brilliant you will be? Sounds corny, but try it. Self-confidence is just as powerful a career change tool as skills, experience or knowledge. The person who makes the picture dark or light is almost entirely you. You can look at the same questions, the same reactions, in terms of light or shadow.

You can learn something from every interview, but don't overinterpret results. Candidates are poor judges of their own performance, and post-interview feedback is often unhelpful. Those conducting interviews are often happy with answers which candidates feel are weak to average.

Have a conversation with the best part of yourself, not the negative voice that's whispering 'you can't do this!', but your better half, the one that's prepared to have a go. Make a deal with yourself to be different in your next interview. Do this by anticipating questions *and* answers. Look at the requirements of the job, known and guessed. Look at surface-level questions relating to the job description, but then dig deeper. Look at the organisation as a whole. Ask around, consulting people who have any kind of knowledge of the organisation, to find out how success is described.

What's the worst question you could ask yourself, knowing your own gaps and weaknesses? Where do you think your skills are inadequate? Where do you lack evidence? Write down rough answers, and edit until they're short and punchy. Practise your answers in front of a mirror, checking that your body language tells the same story as your words. Don't go anywhere near a job interview without trying answers out loud at least three times. Plan the stories you will use, and practise getting each story across in about two minutes.

The six-point structure at the heart of all interview questions

You may be asked several dozen questions during a job interview. It may be helpful to think about the six big question areas.

1. **What brought you to us?** Why did you apply? What is your career plan?
2. **What do you have to offer?** What do you bring to the party? What solutions do you have to offer which match our problems?
3. **How well do you understand us?** Have you worked out how we tick as an organisation? Have you worked out the key result areas of the job?
4. **Who *are* you?** What kind of person are you? Are you like us? Will you fit in? What will you add to a team?

> 5. **Why you?** – rather than one of the many similarly qualified people we are seeing today? What puts you ahead of the pack? What's your unique selling point?
> 6. **What will it take to bring you on board?** What will you cost us? How do we have to motivate and develop you to retain you in the future?

Outcomes and compression

What's the main outcome of a job interview? It is what is being said about you 20 seconds after you leave the room. The exact words you used will be already be fading. An interviewer is already forming a summary of your *evidence* and a judgement about whether you fit the job. There may be 200 pieces of information in your CV and several dozen topics may have come up at interview, but this quick summary determines whether your application goes any further. Rather than be depressed by this rapid filtering, turn this knowledge to your advantage. If a decision is likely to be made around half a dozen key points, make sure you get those six messages across rather than a messy fog of information. Decision makers want to sum you up pretty quickly, and fundamentally they're interested in their problems, not yours.

Rejection

Prepare for rejection. On balance you will be rejected more times than accepted. Even if you don't get the job, you can learn a huge amount about your perceived market value. Remember, there's a job out there for you somewhere. Even in a tough market, a well-planned job search pays off.

It's trite to say that you shouldn't feel rejected if turned down by an employer. It may take a while to bounce back, and that's understandable. However, it's rarely personal: people are rejected for all kinds of arbitrary reasons. In any job search you will receive more rejections than acceptances. You will hear the word 'no' more often than you hear the word 'yes'. This is a neutral statistical fact which has nothing to do with you. Even the very best salespeople in the world work on the basis that they need to hear the word 'no' at least three times before they get a 'yes'. The problem is that when it is 'no' to you, it can knock you off balance. Be careful not to use it as evidence to support 'yes, but' thinking: 'I knew I was unemployable …'.

Shining at the interview

'At interview, be yourself, but the best half of yourself.'
John Courtis

Talk lucky

Interviewers respond well to candidates who view their experience positively. So it does no harm at all to occasionally drop in phrases such as 'I guess I was lucky because …' or 'that turned out well …'. Showing that you have the ability to turn even negative situations around can make the difference between yes and no.

Your pressure points

How will you cope in a crisis or under pressure? It's difficult for an interviewer to gauge this at interview. Some will try to put you under stress during the interview. Better interviewers will seek evidence. Prepare good stories about times when you overcame challenges while working to strict deadlines, or times when everything went wrong and you found some way of coping.

Interpreting interview language

Listen for verbal clues: the snippets of information the interviewer gives you about the job, the questions that are asked. All these things give you huge clues about the job, but also about the language you should use. If the questions are all about targets and performance, match your language.

Listen for checklists

Be aware of the structure of an interview. Some interviewers jump straight in with something like 'tell me about yourself'. Others will have a game of two halves in mind: a first half where they go through a checklist of the things they want to know, and a second half where they probe things more deeply. If you sense a 'checklist' approach, don't go into too much detail with each answer, since it irritates the interviewer. You can always give a brief answer and then offer more detail if invited.

Tell stories

Employers naturally want to hire winners, but at interview most candidates look and sound like everyone else. Describing your experience in the same phrases you use in your CV makes for a dull performance. Trotting out interview clichés reinforces the idea that you are no better than anyone else.

Think about how you package information. We retain stories far longer than we remember information. Learn how to get your best evidence across as short, lively mini-narratives.

Emphasise the whole story

Employers feel comfortable making job offers when they believe three things: you can do the job, you will fit in, and the job makes sense in terms of your career story. Think, and talk about, what you will learn from the role and why you would like it as the next item on your CV. Convince the interviewer that your career story as a whole makes sense: even if you have changed sectors several times you can still explain your career choices in terms of learning opportunities. Leave the selector in no doubt that your career story makes sense, and the role under discussion is the natural next chapter in that story.

> **Top interview tips from Kate Howlett, Managing Consultant for John Lees Associates**
>
> *Given that most people will know to turn up on time, look reasonably smart and sound coherent, I've compiled my alternative 'top ten' list:*
>
> 1. Remember you are the **guest not the host**. Allow the interviewer to play the role of host and enjoy the courtesy afforded to you of being a guest. If you start to put the interviewer on the spot (for example, 'what's your management style?'), they won't enjoy the interview so much. Often candidates have played the role of interviewer more than interviewee and find it hard not to undermine the interviewer. The host needs security of control over the situation and the accolade of being trusted to be the interviewer. The guest needs to be comfortable and looked after – understand this is not a weak position.

2. **People buy from feelings** not from cognitive thoughts. People feel more intensely if you offer pictures not facts. Pitch your achievements through well-told stories – involve and engage the listener, allow them to empathise.

3. **Integrity and enthusiasm are the hardest qualities for any interviewer to resist**. Integrity means that when working with you, they will always know what's going on and can always trust you. You won't undermine their own position or cause them embarrassment. Enthusiasm shows confidence, generates energy and is infectious – they always love offering the role to the person who *really* wants it!

4. **Visualise a time you performed at your best** – play it in your head like a film reel repeatedly a few days before your interview to remind yourself of how brilliant you can be. Allow yourself to believe in your own propaganda. Then at interview perform from the part of you that performed so brilliantly in your 'film reel'.

5. **People watch for things to emulate** – observe and register aspects of other people's personality, performance and appearance and decide which aspects feel right for you to take on board. Decide what the 'grown-up' version of yourself looks like, collecting ideas from colleagues to consciously create a more effective and powerful version of yourself.

6. **Perform from your work head not your home head** – create and project your own brand. Often people feel stripped of their title and brand when they lose their job. You are used to going into meetings with your job title and company brand for validation, and all of a sudden it's just you. Be clear about your own brand – if you were an Operations Manager, you are still an Operations Manager and have years of experience to prove it wherever you work – your brand is

your industry experience. If you go into an interview with your home head on you are more likely to feel far too vulnerable, exposed, overwhelmed and lack clarity of what you are offering. Go in with your work head – clear of your own brand and its appeal in the competitive marketplace.

7. **'What are your weaknesses?'** There is usually something in a job specification you lack or where you lack experience. You could just ignore it at interview, but when the interviewer compares you with other candidates, this hole in your credentials is bound to be discussed. It's better to talk openly about the issue at interview so you can put a positive spin on it and talk about how you plan to overcome this minor gap. For example: 'I have read the job spec carefully and feel very confident in how my experience and qualifications match your requirements. However, I don't have a Prince II Practitioner qualification. I've done some research and know that I can complete a week's course at the end of this month and I have every confidence that with my breadth of experience I would pass first time. I am also happy to fund this myself.'

8. **It's not about giving a good performance but about giving the best performance**. You can pretty much guarantee that the company will have a good selection of strong candidates to interview with the requisite qualifications and experience, all of whom can pull off a decent interview. So, what's the point in being one of the crowd? It's not about taking part, it's about winning – there are no second prizes. Try to challenge yourself throughout the interview to consider not what's a good answer but what's the *best* answer. Ask 'what can I say that nobody else can and how can I put it in a picture so that they *feel* more intensely and I become a compelling candidate?'

9. **Determine three things you'd like them to think about you in the first 90 seconds** and use all your powers of non-verbal communication to portray those three things. Plan it into your appearance, manner, gait and tone. It's amazing that so often people pick up what you're thinking without having to say a word. In fact, only 7% of the impression you make will come down to what you say – everything else is non-verbal.

10. **Don't sell to them.** Don't 'close' – it gives people the creeps and they can see right through it, which makes you a less popular candidate. People on the whole don't like to be sold to. All you have to do is exude your brand and give clear and confident evidence of your achievements with enthusiasm and integrity.

Preparing for specific questions

'What on earth are they going to ask?'

Prepare well, do your homework about the organisation and the job, plan for specific questions, and you can shine at interview. Others will be trying to 'wing it' without thinking the activity through. Begin by adopting the interviewer's point of view. Starting with the key result areas of the job, what questions are almost certain to come up? See my book *Job Interviews: Top Answers to Tough Questions* for a more in-depth analysis of difficult questions. Here are some big ticket items:

- **Tell us about yourself.** Sometimes this is the opening question, and it's deceptively simple. An employer wants to ask questions so will be frustrated if you talk for more than a few minutes. Don't make the mistake of unpacking your entire work history and talking too much. Offer a quick overview of the shape of your career and summarise your key skills, and mention at least one personal thing that will make you easy to remember.

- **Why do you want this job?** Employers like to hear career stories that make sense. Don't apologise for your CV or suggest that it's a series of random events. Rehearse a quick summary of your career which shows how it is one story with different themes which knit together, and then talk about how this job on offer is the perfect next step.

- **How did you handle working with someone you didn't like?** Avoid criticism of past employers or bosses as it will probably rule you out. Everyone's working style is different, so it's best to show how you don't let personality issues get in the way at work; give examples of where you have worked with a range of colleagues and bosses. Explain different strategies you have used to communicate with people you found difficult.

- **What did you like and dislike about your last job?** Likes – make a good match between the things that motivate you in work (for example, people, challenges, new learning) and the key things on offer in this new role. Dislikes – talk about things that frustrated your work performance such as bureaucracy or computer failure rather than talking about individuals.

- **How do you respond to criticism?** Employers don't have time for ruffled feathers or workplace squabbles. Treat this question as if it is really asking about how you respond to feedback. Give examples of times when you have adjusted your working method or tried new approaches. Don't complain that the criticism was unjustified.

- **How do you work with others?** How you work with colleagues and customers may make or break your job performance. Impact can be positive, if you naturally encourage and motivate others, or negative if you are cynical, a gossip, or someone who sees the down side of every situation. Think about what your work colleagues would say about working relationships. Are you a natural persuader and influencer, or are you a relationship builder? There's always something positive to say here – just don't give the impression that you prefer working entirely alone.

- **Where have you used this skill?** Supply evidence. Even relatively sophisticated competence-based interviews are essentially saying 'You say you have skill X. Tell me when you used this skill.' Work out the skills that will make a real difference to the job, and match them to the skills that you know you exercise with ease and enthusiasm. Tell engaging stories to get your skills across – entertain your listener and they will remember more of what you said.

- **How quickly do you pick things up?** Employers want a fairly quick return on the time and money they put into recruitment, so they love fast learners, people who can hit the deck running and can get up to speed with minimal supervision. Talk about a past job (or study experience) where you got on top of a difficult problem quickly, organised your own learning, and got results quicker than expected.

- **What are you most proud of in your working life?** Employers like staff who are proud of what they achieve. Get used to talking about achievements and high points, even if some of them are outside work. Good examples show employers that you are motivated and proud of what you have done. Have at least one good work example where you rescued a situation, delighted a customer, or handled a difficult project.

- **What are your strengths and weaknesses?** This question comes up all the time. Plan to talk about three or four strengths which are required by the job (with good examples ready to hand). If there are any gaps in experience, emphasise that you're a quick learner. Don't linger on weaknesses or talk yourself down – name one skill which you would like to develop further.

- **How do you respond to stress and pressure?** An employer wants to know what you will actually be like in a busy workplace, and how reliable and calm you will be when things start to go wrong. Give examples of times when you have met difficult deadlines or handled tricky people, kept your cool, and got the right result.

- **What kind of person are you?** Handle questions about personality carefully. Rather than say 'I'm an ideas person', talk about a time when you changed things with a good idea.

- **Why are you on the market right now?** An employer wants to know whether you are moving on from choice or circumstances. If you were made redundant, mention this briefly but move on to talk about the work you want to do next. Keep your answer brief and upbeat. If you have been unemployed for some time emphasise your continuing learning and the range of organisations you have looked at. Don't complain about how difficult the market is, or how many rejections you've received. Employers will probe for reasons for job change, so rehearse short, simple, positive 'stories' to cover these points. This is not telling lies, just a simple, positive summary. (See presentation statements on page 84.)

- **Where do you see yourself in five years' time?** If your answer doesn't ring true for you, it won't for anyone else. Talk about career plans, and what you want to learn and achieve in the future.

Competency questions

A 'competency' is a combination of know-how, skills, attitude and demonstrated behaviours, all directed towards outcomes that actively assist an employer. A competency is not just about what you do, but how you do it, and to what level.

Prepare by reading those listed competencies which are considered essential or useful for the job. You may be invited to match your experience against each competency listed. Look back on written examples when you plan your interview. Have one or two fresh ideas up your sleeve so that you don't repeat evidence.

Competency-based questions can come up in any interview. They will usually be flagged by the introductory words 'Tell me about a time when …'. Look at what you believe to be the main competencies required and plan short, upbeat examples of what you have actually done, and when, and what the end results were.

Timeframes and buying signals

We all give out buying signals. If a shop assistant is selling you something, she senses interest when you ask detailed questions, but she knows she has reeled you in when you check how much cash you have in your wallet. The first buying signal in an interview is when the interviewer starts to talk about the present, and then the future. Stay with that, encourage it. The stronger the image in the interviewer's mind of you sitting in a real office at a real desk, the greater the chance it will become reality. Encourage the employer to visualise you in the job by talking about what you hope to deliver. Suggest ideas and possibilities for the employer: it weaves you into the fabric of the organisation's future.

Your closing questions

When asked 'do you have any questions for us?' too many candidates politely say 'no, you've covered everything in great detail, thank you'. Wrong answer! The interviewer feels you have little real interest in the job. Questions will arise from the interview, but prepare three or four good ones in advance. Avoid asking about the selection criteria: this sounds like you're challenging the system or asking for special treatment. Good questions come in two types: questions that show you have thought carefully about key result areas, and questions about the future of the job.

Be clear about the reason for asking questions. It's not to help you decide if you want the job – you can do that thinking later, with appropriate background research. The main purpose of your questions is message reinforcement, not information gathering. Don't waste the interviewer's time by requesting basics you should have learned from the company website. Your task is to leave a final positive impression about your strong interest in the role. The first and last things you say at interview will probably be remembered more than anything else you say, so think particularly about what you say as the interview closes. Before you ask any questions, say something positive about the role. Then your question sounds like your buying signal: you like the job so much you want to know more. Prepare detailed questions about the job and the organisation, for example:

- 'How will the job change?' Show an eagerness to grow as the job grows.
- 'What's coming up in the next 12 months?' Try to work out what time with the company will do for your CV.
- 'How will my performance be measured?' Are there set targets? Is there a formal appraisal system?
- 'What will I learn in this role?' What learning opportunities (courses, qualifications, training) does the job offer?
- 'How much variety is there in the job?'
- 'What will I be expected to deliver in the first three months?' Show that you are aware that you need to hit the deck running.
- 'Is there anything else I can add?' Probe to find out if there are any weak points in your evidence. The question 'is there anything I can add that would help you come to an appointment decision?' might take the employer into buying mode.

Talking money

One major buying signal is when an employer asks how much you will cost – no-one discusses terms unless they're interested. This is not the time to say how little you would settle for; bring the discussion back to the value you can add. Ask the employer what salary they had in mind when they decided to recruit. Only as a last resort should you talk about the salary you'd like, because you're in danger of naming a salary out of line with the employer's expectations (too low or too high). If you name a figure, base it on hard knowledge of what others in similar positions are earning. You should aim to be paid what you are worth to an employing organisation, in relation to the value you add, the professionalism you deliver and the size of the problems you will solve. The final factor is what the market will bear, but at this stage of the process – at this stage only – you have the upper hand. They want you. They are falling in love with you. And just for a fleeting moment you have some leverage.

Interviews with recruitment consultants

Recruitment consultants are professional selectors who make a living finding workers to fill vacancies for client employers (see Chapter 11, particularly the advice on page 181 from Joëlle Warren). A recruitment consultant will not make the final selection decision, but is in a critically important position as a gatekeeper between you and the decision maker, determining whether or not you get on to the interview short-list. You are dealing with an intermediary, someone who can be either broker or barrier. If a recruitment consultant is talking to you, it is likely to be because they hope to place you in a role. Few recruiters will give you an interview otherwise, unless they are hungry for information about your sector.

The consultant acts as the employer's eyes and ears, but will often have more perspective: if there's something unacceptable about your dress code, interview behaviour, CV or qualifications – anything that makes you different from 'vanilla' candidates – the consultant will be highly attuned to it. The reason is simple: a recruitment consultant wants to put forward a safe bet. Therefore, you need to know what buttons you are pressing in terms of safety, reliability or energy and enthusiasm. Get the recruiter to describe to you what he or she is really looking for, and respond to that.

When you deal with recruitment consultants, build relationships by asking for advice on your CV, your interview technique, and market opportunities. Be flexible and available. Don't let any prejudices you hold about recruitment consultancies in general influence this one discussion. Agencies need a flow of enthusiastic, committed candidates. Just as you will show an employer how your presence in the workplace will solve problems, be a problem solver to any intermediaries.

Exercise 14.1 – Shopping list

Find a vacancy that interests you, perhaps through a published advertisement. Obtain a job description.

Take an A4 piece of paper and divide it into two vertical columns. Interrogating the job description, write out in the left-hand column the employer's shopping list, everything the recruiter is looking for.

List all the 'wanted' elements: qualifications, experience, know-how, etc. Work out what's essential, and what's desirable. Use your own industry knowledge to work out all the stuff between the lines: the unstated assumptions.

Now think yourself into the interviewer's shoes. If you were interviewing, what would you really be looking for? What achievements would you recognise?

On the right-hand side of your sheet, write in your matching claims and evidence. These should initially just be bullet points – you can develop detailed examples later. When you seek evidence, look again at the **Skill Clips** exercise (page 80) and the discussion about achievements (see Chapter 6).

Exercise 14.2 – The politician's trick

Listen to a seasoned politician being interviewed on the radio. No matter what questions are asked, the minister always manages to make three or four strong points about government policy. The questions just provide an opportunity: the airtime is being used as a way of getting a particular message across.

You can use the same technique:

- Step 1: look at the key result areas in a job, and ask yourself 'What three points is it vital that I make during this interview?'

- Step 2: write them down, and rehearse a clear, concise way of talking about them.

- Step 3: make sure you get those three points across at interview. Why three points? Politicians know that their listeners can only hold a few ideas in mind at one time. Interviewers are much the same.

'Must do' list – interview reminders

✓ **Preparation.** There is no such thing as enough preparation. Do what you can, but try to do at least four times more than you think is enough. Make sure you know the names of the people who will be interviewing you. Practise saying them if they are complicated. Find out everything you can about the company and what it makes or does. Look for current news – show you are up to date.

✓ **Impact.** What does someone see, hear and experience in the first 15 seconds as you walk in the room? If you wanted to wear a sandwich board into the interview, would it say 'Employ me, I'll fit in' or 'Born to be wild. Please subsidise'? Work hard at creating the right impression: friendly and professional is often the right balance.

- ✓ **Look the part.** If you dress like an executive, you may be employed as an executive and paid an executive salary. If you dress like a new-age traveller ... . Read the signals, and try to look like you're already on the payroll; it's one time in life when conformity really matters. Usually it's best to dress one or two notches smarter than the normal dress code adopted by people already working at the organisation. Leave your coat and briefcase with reception – it helps to reinforce the feeling that you already work there.

- ✓ **Focus on decision makers.** There's little point strutting your stuff in front of someone who has no influence over the appointment decision.

- ✓ **Openings and closings** ... should be clear and positive. Think about what you're going to say. Research suggests that interviewers are most influenced by what you say at the very beginning and very end of the interview.

- ✓ **Think about CV problems in advance.** Don't apologise or hope that an employer hasn't noticed gaps or your lack of relevant experience. Be upfront about the compensating factors you have to offer.

- ✓ **Communicate your experience rather than just listing information.** Explain why your qualifications, training, or experience are directly relevant to the job. If you lack specified qualifications, demonstrate how your experience compensates. If you lack the exact experience required, give examples where you have undertaken something similar, *and* examples of where you have learned quickly.

15

Your first 90 days and beyond

'Built to last now means built to change.'
Stan Davis and Christopher Meyer

This chapter looks at:

- Making an impact in the first 90 days of a new role
- Longer term career management and choices
- Career conversations

Check out cultures before you get on board

At first, new staff are treated like curious strangers, and then the dominant culture starts to assert itself. You quickly learn whether you're in a hostile or supportive environment, and if your face fits. Much of this you can discover well before starting the role – in fact, before you accept the job offer.

The hidden cultures of the workplace have a powerful effect on job success. Your ability to 'read' the office culture can make the difference between walking tall and constantly looking at job boards. Most candidates know too little about working cultures before they take a job. Many people review the employer's website and accept everything that's been said at interview.

Before you take a job, perform a culture check. You don't need to be pushy to do this, and it's probably pointless trying to do it during the interview. Don't accept employer statements about the engaged workforce – most organisations make the same bland claims. Talk to people who know, including past and present employees, contractors and consultants. Find out how long people typically stay and why the previous post holder moved on, and if staff recommend this employer to friends and neighbours as a great place to work.

You can't use the job interview to discover this information. Ask 'what's it like to work here?', and you'll hear positive noises. Two months in, those promises feel like claims from a second-hand car salesman. Now you discover what's going on under the bonnet: high staff turnover, power play, and unhappy staff. Find someone to give you bias-free feedback and help to decode the organisation.

What happens in the first 90 days?

'What do you hope to achieve in your first three months?' is a question often asked at interview. Michael Watkins' *The First 90 Days* (Harvard Business School) reinforces the widely held assumption that judgements made about your performance in the first three months impact hugely on career success. In short, in a high-pressure environment, you have three months to deliver results that convince an employer that hiring you was a good decision.

Six steps towards 90-day success

1. **Do your homework.** Spend time absorbing the language of the organisation, spotting the biggest problems and opportunities. Soak up organisational charts, remembering the names and job titles of people that matter. Keep a notebook. Write down key names, procedures, contact numbers.

2. **Begin by focusing on people.** Your first few weeks have a huge impact on your credibility. Your first strategy is to listen, learn, and ask intelligent questions. Identify the people who will make decisions about your future, the people who can make your job easier. Start by identifying two kinds of people: (a) future allies, for example, key people in IT and finance – find out how their concerns and ambitions impact on yours, and (b) information brokers – the people who know who does what, and who to ask.

3. **Hit the deck running.** You will be judged by the first time you touch every kind of task that comes up in your job: your first report, first meeting, first presentation. Probe the cycle of routine activities: don't be caught napping by a sudden report deadline. Learn as much as you can about procedures and standards. Conformity may be boring, but it keeps you out of trouble in your first few weeks.

4. **Kick-start your networking.** Don't rely just on your day one grand tour to meet new people. Seize opportunities to visit other departments or branches. Ask open questions about the way HR could support your new colleagues – and expect to hear some challenging replies.

5. **Look for quick wins.** What is the biggest impact you can achieve in the shortest time, with the minimum of effort and resources? New HR managers often try to impose a template for change. This takes time, and meets resistance. The best method is to ask around: what gets in the way of productivity? What can be resolved obviously and cheaply?

6. **Catch the wave.** The next step, once you start to become established, is a matter of identifying an area of work that is becoming a strategic focus for the organisation. To do this you need to be tuned in to the overriding needs of the organisation. Offering results that tie into the issues which are top of the agenda at the highest level quickly gets you noticed.

Take control of broadcasting house

Here's a simple test. What is said about you when your name comes up in conversation? You may have 200 pieces of information in your CV, but casual conversations will generally repeat just three or four phrases. Yes, you're pleasant/energetic/committed, but what gets tagged on? A throwaway comment that you're frustrated (or marking time until something better comes along) may travel faster than a summary of your strengths. It's your job to manage the short burst of information that pops up in your absence, and make sure it captures your key messages.

Personal reputations are built on sound bites just as much as brands. Too many individuals try to navigate their careers without having a grip on how they are seen by others, particularly those in their circle of influence. This matters even more if you're trying to build external relationships or if you hope to be visible in the hidden job market. You may worry too much or too little about how you are perceived – either will mislead you unless you get good feedback.

Becoming a known brand

Drop received ideas about how people make progress in organisations. We'd like to believe that people get promoted because of sustained and appraised performance, but this simply flags you up as 'competent'. Advancement is all about being noticed for the right reasons.

Many are perplexed at the 'something extra' they need to put in to be noticed. You work hard and stack up achievements, but the big question is: who notices? You could follow the crowd by working hard and keeping your head down, but will this get you the enhanced career you feel you deserve? And if things falter, how long before you adopt another kind of uniformity by sounding jaded or cynical, and this shapes your water-cooler reputation? Your image isn't shaped by year-round activity, but by flash-moments where you are suddenly seen in a different light by people who matter. This may happen by chance if the CEO happens to be in the room, but well-navigated careers are often built around a conscious decision to create and manage opportunities which enhance visibility, for example attachment to the right project or team.

It's easy to shine in times of unlimited growth just by riding the tiger, but a tight market takes something different. There are plenty of tough cookies out there, driving down cost and shedding resources, which may mean your offering sounds pretty undifferentiated. The individuals who stand out do something different – behaving humanely or imaginatively, perhaps, or transforming dull decline into opportunity.

Don't just work hard, work hard on the things that matter – the topics discussed at the highest level in your organisation. Find a mentor who is senior and wise enough to decode the business for you, and learn the difference between activity and contribution.

Longer term career management

Review everything you've done since you started your current role. Have you progressed, or repeated the same year several times over? Now focus on the past 12 months. What can you do that you couldn't do a year ago? What have you added to your job? What new thinking have you generated or adopted? Some careers are made through managing down times and creatively squeezing thin resources. What's your contribution, and has it been noticed? Find someone encouraging enough to remind you of your successes, but objective enough to ask 'so what?' about your weaker claims.

Follow real leaders

Most successful people have worked around great leaders. Real leaders are not interested in status but are capable of inspiring people. Research from the Work Foundation published in January 2010 showed that many of the best leaders listen to others and are acutely aware of the impact they have on people around them, consciously modelling positive behaviours in the workplace. It's good when old-fashioned ideas come around again.

Record and build

Just as you have catalogued experience and skill for the purposes of making a job change, continue to do this while you hold down a role. It's a useful guide to how much you are learning, and whether the job lives up to its promises. It also helps you to catalogue achievements which are vital for career conversations (see below).

Career conversations

All work is a deal, a compromise between what you want out of life and what an employer wants to get out of you. Every deal needs a regular review of terms. Adding new content to your job mix and new learning opportunities can refresh your week. Learning how to initiate career conversations can make the difference between stagnation and growth. It often pays to ask for a career conversation outside the normal process of appraisal and role review. Say that you'd like a chance to think about career growth within your organisation. See the list at the end of this chapter for a script.

When you suggest change, make sure it doesn't sound like a complaint. Career conversations don't work if you expect to be given all the answers. Be specific about what you want, and shape it as a concrete offer with realistic wins on both sides. Research your current employer as carefully as if it was a major new customer you were trying to win.

Ask for a promotion if you think one might be possible, but make sure you already look the part. Almost everyone today has been asked to take on more at work, so claiming extra workload or increased responsibility doesn't cut it. Show how you are doing relatively complicated things that make a big difference to the organisation.

Be ready to think on your feet if you don't get everything you want. Probe alternatives such as learning opportunities, extending the range of your job, secondments to other teams. Ask for an early review date.

Don't threaten to look at jobs elsewhere – that simply sidelines you until you move out. Keep offering potential solutions, looking for opportunities to make your job grow, and (often after asking more than once) you'll start to get a little more of what you want, shaping your job rather than rushing to the job market for a much more random result.

When is it right to move on?

There's a golden rule in career change: the attraction of the new should be greater than the repulsion of the old. You should have a better reason for *moving to* than *moving from*. Before you jump ship, look at what you can fix in your current role. If you want to adjust something, is it the role, the organisation, or your boss? You may need to find more reasons to love the job you've got, but you probably have more power than you think to shape your role.

So, when you think of the word 'career', don't think of job moves but do think of managing your working life within the role, creating new opportunities and sculpting your job so it's a better fit for you and the organisation. This will be even more powerful if you also take account of the way others see you, as outlined above.

'Must do' list

Plan for your next career conversation with your line manager or HR. Use this checklist to prepare.

- ✓ Think about the person you will be talking to. Do they prefer information in writing, with time to think? If so, send a summary of your thoughts in advance.
- ✓ Keep talking to colleagues in other parts of the organisation so you are up to date on current projects and priorities.
- ✓ Prepare a short summary of where you have added value in your current role.
- ✓ Talk about what you have learned in the role already, and how you want to build on that.
- ✓ Rehearse a brief but punchy summary of your most useful skills (see Chapter 6).
- ✓ Offer concrete ideas for reshaping your role.
- ✓ Make sure that what you offer benefits the organisation as well as yourself.
- ✓ Have a plan B in mind if you can't get the promotion or role definition that you're asking for.

From part-time to portfolio: rethinking career choice

'If you can fall in love with what you are going to do for a living, you've got it made.' **George Burns**

This chapter looks at:

- Rebalancing and refreshing your career
- New choices in working arrangements
- Building a portfolio career
- Temporary, interim and flexible working arrangements

Changing the way you think of your career

Two generations ago we enjoyed an unusually high degree of job security in return for company loyalty. Workers of the twenty-first century face a very different world. Jobs are created and lost at great speed as organisations restructure themselves frequently. A career no longer seems a simple path; it will probably be built of several strands and multiple experiences.

Management writer Charles Handy predicted 'the end of the employee society' – a decline of the conventional full-time role and an increase in both flexible working (interim, contract, flexi-hours) and self-employment. Work no longer makes sense in traditional terms. Workers today are, for example, likely to find themselves in occupations which are not closely related to their prior qualifications and training.

Even though everyone knows that jobs are no longer for life, it still comes as a surprise to have to reinvent yourself. Each year more individuals discover they have to draw their own maps.

Career refreshment

This is a book that acknowledges the importance of finding the right kind of work. However, the job you love now may not be a job you want to do forever. Our motivations for work and our sense of the rewards we get out of it change as we grow older. Careers need refreshing from time to time. We are becoming increasingly attuned to the idea that we will probably change career paths several times during a working lifetime. In other words, your long-term focus may not just be on getting a job you'll love, but on getting a series of jobs you'll love, and perhaps doing some of those jobs at the same time.

Working options

Organisations and workers are both learning to think differently about how projects are completed and work is delivered. We're all learning to think less about jobs and more about problems. Increasingly, the emphasis is on the task or project, which might be delivered entirely through external or internal staff resources, or a mix of both. As this chapter will explain, the market is increasingly less focused on job-shaped objects. Don't overestimate the impact of this: most workers are still in conventional salaried employment. The Office for National Statistics recorded that at June 2012, there were an estimated 4.2 million (14% of those in work) self-employed people, compared to 25 million working for someone else. Self-employed people tend to be older and male.

Whatever the totals, many workers, particularly at a professional level, have learned to think and talk about their careers not as a series of jobs, but as a series of projects, rather than as long-term relationships. Hence the rise of terms like 'giga-nomics': when work feels more like a 'gig' or a one-off task, your focus is on multiple clients rather than a single employer. In addition, we have seen a growth in unpaid internships, interim positions, fixed term roles and zero-hour contracts.

Temporary and contract working

A significant slice of work is available on a **temporary** basis, largely through recruitment agencies. Although there are few sectors which do not use temporary staff, most of the work available is in relatively conventional areas. So, for example, many office and reception roles are filled on a temp basis, as are a number of factory, warehouse and processing jobs. There are defined contract markets in health, education and transport. In other areas it's more common for work to be provided on **contract**, sometimes for several months, particularly in fields such as IT. Temp work can be a good door opener by giving you knowledge of new sectors or what it's like to work in a large organisation. You may not get access to training and career development opportunities.

If you are going to take temporary or contract work, think about what it will add to your CV. You will subsequently be asked about your choices, and to make sure that you don't get stuck in temp roles for a long period, it's important to look at the learning value of each appointment. Remember also that undertaking work on a short-term basis is often an extended audition: because your performance is a known quantity there's often a pretty good chance that you will be offered a permanent role.

However, be aware that agencies match candidates and roles very rapidly, and it's easy to be pigeon-holed in the wrong way, for example, being offered a series of repetitive temp roles that don't stretch you. Agencies often assume you want to do what you have done before. Ask for different kinds of work assignments and negotiate learning opportunities.

Those recently qualified, and some career changers, find that paid or unpaid internships offer a useful form of short-term working arrangement. See Chapter 17 for more advice.

Interim work

Interim work is essentially a form of short-term contract for more experienced staff. The work is provided through a wide range of interim agencies who regularly seek professionals with specialist expertise or extensive management or functional experience. The daily rate depends very much on the seniority of the last permanent job you held.

Interims can cover a short-term problem or can be retained for more than a year. Unlike a consultant, your role is not just to make recommendations, but to implement them. There is now a wide range of interim management consultancies in the UK, and if you are thinking of working in this field, investigate what they have to offer. However, the best course of action is to talk to someone who is currently undertaking an interim assignment. Remember, too, that your most likely source of interim work is with an employer you already know.

An interim assignment is often a good way of gaining sector expertise that will allow you do move into a senior role in a new sector. These types of assignment offer a great deal of flexibility for those who want to work for part of the year and take extended breaks. The negatives are that you may have to work some distance away from home, and it's easy to become known as a 'career' interim and lose credibility as a permanent candidate.

Flexible working

Even in a recession, employers have become far more positive about flexible working, including some degree of home working, largely because of advances in technology. You may want flexible working hours because of family responsibilities, commuting stress, or to free up time for other activities. Part-time working can assist with life–work balance, but you will probably put in more hours than you are paid for. In addition, you may be underexposed in the company and so not have a high profile with decision makers, and therefore miss opportunities for promotion and career development offered to full-time colleagues.

Remember that a great many part-time jobs are negotiated rather than advertised, and these roles are often filled by word of mouth. Alternatively, a job that is first conceived as a full-time position may sometimes be renegotiated into a part-time role once you have proven your value.

Job shares can sometimes be the answer. However, it's near-impossible to persuade an employer to agree to a job share unless you and your colleague are already working for the organisation. Employers are wary of set-up work and the complexity of managing job sharers. Like part-time staff, job sharers sometimes find they are overlooked in career development terms. If your job-share partner leaves, you may find it difficult to find someone else to fill the role.

Mixed mode: employed and self-employed

Some workers mix salaried and self-employed work. A few have more than one employer. You may gain an income from freelance or session work. Investigate alternative careers by trying out something different. This might be at the weekend, or during the evening (what some people call the **5 to 9 week** rather than the 9 to 5 week). Others start businesses on a part-time basis, phasing one kind of work in and another out as the business grows.

Is self-employment right for you?

1. Work out what **draws you** towards self-employment (for example, freedom of action, being your own boss, performing tasks you enjoy and working with stimulating people).
2. Look seriously at how many of these drivers you could achieve in a **conventional job** (for example, running your own profit centre within a larger organisation).
3. Then work out what **pushes you away** (for example, having to sell your services, uncertain income, lack of contact with co-workers). Look at ways of fixing these negatives, for example, by working in partnership with others, or moving into an existing business.
4. **Look before you leap**. Find people who have made a similar move.
5. If it's a competitive field, find people to talk to in other parts of the country.
6. Think hard about how you are going to **promote yourself**. How will people find you?
7. Plan ahead for **isolation** – recruit friends and mentors to support you, and network with people doing the same kind of work to swap stories and exchange ideas.
8. Focus on your **offering** – what product or service will you offer? How will it be different (cheaper, better, quicker, smarter) than others available?
9. **Don't get hung up on the frills**. It's great fun equipping your office, printing your own business cards and setting up your own website, but none of this matters as much as your first piece of work. Look hard at where your first business transactions are going to come from.

10. Pin down your **first three clients**. If you have three customers lined up who will pay for your services, no questions asked, you probably have a business. Don't get hooked on the business idea: look for an income stream.

Negotiating something which isn't a conventional full-time job

When candidates are talking to organisations they often learn that it's best not to talk about **job-shaped objects**. In other words, focus on the problem to be solved rather than the way the job is conceived.

When talking to an organisation don't put your needs first. If you start by saying 'I am only interested in a job that is part-time/interim/short-term …' you are putting the focus on the time you won't be delivering. Often this is enough to exclude you. Your main motivation to get hired appears to be finding a job that fits your lifestyle, not focusing on the needs of the organisation. Begin by finding out what an employer needs and make your usefulness clear. If the employer is interested, you *may* have the opportunity to negotiate different working arrangements to those stated. Some employers would rather have someone on a flexible basis than miss out on the right skills; others are attracted by the ability to reduce overhead costs. If they want you, things become negotiable, including working conditions.

Portfolio careers

What is a 'portfolio' career? The term is used to describe a deliberate choice to mix and match different work modes to find an effective balance. In the past, well-funded company pension schemes allowed executives to retire early and build a portfolio to keep them active during their final decade or so of working. Today's portfolio worker may have several drivers including income, variety, and the difficulties and restrictions of salaried roles. Some hold down three or four appointments simultaneously; for example, an IT consultant who also works as a board member of a health trust, a non-executive director of a publishing company and a charity trustee. Some use high-paid working days to subsidise other work, for example, a marketing specialist who works for two days a week at corporate rates, the rest as a lecturer. Examples vary enormously: a self-employed joiner who buys and sells antiques as a sideline, a part-time HR specialist who works as a freelance book editor, an in-house lawyer who runs her own business as an equal opportunities trainer. Some of these people might not automatically recognise themselves as 'portfolio workers', but they are living examples of a new, pragmatic and highly inventive method of working.

In recent years portfolio working has become something that far more people think about. Surveys suggest that self-employment is growing (in the UK the number of workers self-employed in their main job rose by 367,000 between 2008 and 2012; 84% of this increase in self-employment was for those aged 50 and above). In the early 1990s only about 10% of executive career changers I was working with were interested in portfolio working. Today it's more like 50% of men and women in this client group over the age of 50. Younger people, too, are adopting the approach – sometimes out of necessity – as Barrie Hopson and Katie Ledger make clear in their excellent book *And What Do You Do? 10 Steps to Creating a Portfolio Career* (Black, 2009).

What kind of people benefit from this new working method? People who enjoy variety and change. People who have become dispirited by the constraints of a conventional career, lack of variety or growth. One of the great advantages of portfolio work is that you're not at the whim of a single organisation. You probably won't be made redundant, and if one income stream stops you have others already in place. The exciting thing about portfolio work is its unpredictability: you never know what kind of project or enquiry is coming in next, and you may be doing an entirely different mix of work in 12 months' time.

Beginning a portfolio career

The market doesn't offer you the chance of becoming a portfolio worker. It's not a role you can apply for. You might, however, begin a portfolio career as a result of a single request: if an organisation wants some of your time on a day-rate basis, you can start to think about how you are going to fill the rest of your week. This might not just be all about work – personal development and family time might be important ingredients too.

Dig deep in terms of possible elements in the mix. If you are already used to changing jobs rapidly and coping with varied income levels the transition may be relatively painless. Think now, at the start of your exploration, about how you will fill your dance card so that you are busy and earning enough. If you plan it right, the work will find you, but that means you have to invest a great deal of time and energy initially into making a great range of contacts (see Chapter 13 for more tips on networking). You will have to learn how to talk about what you do: explaining your distinctive work mix, and actively seeking out people who can help you to find customers and other kinds of contact.

Talk to people who have made the journey before you. Talk to people who have successfully reinvented the work they do. The reality may not be as glamorous as you think. If you are head over heels in love with an idea, speak to at least one person who is thinking of getting out of that line of business. Find out why, then match that with a balancing conversation with someone who loves their new career. If you want to move back into permanent work later in your career you will need to prepare a good interview answer about this segment of your work history.

Exercise 16.1 – Force field analysis

Kurt Lewin's force field analysis presents a variation on traditional problem-solving techniques. Lewin argues that change happens when the forces driving it are greater than the restraining forces. Driving forces are often positive, restraining forces often emotional.

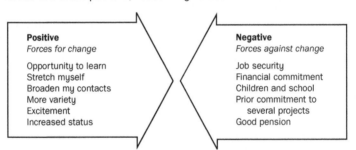

Positive
Forces for change

Opportunity to learn
Stretch myself
Broaden my contacts
More variety
Excitement
Increased status

Negative
Forces against change

Job security
Financial commitment
Children and school
Prior commitment to
    several projects
Good pension

The above diagram shows typical forces pushing you towards and against career change. Until restraining forces are addressed, change becomes increasingly difficult. It's like pushing against a coiled spring: at first it's easy, but the harder you push, the greater the resistance.

Draw up your two force fields. In the first, list the benefits of career refreshment (which might mean renegotiating your job or changing it). In the second, list forces against change.

Look in detail at your negative forces. How real are they? Give each factor a score from 1 (weak) to 5 (strong). Add up the total score on each side: which side is stronger at the moment?

See if you can strengthen any of your positive forces. If 'opportunity to learn' is a positive factor encouraging change, then ask yourself what your job will be like if this is taken away from you. This might mean that you increase the score for factors which are really important. Can you add any new positive factors? Now see if you can reduce the negative forces in any way, or even turn them into positives. Is your present job really as secure as it seems? If you are worried about the effect of change on your family, what would be the effect if you do nothing and remain unfulfilled? If you have given them strong scores, look at times in the past when you have overcome these difficulties, for example, managing insecurity, learning new tasks quickly.

Once you have a final score, talk your exercise through with someone you trust. What have you missed? How do you really feel about not making a change?

'Must do' list: exploring a portfolio career

- ✓ Describe your ideal portfolio career. Write down what you would be doing during a typical month.
- ✓ Focus on the steps you would need to take to make it happen.
- ✓ Research your escape route: talk to people who have left your profession recently.
- ✓ Be better informed about key changes in the way people work, and the impact of new technology and new working methods.
- ✓ Think again about what you recognise as a career and a 'proper' job.
- ✓ Investigate the different routes others have taken towards portfolio careers.
- ✓ Talk to people who have made the journey before you. Talk to people who have successfully reinvented the work they do. Use the REVEAL method of information interviews (see page 215).
- ✓ Ignore job myths. Find out for yourself.
- ✓ Weigh up the real pros and cons of change. How can you minimise the risk and maximise your return?
- ✓ Watch out (here as much as anywhere) for the overwhelming, crippling power of 'yes, but' thinking.
- ✓ Distinguish dream from reality. If a new career or enterprise interests you, find out what you will be doing most of the time.

Starting your career after finishing study

'Of course, it is very important to be sober when you take an exam. Many worthwhile careers in the street-cleansing, fruit-picking and subway-guitar-playing industries have been founded on a lack of understanding of this simple fact.'

Terry Pratchett

This chapter looks at ways of:

- Using this book if you're leaving school, college or university soon
- Building on your academic achievement
- Composing a CV when you have little or no work experience
- Translating what you know and can do into employer language

Thinking through your options

Choices apart from finding a job

Undertaking two or three years' **further study** may seem like the most comfortable option. Indeed, many students choose this as the 'default' mode, but is this the right step? Taking a higher qualification may give you a late start on the salary ladder, so is it an essential requirement for the career you have in mind? Ask yourself about your real motives for continuing your studies. Are you continuing simply because you have been offered a grant or a place, or because you don't know what else to do?

Choose your subjects for further study carefully. Avoid being press-ganged into a subject because someone else thinks it's a good idea. Areas of further study should meet two benchmarks: (a) the qualification will be a reasonable stepping stone, and (b) you will be motivated to study the topic (this works best if you really enjoy what you are studying).

Taking time out may also appeal. Again, the question is whether you want to delay your career start merely to indulge yourself, to put off a decision, or whether there are things you really want to do. There is probably no other time in your life when you will be able to travel with so few restrictions, but think hard about what you will learn from the experience. Employers need to see the relevance of your time out, and what you learned from the experience. Sometimes you can successfully combine travel with work.

For many people this is the moment to seek a new job. This might be your very first role, or the next job after a study break.

First steps into the shark tank

If you're at the end of full-time education or you've taken time out for study, finding a job may seem like a very dull task compared to study. After stretching your brain, committing yourself to routine tasks like filling in online forms and finalising your CV may seem very tame. This is of course why many of our smartest market entrants have weak CVs and unpractised interview skills: market readiness seems so easy, they don't do it.

There are several basic problems facing you if you've just finished a course of study:

- Are you looking for any kind of job to start repaying your student loan, or are you trying to build the kind of CV you'll be able to talk about with confidence in ten years' time?
- What kinds of roles might you be equipped to do, both immediately and in the future?
- Where are the jobs? How do you set about looking for them?
- What are the channels to finding jobs? Is it all about advertised positions, job boards, or networking?
- How do you apply the skills and knowledge you've learned in your studies? How do you talk about your qualifications in ways that employers find meaningful?

Getting more out of times you have seen work happening

Look at times you have had exposure to work: placements during a sandwich course, overseas work while travelling, paid work during term time, work experience while studying, holiday jobs, even workplace visits.

For any kind of work, paid or unpaid, keep good records of what you have done, including details of your role, the company, the contribution you made and where you made a difference.

What to say if you have little or no work experience

When you are leaving full-time education, finding good-quality evidence for your CV can feel like a tough job. You may feel you don't have many skills, or you are not sure what an employer finds valuable. You may have a fairly good idea of your personal strengths and feel that these are the only things you can write about. You probably haven't yet really understood how to communicate your skills to an employer, and although you know that employers are interested in evidence of achievements, you don't feel you have many worth mentioning.

For all the reasons mentioned above, most school, college and university leavers write an upside-down CV, where all the important messages are at the wrong end. You can read more about what goes wrong in my book *Knockout CV*, but the main point is that too many CVs major on recent academic success. These documents don't say anything about skills, know-how and achievements until page 2, when a rather thin-looking work history is presented. Such a CV shouts out 'I am a student who has had the occasional job' or 'I have little experience but some potential', rather than showing that you already have the skills to hit the deck running.

What every school leaver should know about finding a job

1. Your education may be the biggest recent event, but employers are only interested in your studies if they demonstrate useful skills or a high level of commitment. Explain your qualifications by showing how they taught you skills and knowledge that an employer can use.
2. Don't fill your CV with clichés and adjectives which scream out 'no experience, but great potential'.
3. When communicating to employers match claims with evidence. Give solid examples.
4. Catalogue any kind of experience that is work related including placements and volunteering. Look hard at the skills you used and where you made a difference.

Use temporary work as a way of gaining skills and relevant experience.

5. Don't oversell your experience, but explain it. Write and talk about what you did, not what your job description listed.

6. Plan for job interviews, don't wing it. List the requirements of a job and practise talking about your matching strengths.

7. Find someone with hiring experience to give your CV a cold read and to give you a general, introductory job interview. Prepare for it as if it's the real thing.

8. Reach out to people early in your job search. Ask around for ideas, leads, advice on your marketability. Talk to anyone who can move you closer to job-related information or a decision maker.

9. Don't rely on job boards and advertised vacancies to help you find a job. You're far more likely to land your first role or useful work experience through word of mouth.

10. Take advice from people who regularly make short-listing decisions, not websites or the opinions of friends and family.

Returning to a career after a study break

Those who have taken a career break to take a full-time course need to plan carefully when trying to return to the workplace. Taking time out to study places a gap in your CV, and doesn't always communicate employability; for a start, you have to convince an employer that you really are motivated to return to paid employment.

The key thing to remember is that you need short, focused answers to three questions:

1. Why did you decide to give up work to take this qualification?
2. What did you get out of it?
3. What do you hope to do next as a direct result of your studies?

If you fail to give an adequate answer to question 1, a recruiter starts to worry that you make random decisions in your career, or that you might be in danger of becoming a lifelong student. Question 2 requires you to think about *translation* (see below), but also requires you to talk with enthusiasm about what you enjoyed while studying (after all, if you didn't enjoy it, why did you do it?). The third question requires you to communicate a clear, straightforward data-burst about the way this recent experience adds to your CV and has helped to reshape your career path.

'I don't know what kind of work I want to do'

If you add up the thousands of hours students put into getting qualified, it's rather surprising how little attention they give to figuring out how they can apply their studies in work.

You may feel you are facing a bewildering range of choices regarding possible jobs and careers. Your problem may in fact be that you don't know enough about work to know which parts you are going to dislike. You may have little experience of work, or you may feel that your experience is not appropriate or useful to the new career you are hoping to begin.

Stuck for a career idea? Begin by looking at two big areas of life for clues: (a) what you enjoy doing (how do you spend your free time and what activities motivate you?) and (b) what do you enjoy thinking/talking/learning about? Look at what you love doing and try to find the opportunity to try it out on a work experience basis. Throw in some background thinking:

- Look at all the subjects that have interested you, and translate them into potential fields of work using Chapter 9.
- Look at all your experience of work to date. What has motivated you or excited you? Where have you been fully absorbed in your work?
- Look at the subjects you have just studied. What would you like to know more about? What skills have you developed while studying? Be very clear about your qualifications: why did you study them, what are they, what did they cover and what are your grades? But when you apply for a job, list them after your skills and work experience, however limited that is.
- Take work experience and short-term work assignments seriously. Write down the skills you use and what you have learned.
- Conduct an audit: what do you actually know about work? How can you find out more? Who can you talk to? Chapter 13 shows you how you can use REVEAL interviews to help.

Finding out

Don't miss out on obvious sources of information. If you have studied at university you will have access to a university careers service. In a society where funding is largely being cut from careers services, the university sector maintains high standards of support and guidance. You will get more out of your service if you go to all the careers events on offer and, when you have a one-to-one session, if you have specific questions about areas of investigation.

Lecturers and subject specialists can sometimes help with industry contacts, but one of the best sources of help for graduates, even if you left university some years ago, is the wide range of alumni associations available.

Few *current* students seem to make use of alumni associations. The great thing about these associations is that alumni of universities who have agreed to help those leaving study after them have effectively pre-contracted to provide help. You don't have to say much about who you are or why you're asking – simply mentioning that you're a member of an alumni group is usually enough of a door opener. An efficient association should be able to put you in touch with former students. Talk to students a year or two ahead of you who studied a similar subject and who have found work in sectors you find interesting. Send an email to establish contact, but see if you can get a face-to-face meeting, or at least a phone call. Ask members of your alumni association to be your first point of contact for information interviews (see Chapter 13).

Accept all ideas for career pathways gratefully, but make up your own mind based on evidence. Talk to anyone you can reach out to who is doing work which looks interesting. Where your studies are related to work, use them as a platform for your investigation. Most organisations will speak to you, for example, if you are carrying out a research programme, as long as your questions are not too extensive.

Thinking rather than drifting

Many people in their forties and fifties say 'I wish I'd thought more carefully about career choice when I was young'. Your first full-time job makes a big impact on your career.

Many people take 'fill-in' jobs after qualifying. If you start that way the danger is that you become a job hopper, snatching opportunities every time you feel dissatisfied, but never thinking about the overall shape and direction of your career. This experience can quickly lead to the idea that 'this is all there is' or 'this is what work is like'. You may convince yourself that the work you do will never be linked in any way to your studies. 'Fill-in' jobs can quickly become permanent posts unless you keep your goals in mind.

If you have little work experience, it's difficult to know what job satisfaction feels like. You don't get a sense of what motivates you until you've sampled work and experienced what 'fit' feels like. The advantage of traditional graduate programmes was that they allowed entrants to experience different parts of a business before choosing to specialise. The number of schemes has decreased significantly, but you can still adopt the career strategy of trying to replicate for yourself the opportunities provided by a good graduate scheme. Look for variety and range, particularly where you undertake unpaid work experience (see page 276).

Be clear about what you have to offer

The list below outlines a range of career management skills seen by employers as vital for workers competing in the twenty-first century labour market. The information comes from the Association of Graduate Recruiters, but this list of skills and qualities is useful to anyone beginning a career.

- **Self-awareness** – being able to identify your own skills, values, interests and strengths, seek feedback from others, and seek opportunities for personal growth.
- **Self-promotion** – defining and promoting your own agenda, shaping your personal reputation and brand.
- **Exploring and creating opportunities** – being able to identify, create, investigate and seize opportunities.
- **Action planning** – goal-setting, organising your time effectively, and preparing contingency plans along the way to achieving goals and targets.
- **Networking** – being able to define, develop and maintain a support network for advice and information.

- **Matching and decision making** – finding a match between opportunities you meet and your own core skills and knowledge; making informed decisions based on constraints and opportunities.
- **Negotiation** – negotiating the psychological contract to achieve win/win.
- **Political awareness** – being aware of hidden tensions and power struggles within organisations (sometimes defined as spotting the person most likely to stab you in the back).
- **Coping with uncertainty** – adapting goals and your mindset in the light of changing circumstances.
- **Development focus** – being committed to lifelong learning and your own personal development.
- **Transferable skills** – applying your skills, and communicating them, to new contexts (see 'Translation', below).
- **Self-confidence** – having an underlying confidence in your abilities, in terms of both past success and your innate qualities.

(Adapted from *Skills for Graduates in the 21st Century*, reprinted with permission from the Association of Graduate Recruiters (AGR).)

Former AGR Chief Executive Carl Gilleard wrote in support of these definitions: 'We asked our members what skills they are looking for in graduates. Top of the list come interpersonal skills and the ability to communicate effectively, the ability to work in teams and customer awareness. We also find that employers very much look for candidates who have had work experience; that carries a high premium these days. And let's not forget the old-fashioned attributes of enthusiasm, motivation and commitment – all of these things still carry a lot of weight with employers.'

Translation

The single biggest problem with CVs of university or college leavers is a failure to translate qualities, know-how and experience into terms that are meaningful to an employer. This isn't just a problem for people leaving full-time education; it's very difficult for people to leave teaching, the health service or the armed forces for exactly the same reason. You find yourself immersed in a particular language, and then fail to perceive the need to help others to understand what these terms mean.

Get in the habit of 'bridge thinking'. Busy recruiters don't have time to make connections unless they're obvious. It's your job to form a bridge between your experience and the world of the hiring company. Get an employer to see not just skills, but *transferable* skills – and they only become transferable when you communicate them *in terms an employer will get excited about*. For example, if you write that you produced a 6000-word dissertation on a topic, you will get minimal response. If, however, you talk about the problems of gathering data, interviewing people, keeping up with the latest developments in your subject area, and working under pressure to achieve the project by a fixed deadline, then your interviewer starts to get interested. You have started to talk the same language.

Identifying achievements

Employers get tired of hearing empty claims about the abilities of candidates, but they get interested when you can provide hard evidence, especially if you've achieved something. This doesn't have to be earth-shattering like climbing Everest or winning an Olympic medal. Achievement evidence shows an employer that you like to get things done, and produce results which assist an organisation and add to your CV.

Your recent studies may provide useful material. Some academic subjects mean little to employers, so explain why the topics you studied are relevant to a modern workplace. Talk about what you most enjoyed in study, what it taught you in terms of life skills, what special projects you undertook. Even if you studied something fairly abstract, you will have gained considerable experience of researching, organising and analysing data, consulting experts and presenting information concisely and coherently in speech and in writing.

Look at all of your experience for evidence of skills, learning quickly, and having the right attitude at work. Look at your activities outside study. Perhaps you organised complicated or exciting social events, competitions or sporting activities, or you may have been a member of a society or club. Think about the transferable skills that you acquired from these experiences, and make sure that they are mentioned in your CV.

Taking unpaid work to build CV evidence

If you find it difficult to get a paid role, you'll almost certainly be offered opportunities to work for nothing to help you reach the first rung of the career ladder. This may be classed as work experience or an internship. At one time such opportunities were confined to highly competitive fields such as fashion or media, but now most large organisations have structured volunteer programmes. What impact does volunteering have on your career prospects? Does it make you look like a go-getter or a doormat?

Let's look at the downside. Even though you're working for an organisation with great values and purposes you may still be stuck in a back room stuffing envelopes all day. With senior appointments the risk is that organisations place less value on your contribution and advice because they haven't paid for it. If you don't manage the event carefully or move on quickly enough you can easily find yourself underchallenged.

You may give yourself CV problems if you stay too long or take too many internships. Do your research to find out what your sector considers to be a reasonable length of time for an internship, and how many unpaid roles you can take without it looking like you are unable to secure a paid role. Keep in mind that while you are working it may be harder to find time for an active job search. If there really are no paid jobs in your sector, you might be better off gaining experience in another, related, sector for a couple of years.

One pitfall in working for nothing is that employers may leave you unsupervised while you undertake only low-level tasks. The critical question is what volunteering will add to your skills and whether it will enhance your value to future employers. Better placements include supervision, feedback and development. Volunteer workers often recognise that they have a 'foot in the door': if a paid post comes up you are a known quantity with a distinct advantage over external candidates.

All work is a deal, whether it's paid or unpaid. You may feel the deal is entirely one-sided as you're working for free, but it's still possible to seek a trade-off between your contribution and any non-financial benefits available. Spot them in advance and negotiate the ones that matter most to you. Always seek something in return: your contribution will be valued more. One of the greatest spin-offs can be exposure to new contexts and people. Benefits you can negotiate as a volunteer include learning and development, but don't take this for granted, it may only happen if you ask for it. Seek opportunities to develop skills, even for short bursts of activity. In job interviews, don't say 'it was just voluntary work'. Good volunteering experiences can add significantly to your employability.

From the outset, think of each volunteer post as a project. Before committing yourself, negotiate regular feedback on your performance, a reference at the end of the assignment and introductions to key people. Take every chance you get to meet new people inside and outside the organisation. Your natural curiosity may prove to be a door opener.

If you apply for a job and you're asked to work without pay for a period of time, don't be offended by the suggestion. Continue to show strong interest in the organisation. You might indicate that this mode of working isn't right for you at the moment, but you'd like to be considered for any paid roles that come up in the future.

'Must do' list: ten steps forward if you're new to work

1. **Build evidence of your employability while studying.** You will find that your job search will be easier if you are able to offer concrete evidence of skills and achievements. Increasing numbers of students are working while studying. Sometimes this is just during vacations, sometimes students work up to 20 hours a week or more during term time. Again, do more than mention job titles – talk about problems you solved, skills you used, and where you made a meaningful contribution. While you are doing the work seek opportunities to enlarge your skill set, and learn to communicate these skills to employers.

2. **Think about how you are going to choose your career.** Draw up a shortlist of ideas, and then talk to as many people as you can. A small amount of time now spent seriously thinking about career possibilities will have an enormous impact on your future life. Find out what careers other people like you have gone into, and ask them how they got there, what they enjoy, and what hirers are looking for. What negative thoughts are holding you back? How many of them come from other people? How

much of your thinking is informed by objective information about the real marketplace?

3. **Think about your experience** and how you will make it relevant. An employer is trying to measure potential, but provide what information you can about relevant experience (for example, work, travel, time out). Learn to describe your work history more dynamically. What did you actually do? What problems did you solve?

4. **What do you have to offer?** Look seriously at your skills. Build carefully, based on what you have done and the work that becomes available to you in the short term. Catalogue the skills and achievements you have acquired from *all* parts of your life. Almost any kind of work experience is valuable at this stage for you for experiment and work out your preferences. Think about the support skills you can offer, and an employer's expectations (for example, IT, word-processing, customer service or sales skills).

5. **Describe your strengths**, but be realistic about how far you should 'sell' what you can do. This means avoiding empty claims, but also avoiding undue modesty. Name your skills and say what happened when you used them, with concrete examples.

6. **Catalogue your accomplishments** from different contexts: study, work, leisure time, voluntary activities. Try to present your achievements in interesting terms, explaining them as mini-narratives if necessary (see Chapter 6 for further details).

7. **Explain your qualifications.** Don't assume that an employer is automatically interested in your academic achievements. Translate your studies into

language an employer finds not only meaningful but exciting.

8. **Be clear about what motivates you** inside and outside work. Examine your career hot buttons (Chapter 5) and draw up your personal wish list. You may find it important to think about the likely values of organisations you will be talking to.

9. **Get your message right.** Work hard on your CV and LinkedIn page before you try to gain traction in the job market. Look hard at the first 30 words of an paper or online profile to ensure it captures your key experience to date and what you can offer an employer. Avoid flowery adjectives or claims you can't support. See Appendix 1 for a model CV and a range of tips.

10. Prepare now for **interviews**. Don't believe that interviews are a matter of luck. Prepare. Work out what the employer is really looking for, and work hard to communicate your matching abilities. Show employers that you really want to work in their field, not that they happen to be the first to have a vacancy.

CV and covering letter tips

Designing a winning CV

There are many different ways of setting out a CV. The most important thing to remember is that your CV will only receive a few seconds of someone's attention before they decide whether to read further. This means that it is the first page of your CV that does most of the work.

Look critically at the first 30 words or so. What do they say about you? What conclusions do you expect a reader will draw from those words? If you start with a cliché such as 'A reliable, hard-working motivated worker ...' you've already categorised yourself as being the same as a wide range of other candidates.

Think about whether you need a profile or not at the beginning of your CV. In general, if you are happy to stay in the sector you're already in, and just want the next big job along, you may not need a profile but you can start with your most recent (or current) job. However, if you want to make a career change, you will probably need a profile to make sure the reader interprets your history in the right way. It says pretty much what you would say if you were in the room handing the document over.

What to put on the first page of your CV

1. Remember your CV will be screened into a 'yes' or 'no' pile. Do everything you can on page 1 to end up in the 'yes' pile.
2. A reader will probably have made a decision about you before getting to the end of your first page. Make sure any *key information* is here.
3. Think of the first page of your CV as a **one-page advertisement**, which should be strong enough to stand alone.
4. Don't put anything on the front page that strikes a negative note, such as difficulties you had with a past employer, or a failed course.
5. Include your contact details at the top of page 1. Include an email address, and make sure it is businesslike. Something like 'PleasureAddict@slaphead.org.uk' might convey the wrong impression.
6. Use summary words such as 'qualified' or 'graduate' to get your message across in the profile.
7. Don't include **empty adjectives**. Almost everyone is creative, dynamic, enthusiastic …. Focus on what you can do well.
8. Include any **important qualifications** on page 1 if you know an employer will be attracted by what they represent.
9. Match your evidence to the top five or six items required by the job.
10. Look hard at your **profile**, particularly if you use a job title to summarise what you do.

Other things to remember in a CV

1. A CV only has one function: to get you an interview. **Don't overcomplicate it.**

2. Make your CV immediately **interesting**. The first 30 words matter.
3. Keep ɩ **concise**. It isn't your life story.
4. Your CV should make **claims** about who you are and what you can do, and then provide evidence to back up those claims.
5. **Translate** what you know and can do into terms that will appeal to a recruiter. Talk about solving problems, making a difference, etc.
6. Try to say something interesting about your **academic history**. Relate it to an employer's needs rather than regurgitating the syllabus; for example, if you led a seminar or gave a talk, write about your facilitation or presentation skills.
7. It's all very well being the best thing since sliced bread. **Be specific**: try to express **achievements** in terms of awards, money, time or percentages.
8. If you recently qualified, don't go overboard about your qualifications. Make sure you include information on page 1 about your work skills.
9. Include something under 'interests' that is neither bland nor run of the mill. Include interests that make you appear a rounded person, and those that have some relevance to the job. Make sure you can talk enthusiastically about any interest you mention.
10. Take some time to make the layout attractive, with plenty of white space. Don't print text so small that it's painful to read.

Example CV

You can see on the following pages a good working example of a CV in the style recommended by *Knockout CV*, which covers CV preparation in depth.

Jo Hope

Location: Newtown | m: 07777 000000 | e: jhope@example.com
LI: uk.linkedin.com/jhope27

A graduate information management professional with B2B experience focused on the information security needs of the insurance sector and a track record of achievement in building customer relationships:

- **First line technical support to business users.**
- **Redesigned user manuals and online customer support materials.**
- **Introduced customer satisfaction measurement.**

EMPLOYMENT HISTORY

Information Security Manager –   Nov 2012–Present
ZZ Technical Industry Group

Responsible for a team of 5 colleagues providing first line customer response around data management and security.

- Improved customer satisfaction scores focused on my department's work by 38% in the year to April 2014.
- Designed intranet staff training pages on internet security.
- Rewrote staff training manual.
- Seconded on in-house data security project for BigChain Plc in Q3 of 2013.

Assistant Information Manager –   Jan 2009–Nov 2012
ZZ Technical Industry Group

Appointed to work alongside Information Security Manager in a new department rolling out a range of new service products.

- Key input into product range launched March 2010.
- Commissioned web tools from outside providers.
- Recruited, trained and coached new appointments, all retained as of 2014.

Customer Services Manager – 2008–2012
New Bubble Design

Taken on to provide and manage a range of customer service
functions including:

- Liaison with clients about design needs.
- Managing a team of freelance designers.
- Keeping projects on target and on budget.

Trainee Designer – AZ Holdings 2007–2008

Secured initial position against extensive competition as a trainee
in a prestigious major organisation offering B2B interior design and
shop fitting solutions.

- Extensive client visits and consultations.
- My design for BetterShops front of sale literature featured in
  Print.
- Offered senior position but chose to move into consultancy
  work.

QUALIFICATIONS

BA, Fine Art, Newtown University, 2.1, 2007

Diploma in Marketing, Newtown College, 2010

A Levels, Newtown Sixth Form College, History (A), English (B),
Art (A), 2004

INTERESTS/VOLUNTARY COMMITMENTS

Helped organise DesignFest fun run 2013, raising money for
children's charities.

Active member of community group teaching digital photography/
Photoshop skills to retired groups.

Wardrobe Manager, Green Room players, Newtown, since 2011.

Features from the example CV

- The opening is brief and uncluttered. Do not title your document 'Curriculum Vitae', which sounds very old fashioned.
- It begins with the most user-friendly version of the candidate's name.
- In line with up-to-date formats, the CV does not include a full postal address but does include an email address and LinkedIn URL.
- There is just one phone number provided.
- It uses the word 'graduate' in the first line and saves more details about qualifications for later in the document.
- The profile avoids flowery language, too many adjectives and unsubstantiated claims. It shows what this candidate might be doing next and points to measurable achievements which will be set out later in the document.
- A short number of bullet points are used immediately after the profile to give early prominence to key areas of experience.
- It does not say 'I' or 'he' but adopts an abbreviated, punchy style aimed to assist a reader to quickly get to relevant evidence.
- It uses bullet points throughout; most begin with a strong verb.
- Bold text is used sparingly to emphasise the profile and job titles.
- A short summary of the organisation and role is provided, leading quickly into more evidence of skills and achievements.
- It does not repeat obvious or dull information about past jobs, but emphasises hard evidence of added value.
- It pitches a strong message in the first half page.

What you should *not* do with your CV

1. **Don't** put any information on page 1 unless it says something important about you that might get you an interview.
2. **Don't** provide huge amounts of detail about jobs you did more than ten years ago.
3. **Don't** put yourself down, or try irony or humour. It rarely reads the way you want it to.
4. **Don't** give the names and addresses of referees. You can provide them if they are requested, but you should brief your referees carefully about who they may be talking to, and what the potential job is all about.
5. **Don't** use obscure abbreviations or jargon.
6. **Don't** include your age or your date of birth.
7. **Don't** disclose your salary unless you think this is going to be specifically helpful to an employer. It's generally best to deal with this at interview or, if you have to, in a covering letter.
8. **Don't** include non-essential personal information, for example, height, weight, names of your children, or your religious or political beliefs.
9. **Don't** send out poor photocopies. Print on good-quality paper if you are posting or delivering a copy.
10. **Don't** include your reasons for leaving jobs, but be prepared to discuss this at interview in a positive way.

The essentials of a great covering letter

Again, see *Knockout CV* for detailed advice on letter construction and some examples.

- The only function of a covering letter is to get your CV read, and to get you a meeting. Think of your letter like the first page of your CV, as a one-page **advertisement** for you. Make your letter **brief, enthusiastic and interesting**.

- Work out the top three or four **strengths required by the role**, and match them with short, punchy bullet points in your letter.
- Try not to begin every sentence and paragraph with 'I'. Focus on the **reader** of the letter and his or her perspective.
- **Research** – refer to the problems, opportunities and headaches that your target company is facing. Work out the main three or four requirements of the job, and provide matching evidence.
- Indicate in brief paragraphs **what** you are applying for, **who** you are, **why** you are interested, and **what** you have to offer. Don't oversell. State briefly why you are a good **match** for the job.
- Refer the reader to your enclosed CV. Discuss three or four of your top **achievements** which match the job, using different terms from the way you have expressed them in your CV.
- Don't put anything in your covering letter that gives the reader an excuse to put the letter aside, for example, apologising for your lack of a particular requirement, or mentioning your age, or referring to negative aspects such as why you left your last job.
- If your letter is a **speculative** approach (that is, to a company that isn't currently advertising a job), try to ensure that your letter is read by a **named decision-maker**.
- Think carefully what **action** you are asking for. If you are seeking a meeting, ask for one.
- **Telephone to check** that your letter has been received by the intended recipient. Ask one relevant question, or mention one reason why you might be able to help the employer, and try to sound relaxed about the process.

People who have transformed their careers

The case studies set out below are from clients who have worked with John Lees Associates and built their career change around ideas contained in this book.

Melissa Carr, assistant operations manager, third sector

Melissa studied Archaeology and Classical Civilisation at Nottingham University. After leaving university she felt 'lost', not knowing what direction to take. She began a career within the ambulance service, which was not right for her but provided an early indication that she wanted a career where she could 'give something back and do some good'.

Melissa then moved from working in healthcare to child-care. After working in a school for children with learning disabilities she felt she had found her niche. She writes: 'I loved going into school every day and working with the children. However I did not want to go back to university to study teaching and I wanted more responsibility than being a teaching assistant. When I couldn't settle and decide what to do I decided to travel and work abroad, moving to Australia for two years. In hindsight this was perhaps an attempt to escape the real world of work and finding my career! I do not regret my time spent away and I had some excellent work experiences, but when I returned to the UK I felt more lost career wise than ever!'

Melissa worked with JLA coach Gill Best, who asked for an outline of her dream job. Melissa writes: 'I just had to find it! I received guidance on creating a CV that would get me into an interview. Gill encouraged me to network rather than sit trawling through internet job sites. During this time I was temping as a waitress in a university, far removed from where I wanted to be! I felt demoralised when several job applications were rejected. I began to network in the university and through this I was given the details for the agency where I now work. I sent my CV, which I wrote using the advice in *Knockout CV*. Within a week I had an interview and within two weeks I was working as a support worker for children with autism. After two months I was promoted to management. I had found a job where I was giving something back but it also gave me the responsibility that I had craved.'

Melissa adds: 'I believe that having a clear idea of what I wanted from a job came across to my employers. They could see how passionate I was about working with children with learning disabilities. I have no doubt that this is my dream job and where I am supposed to be. I can safely say that I go into work each day with a smile on my face.'

Mary Wilson, musician and careers counsellor

Following a degree in Social Anthropology at Cambridge and an enduring curiosity in what makes people tick, work cultures and how people behave in groups and individually, Mary was drawn to working in the advice/counselling sector and enjoyed developing her skills as a one-to-one adviser and group trainer in a number of different fields including the Citizens Advice Bureau, a national charity, higher education and a psychology consultancy. Weaving through this time after hours and at weekends, she was also a musician performing in a band at clubs and festivals.

Taking a few years away from the job market, Mary brought up two children while continuing to perform in her band. The time came to think about a return to work and Mary spent a few months working through *How to Get a Job You'll Love*, having attended John Lees' career coach masterclass. While Mary was comfortable with the idea of networking and talking to people about what they do, she needed some time to focus internally on what really mattered to her and work out what she wanted to do next. 'I felt as if I was drowning in a sea of creative ideas and didn't know which direction to follow.'

'Working through all the exercises in the book gave me a space to think through my ideas and even encouraged me to have some more! The book does not force you to make decisions too early but allows for lots of blue-sky thinking before laying out all the exercises on a giant sheet of flipchart paper. It was during this final process that breakthrough occurred and I realised that I didn't have to decide between psychology and music but could see the links between them and gradually a vision emerged. I would be able to pursue a portfolio flexible career that also fitted around the needs of my growing family.'

After using the **JLA Skills Cards** Mary commented: 'Although I have highly developed people skills, I am most inspired by taking a fusion of concepts/ideas/sounds into a forum where I am in command. I need to be out there being radiant, full of warmth and empathy with a box of delights at my finger-tips. The toolkit needs to be maintained from the inside (requires time alone) and is full of musical instruments, imagination, psychological concepts and tools and ideas.'

Two years on from this process Mary enjoys a portfolio career, mixing family life, freelance career coaching and regularly performing in her band – and she also devises and runs lively music groups for babies and toddlers.

Will Beale, head of programme management, World Wide Fund for Nature

Will studied Natural Sciences and Chemical Engineering before joining Unilever. He worked in research, manufacturing and new product development, but after ten years had a strong impulse to find his ideal career path. Will began by feeling apprehensive, but threw himself positively into the process: 'I spent three months undertaking Information interviews with about 40 people in my target fields. I learned a lot but it was also quite a tough time, especially for my family.'

Will applied for a wide range of jobs – business, NGOs, public sector. His dream was to work for an organisation actively contributing to environmental and animal protection. When a job at the World Wide Fund for Nature (WWF) entered his sights he felt he had found the perfect match: 'It seemed ideal but honestly I did not expect to get it. However, by this time my application, interview and negotiation skills were well practised, and I knew how to sell the positive about myself.'

At WWF Will has moved from quality management to building excellence in conservation management. Will continues to enjoy his work enormously, and recognises that the change he has made is part of deeper life choices – 'it's an analytical role but requires a lot of people skills. I have travelled widely (while endeavouring to minimise flights) and have a much broader perspective on the world. Through the whole process of change, my personal faith and my prayer life were very important in sustaining me towards finding my mission in life.'

Chris Webb, graphic designer

Although Chris was studying Classics at university, working on the university newspaper revealed a talent for design, so after graduating he found a job as a graphic designer working for an engineering company. When the recession hit he was made redundant, still in his early twenties. Everyone advised Chris that this was a time to get a 'sensible' job, and that there was no point applying for jobs in the graphic design field. Chris considered alternative career paths, even though they were far less interesting to him. Chris found from using the JLA Skill Cards that 'I really was drawn to creative work, but I also had people and analytical skills'. When asked what he would do if all jobs paid the same, it was clear that Chris wanted to explore the world of illustration.

The next step was to rethink his job search at a time when the market was laying off graphic designers every day. Chris reveals how the hidden job market opened up: 'I learned not to look for advertised jobs, but to find people who are doing interesting things and may need help.' By making direct approaches to organisations who were not advertising, and demonstrating both skill and enthusiasm, Chris had two job offers within a fortnight of his change of strategy. Twelve months later Chris had gained experience of both in-house work and freelance work as an illustrator and cartoonist, and as Chris 'Curis' Webb he wrote his first graphic novel *Punishment of the Dice Gods*. His Amazon.co.uk biography reads: 'To Curis, cartoons are the best way to interact with the world. They got him into trouble at school, into print at university and into minor celebdom in the world of miniature wargaming. Curis' favourite resignation letter took the form of a three-panel cartoon, and his close associates regularly get weird doodles passing as birthday cards, or passive-aggressive notes about doing the washing up.'

Since then Chris has worked as a web developer but is now in an exciting role at www.manticgames.com where he is responsible for designing game and painting figures, product and packaging design, publications and point-of-sale/ publicity material. He gets a great buzz from coming up with new character and gaming concepts and seeing them turn into commercial products. Chris shows how you can turn a teenage obsession into a professional career.

Beth Grant, practice administrator, West Sussex

When she first came to JLA, Beth had been unable to work for three years following an accident at work resulting in a long-term shoulder problem. Initially, she could see very few work options and was worried about the kind of reception she would get from employers as a job seeker with long-term health problems and a long period out of the labour market.

Beth worked with JLA consultant Caroline Humphries. Beth was encouraged by the fact that the exercises she was offered were tailored to her particular circumstances: 'All of the exercises completed were incredibly thought provoking and were excellent in really helping you to think about what it is you want from a job and from life. Even though some of these were testing, with the amazing support I was fortunate enough to have, the end results far outweigh the difficult soul-searching moments.'

Not only that, the work she did boosted her confidence: 'At all stages we celebrated the progress I had made and it was refreshing to be reminded of how far I had come.' With her consultant's knowledge, advice, encouragement and guidance Beth found herself in a position to start looking at retraining and returning to work with a clearer understanding of her skills and the messages she needs to communicate to employers.

Beth learned to place the focus on what she can do rather than on her limitations, and in 2011 moved into the first permanent role since her accident, working as practice administrator in a busy, thriving orthodontic practice. Today, she describes herself as fortunate to have found an employer who values staff and customers equally, but also rewards hard work. She enjoyed the opportunity to return to work after the birth of her first child.

Beth adds: 'My self-confidence and self-belief has rocketed and using techniques I have learnt through my journey with Caroline I have confidence I will eventually find the right job for me at the right time. When I first met with Caroline I was struggling to even contemplate the thought of returning to some form of work and did not believe it would be possible to change this. I am delighted to say I was proved wrong!'

Simon Barber, chief executive, 5 Boroughs Partnership NHS Trust

Chartered accountant Simon Barber left United Utilities and a long career in the commercial world, after undertaking a senior role in Your Communications. He felt his skills and experience could be useful to the public sector but added: 'It seemed a tall order to move role and sector.'

A strategy developed: 'I learned the power of developing a network – of simply picking up the phone or sending a short letter to ask how I might help in my target sector. This took me outside my comfort zone – I had been very confident in the internal network of United Utilities but I was very reluctant to approach people I didn't know.' Simon learned a great deal from new contacts inside the sector, who pointed to the value of short-term assignments. The turning point came when Simon received a 'no' letter on a permanent job at Christie's Hospital, then turned it into a conversation about the organisation's needs and into a breakthrough short-term assignment.

For Simon 'that moved the conversation from the theoretical to the specific'. Simon focused on the way health authorities were required to make radical changes by the Department of Health, and became appointed as the turnaround director for a high-profile primary care trust. Having started with recruiters telling him that a move into the health sector was all uphill, Simon became chief executive of 5 Boroughs Partnership Trust (a specialist mental health trust covering Warrington, St Helens, Knowsley, Wigan and Halton), beating 50 other applicants to the job, many of whom had far more health sector experience.

Six and a half years later Simon is still CEO at 5 Boroughs, having successfully led to foundation trust status. In addition, Simon has held a number of regional roles. He chairs the North West Mental Health CEO Group and has been the North West strategic lead for mental health and been seconded two days a week to the North West provider development Team.

Simon Ryan, aspiring TV location manager

Following a 12-month sabbatical after the birth of his son, Simon felt that he had reached an important crossroads in his working life. Having graduated with a construction degree, he'd worked across numerous business sectors including construction, health and safety, event management and property finance. His last position was working as a mortgage broker in central London. The thought of returning to finance did not appeal, so Simon decided to investigate other options based on his skill set and experience. After a couple of unsuccessful meetings with recruitment consultants, he realised that assistance from a specialist in career redirection would be beneficial. Simon writes: 'I remember our first meeting and John asking me a question: when you're driving home from this meeting, what do you want to have happened to make you feel that it was worthwhile?'

The answer presented itself as their discussions progressed, and they explored areas that interested Simon, and also importantly areas that hadn't in the past. They discovered that his interest in buildings and property could be transferred to the TV and film industry, particularly finding locations for filming. Simon decided that he would explore this idea further, and set about researching location management.

Simon continues: 'From the outside, the TV industry can be perceived as a closed shop that can't be entered unless you are in the know, but if you are determined enough, you can find a way in.' A chance conversation with a family member opened a door, and Simon started to make contact with various location managers. The process was challenging: 'I gathered a list of people working in the area and contacted everybody in turn, with the initial purpose of asking them about their work, and any tips they could offer going forward, using the information interviews technique recommended. I was pretty much cold calling which in itself was tough, but I persevered and it paid off.'

Simon began to form relationships within the business, and after four months he got his first job as a location assistant on a production for the BBC. Seven months later he's on his sixth position, and more doors keep opening. He adds: 'I'm still in the early stages of my new career, but feel that I'm on the right path to finding a job I'll love.'

Useful websites

This appendix lists a wide selection of interesting and useful websites. As addresses change regularly, you can find additional and updated links at www.johnleescareers.com.

Job boards

www.alljobsuk.com
Job board portal, listing the major and specialist job board sites and a list of the top UK job boards. The site also contains a database of recruitment agencies in the UK searchable by location and function.

www.indeed.co.uk
A job board aggregator that collects jobs from jobsites, newspapers, associations and company career pages. The advanced search option gives you a broader range of search criteria that will help you to refine your search.

www.simplyhired.co.uk
Consolidates jobs from the top job boards, content sites, newspapers, organisations and company career sites.

www.workhound.co.uk
A large search engine which lists job offers sourced from job boards, employment services and company job postings.

www.cv-library.co.uk
Covers jobs from 70 industries in the UK sourced from a range of recruitment agencies and employers.

www.reed.co.uk
Features over 150,000 live jobs across 42 industry specialisms with vacancies from over 10,000 recruiters.

www.totaljobs.com
Leading UK job board which contains useful job search tips and jobs databases.

http://msn.careerbuilder.co.uk
This jobsite contains a wide range of useful articles.

www.jobmarketsuccess.com
Clare Whitmell's web page, full of valuable information, especially on CV writing.

Careers information and exploration

The links below provide information about a wide range of career paths.

www.prospects.ac.uk
Aimed at graduates but a useful resource for anyone exploring sectors, entry routes and training opportunities, and links between job families.

www.workingforacharity.com
Promotes the voluntary sector as a positive career option for those seeking paid employment.

**https://nationalcareersservice.direct.gov.uk/Pages/
Home.aspx**
Contains a wealth of career tools, information and advice.
The site also contains the latest regional job market information, skills health check tool and information on hundreds
of different careers. To use the career tools you will need to
register and create a free lifelong learning account.

www.open.edu/openlearn/about-openlearn/try
The Open University offers 650 free courses on a range of
subjects and topics to help you explore new areas or brush up
on existing skills.

www.jobhuntersbible.com
A compendium of job-hunting tips from Richard Nelson
Bolles, author of *What Color Is Your Parachute?*

http://careers.theguardian.com
Articles and blogs on career matters from *The Guardian*.

Social media

The explosion of usage on social media over the past few years
makes it an interesting space for job searchers and career transition. Social media tools can be helpful in researching people,
companies and sectors, and increase your online presence.

**www.dummies.com/how-to/content/job-searching-with-
social-media-for-dummies-cheat-.html**
Overview of using social media for job searching from the
popular *Dummies* guides.

http://learn.linkedin.com/job-seekers
LinkedIn help pages with useful tips on how to use LinkedIn in a job search.

www.social-hire.com
A site that joins together recruiters and job seekers, launched in 2012. It allows job seekers to be anonymous so they can job search discreetly. It also contains a wealth of articles and tips on job searching and using social media to help in the job search process.

http://theundercoverrecruiter.com
A useful blog on careers and job search techniques.

www.zoominfo.com
Gathers publicly available business information from the web and compiles it into profiles. This site caches pages, which enables you to see websites from earlier versions of the site. This is helpful when researching individuals' backgrounds.

Self-employment

www.gov.uk/business
Start-up advice and links to further information from the British government.

www.mentorsme.co.uk
An online gateway that connects business mentors with organisations to help them grow.

http://trendwatching.com
Scans the world for new consumer trends and innovations, reported in a monthly briefing.

www.peopleperhour.com
Helps people to connect with independent freelancers. Jobs are posted by businesses looking for people with specific skills set to complete variety of projects, and freelancers then can tender for the work on offer.

Other useful websites

www.gov.uk/browse/working
Information from the British government on employment topics ranging from finding a job to pensions.

www.disabilityrightsuk.org
Includes specialist advice on the rights of disabled workers and state benefits available to them.

www.volunteering.org.uk
Volunteering England is the national development agency for volunteering. The site contains information on volunteering in different sectors and multiple links.

www.reachskills.org.uk
Reach is a skilled volunteering charity, helping charities to find skilled volunteers. The site has a searchable database of skilled volunteering vacancies.

www.adviceguide.org.uk
Online help from the Citizens Advice Bureau network covering a wide range of topics.

www.hays.co.uk/salary-guides/index.htm
Salary guide from Hays: a useful site for comparing salary rates.

www.assessmentday.co.uk
A wide variety of free practice tests covering numerical, verbal, inductive reason, psychometric tests.

www.rec.uk.com/membership/member-directory
A directory of recruitment agencies from the Recruitment and Employment Confederation.

www.reed.co.uk/jobindex
Provides information on the jobs market including statistics on the growth areas.

http://hiring.monster.co.uk/hr/hr-best-practices/market-intelligence.aspx
Market intelligence on the UK jobs market.

www.statistics.gov.uk/hub/labour-market/index.html
Labour market statistics from the Office for National Statistics.

Index

70% overlap 53–54
A to Z thinking 45–46
achievements 83, 100, 275
adaptability 35–36
ADEPT model 186–187
age, and employment, age
 discrimination 23
agencies, employment, *see* recruitment
 agencies, consultants
alumni associations 272
anxiety, nerves at interview 225–227
Aristotle 150
Association of Graduate Recruiters
 273–274

behaviour and belief 49–50
Best, Gill 129, 152, 290
Boateng, Ozwald 53
Bolles, Richard Nelson iii, vi, 20, 49,
 136, 215
Boorstin, Daniel J. 206
brand, personal 247–249
Brett, Marie 21
Briggs, Johnny 148
Bright, Jim 138
Brower, Charles 78
Brown, Eva May 184
Browne, H. Jackson 121
Burns, George 253
Buzan, Tony 42

career break, time out 266
career conversations 250–251
Career Motivation Indicator 68

Career Triangles Exercise 40
chaos theory in careers 138
Childs, Julian 200
Chartered Institute of Personnel and
 Development 3, 15
competence-based interview questions
 237–238
confidence 135
Connections Game Exercise 222
constraints, personal barriers 28–29
Courtis, John 23, 229
covering letters 287–288
Covey, Stephen 51
creativity, creative thinking 33,
 45–48
Csikszentmihalyi, Mihaly 52
CV writing 281–287

Davis, Stan 245
de Bono, Edward 46, 105, 164
decision making 36, 48

Economic and Social Research
 Council 9
Edison, Thomas 99
Einstein, Albert 135, 144
emotional intelligence 120
engagement 15
Escher, M.C. 90
experiment 39

Facebook, *see* social media
Feist, Matthias 202–203
Fennah, Peter 110

Ferguson, Marilyn 40
Field Generator 160–163
flow 52
Ford, Henry 49
Forster, E.M. 189
Frost, Robert 41, 161
Fuller, Buckminster 14

gap year, *see* career break
Gardner, Howard 110
giganomics 255
Gilleard, Carl 274
goals, setting, problems 48
Goodman, Ellen 20
graduates 273–274
Guardian, The 2
Guare, John 210

Haldane, Bernard 207
Halverson, Kate 96
Handy, Charles 253
happiness 7–11, 16–17, 52
Herrmann, Ned 19
Hopson, Barrie 260
Howlett, Kate 225, 231–234
Humphries, Caroline 294

Ibarra, Herminia 137–138
Ideas Grid Exercise 56
imposter syndrome 26
information interviews 214–221
intelligences, multiple 110–119
interests, on your CV 279, 283
interim work 256
internet job search 189–191,
    204–205
internships, *see* volunteering
interviews
    questions to ask prospective
        employers 238–239
    tough questions 234–237

Jigsaw Job Exercise 61
job-hunting
    first time mistakes 167
    myths 171–172

jobs
    hidden market 184–186
    multi-strategy search 170–171
    sharing 257
Johannesburg 37
Johnson, Lisa 136–137
Johnson, Samuel 226
Jung, Carl 54, 108

Kay, Alan 127
Kelly, Kevin 127
Knowdell, Richard 146

Lawrence, D.H. 1
Layard, Richard 9, 11, 52
leadership 249
Ledger, Katie 260
Lennon, John 135
Lewin, Kurt 262
Lincoln, Abraham 135
Lindenfield, Gael & Stuart 209, 212
LinkedIn 192–201
Lore, Nicholas 44
luck 38–39

Maslow, Abraham 106
Master Sheet 142
McPherson, Colin 94
media, influence on career choice
    147–148
message, two-breath 209
Meyer, Christopher 245
mind mapping 42–43
money and pay 59–60,
    240
Myers–Briggs Type Indicator (MBTI)
    test 108

networking 174, 207–209, 246
New York Times 121

Office for National Statistics 7, 254,
    260
older workers, *see* age

part-time work 256–257
Paths Not Taken Exercise 41

Pauling, Linus 47
Pearce, Bernard 84
Pemberton, Carole 8
personal barriers, *see* constraints
personality tests 106–110
Politician's Trick Exercise 242
Porot, Daniel 213, 215
portfolio careers 259–262
Pratchett, Terry 265
presentation statements 84–85
Pryor, Robert 138

qualifications 24, 172, 243, 279, 283

rat race 26
Reade, Charles 70
realistic 103
recession 2, 5, 15, 20, 38
recruitment agencies, consultants 3,
    176, 180–183, 240–241
rejection 228–229
reputation, *see* personal brand
retirement 22
retraining 25
REVEAL method of information
    interviews 215–221
Ruskin, John 58
Russell, Bertrand 9

safety habits, employer 175–176
Sarnoff, David 102
school leavers 268–269
self-employment 254, 257–259
Seneca 59
shopping list, employer 241
Sinclair, Peter 156
six degrees of separation 210
Skill Cards, JLA 89, 291, 293
skills
    categories 72
    motivated 86
    transferable 73, 275

Skill Clips Exercise 870
Skills Catalogue Exercise 71
Skills Circle 87
social media 192–203
stories, at interview 230–231
strengths and weaknesses 233, 236
study, further 265–266
support team, trios 55–56

temporary work 255–256
Terkel, Studs 15
Three Career Circles 149
Time Balance exercise 11
Tomlin, Lily 26
Twain, Mark 94, 136
Twitter 201–203

UK Commission for Employment &
    Skills 174–175
university careers services 271

values 152–155
Van Oech, Roger 164
velvet rut 48
vocations 155–157
volunteering 276–278

Warren, Joëlle 181–183
Watkins, Michael 245
Watson, Thomas 99
Whitehorn, Katherine 224
Williams, H.H. 31
Williams, Rowan 157
Wiseman, Richard 159
Work Foundation 249
Work Themes Exercise 131
work, time spent in 6, 7

yes, but ... thinking 19, 56, 104, 143,
    229
Young, James Webb 166